[by Apostolo, Giorgio and Giorgio Bignozzi]

COLOR PROFILES OF WORLD WAR I COMBAT PLANES

TRANSLATED FROM THE ITALIAN BY
DALE McADOO,

WITH AN INTRODUCTION BY
WILLIAM GREEN

CRESCENT BOOKS, NEW YORK

INTRODUCTION

"When my brother and I built and flew the first man-carrying flying machine, we thought that we were introducing into the world an invention which would make further wars practically impossible." So wrote Orville Wright in 1917, fourteen years after he and his brother, Wilbur, had succeeded in making the first powered, sustained and controlled aeroplane flights in history. If, indeed, the Wright brothers truly entertained such a belief as they performed their experiments on the Kill Devil sand hills near Kitty Hawk, their inconceivable naïveté was not shared by others who saw in the aeroplane an obvious instrument of war. In fact, in 1899, while Wilbur Wright was flying his first kite embodying a system of wing-warping, and before any navigable lighter-than-air or heavier-than-air vehicle of proven practicability existed, an internationally-agreed Hague Declaration had formally banned the launching of all forms of projectiles or explosives from any form of aerial vessel.

The use in warfare of manned aerial vehicles had been prophesied for hundreds of years, and lighter-than-air craft had made a successful military début as early as 26 June 1794, when the manned balloons of the military Company of *Aérostiers* were employed during the Battle of Fleurus. For observation and reconnaissance tasks, the balloon continued to be used, seeing service in both the American Civil War and the Boer War, but lacking means of propulsion or steering it was an impracticable vehicle for offensive operations. The possibility of attacking an enemy from the air, for long considered, had perforce to await the birth of a navigable aerial vehicle, and such came with the dawn of the twentieth century: the flight in 1900 of Graf Ferdin—and von Zeppelin's first giant dirigible airship over Lake Constance. The military potentialities of Zeppelin's dirigible were all too obvious, as were also those of the aeroplane once its practicability had been proven, and thus, by the end of the twentieth century's first decade, widespread and official concern was being evinced in the rôle of the aircraft in warfare, although only a few visionaries foresaw that it would revolutionise all future conflict.

During the course of 1911, the first *Concours Militaire*, a display of aircraft that could be utilized in warfare, took place at Reims, but prior to this event the first live bombing trials had taken place in the USA, and while it is not possible to state with certainty today which aeroplane type was first adapted for warlike use, rifles and machine guns were being carried experimentally by various aircraft. But the use of aircraft in warfare had progressed beyond theory when, on 23 October 1911, a Blériot XI of the Italian Army participated in the Italo-Turkish War by reconnoitring the Turkish lines near Azizia, and, a week later, on 1 November, another aircraft performed the first recorded bombing raid when its pilot dropped grenades on Ain Zara and Taguira.

The aircraft had been used as an offensive weapon for the first time, and in a prophetic speech to a technical sub-committee of the Committee of Imperial Defense on 5 February 1912, Captain Murray F. Sueter, R.N., said: "In the case of a European war between two countries, both sides would be equipped with a large corps of aeroplanes, each trying to obtain information of the other and to hide its own movements. The effort which each would exert in order to hinder or prevent the enemy from obtaining information would lead to the inevitable result of a war in the air, for the supremacy of the air, by armed aeroplanes against each other. This fight for the supremacy of the air in future wars will be of the first and greatest importance . . ."

By the time the first shots of World War One were fired there was, nevertheless, still no real appreciation of the aeroplanes as a weapon; the heterogeneous collection of monoplanes and biplanes, tractors and pushers, fielded by the combatants was regarded almost exclusively as a source of reconnaissance information. But the seeds that had been first sown over Tripolitania by aeroplanes of the Italian Army, if slow to germinate, were soon to grow at a fantastic rate under the exigencies of war; aircraft for specialized rôles rapidly emerged and the pattern of aerial warfare constantly changed; the foundations of military air power were laid.

The development of combat aircraft in World War One was more a process of refinement than one of constant innovation, more powerful engines being progressively applied to ever more robust airframes, although there were the brilliant exceptions. Completeness is an absolute quality admitting of no degrees, and let it be said at the outset that this book has presented a major task of omission rather than one of commission. The two dozen plus basic aircraft types featured in the pages that follow, orthodox or innovatory at the time of their début, each made, in the view of the editorial team, an important contribution to this, the first major conflict in which aviation played a rôle. The reader may feel that some of the aircraft included were less worthy than some omitted, but in endeavouring to provide a broad cross section of the earliest to the last aeroplanes employed during the conflict as well as examples of each of the principal combat aircraft categories, the editorial team has unashamedly exercised its personal preferences and has endeavoured to capture on the pages of this book something of the "feel" of that period with which the annals of aerial warfare opened.

WILLIAM GREEN

Co-ordinator:

Giuseppe Dicorato

Text by:

Giorgio Apostolo
Giorgio Bignozzi

With the collaboration of:

Baldassare Catalanotto
Cesare Falessi

Illustrations by:

Vincenzo Cosentino
Pino Dell'Orco
Amedeo Gigli
Marcello Ralli
Roberto Terrinoni

Technical consultant:

Gianfranco Rotondi

INDEXES

INDEX OF CONTENTS

analytical index

The words and letters in heavy type refer to the names and abbreviations of the aircraft; the names in italics refer to engines; the numbers in italics indicate the page on which illustrations are to be found; the symbol 5v stands for five-view illustrations; the symbol pr stands for profiles.

7

NIEUPORT Ni.17 C.1

Specifications

The Nieuport 11, the famous Bébé, *gained its nickname from its small size. Here it is shown maneuvering above the Centocelle military airport near Rome* (Aeronautica Militare Italiana).

	Ni.11	Ni.17	Ni.24 *bis*	Ni.27
Power plant	Le Rhône 9C 80 hp	Le Rhône 9J 110 hp	Le Rhône 9Jb 120 hp	Le Rhône 9Jb 120 hp
Span, *m*	7·55	8·22	8·20	8·20
Total length, *m*	5·80	5·74	5·85	5·85
Height, *m*	2·45	2·33	2·42	2·42
Wing area, *m²*	13·00	15·00	—	—
Weight, empty, *kg*	352	374	354	354
Weight, loaded, *kg*	480	565	544	585
Maximum speed, *km/h*	156	177	186	186
Climb, *m in min-sec*	3000 18:30	4000 19:30	5000 21:40	5000 21:40
Service ceiling, *m*	4600	5300	5550	5550
Flight endurance, *hrs-min*	2:30	2:00	1:30	1:30

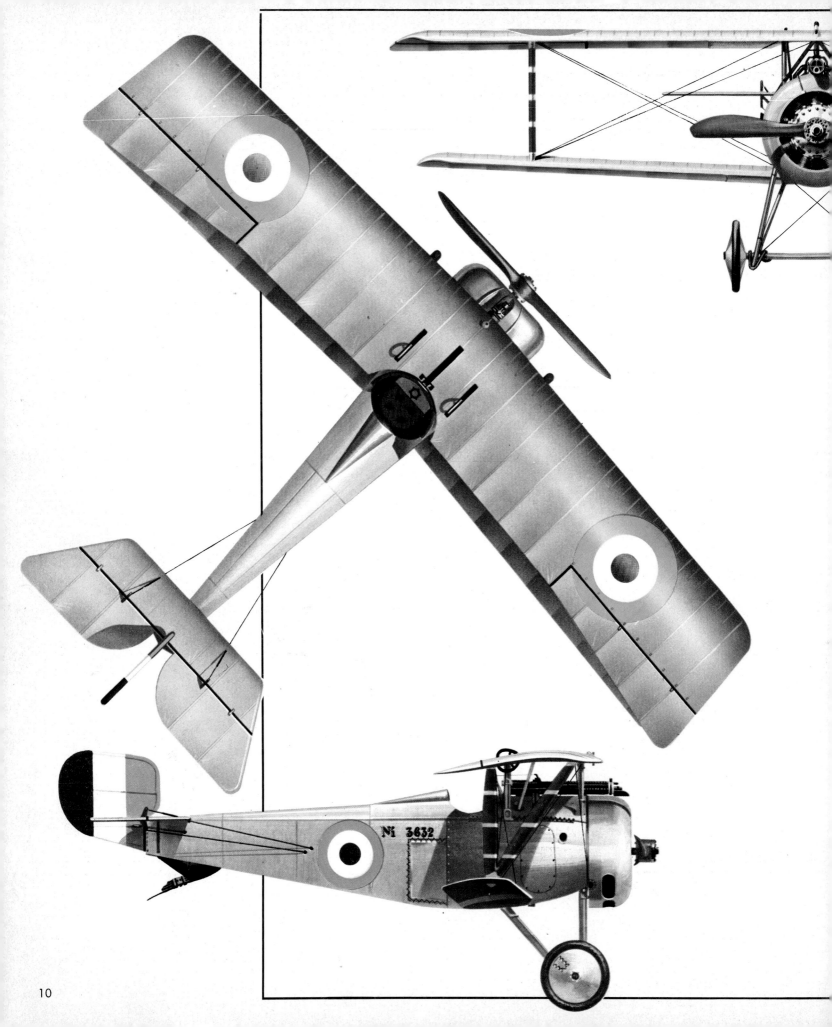

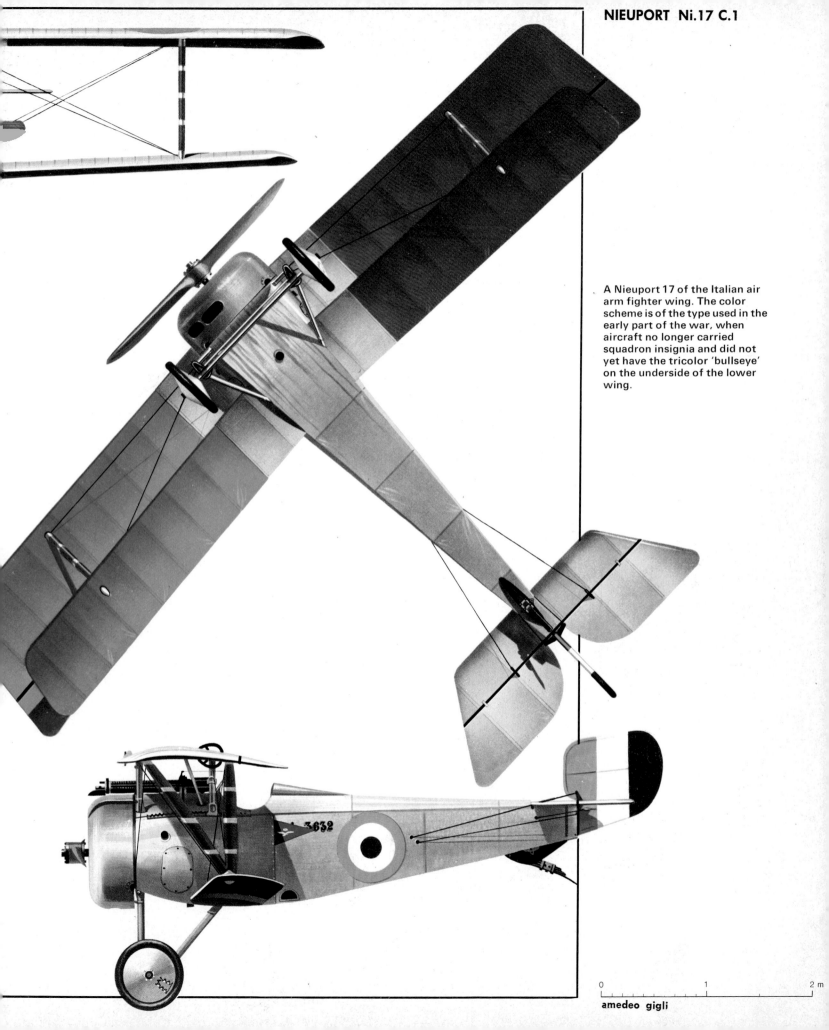

A Nieuport 17 of the Italian air arm fighter wing. The color scheme is of the type used in the early part of the war, when aircraft no longer carried squadron insignia and did not yet have the tricolor 'bullseye' on the underside of the lower wing.

0   1   2 m

amedeo gigli

The Nieuport 11—the Bébé—was used by the air arms of all the Allies. It was built under licensing arrangements in various countries. Together with the Hanriot it formed the basic working equipment of many squadrons and notched up a fine record of kills. It was flown by nearly all Allied aces, including Ancillotto,, who was the first to fire Le Prieur rockets ignited electrically.
In Italy, between 1916 and the end of the war, 646 of these aircraft were built, powered by 80-hp Gnôme engines. These photographs show Nieuport Bébés in various activities The group at upper right includes some Ni.17s.

The Nieuport Ni.17 C1 was one of the most famous fighter planes to see action in World War I. A description of the Ni.17 alone does not suffice, however; historical accuracy calls for consideration of the entire series of sesquiplanes ('one-and-a-half-winger's) which the Issy-les-Moulineaux factory developed with original designs beginning in 1914, when the Nieuport Ni.10 made its maiden flight. This series was a 'family', of which about 7,000 machines were produced between 1915 and 1918.

The sesquiplane formula was intended to combine the structural rigidity of the trussed biplane airframe with the advantages offered by the monoplane configuration, especially in regard to visibility. These planes were, then, high-wing parasol monoplanes with normal double-wing-spar structure provided with a second, lower wing of reduced chord and single spar.

The Ni.10 appeared at the front early in the summer of 1915 and was a two-seater scout (fast reconnaissance) plane. Designed by Gustave Delage, the Ni.10 was produced in two versions, differing in the observer's position, which could be either fore or aft of the pilot's cockpit. Unarmed at first, it later carried a Hotchkiss or Lewis machine gun fired through a cutout in the upper wing. The power plant was an 80-hp rotary Gnôme or Le Rhône engine. The Ni.10 was issued to British, Belgian and Italian squadrons. In Italy it was manufactured under license by the Nieuport-Macchi factory in Varese.

With increased operational use the various versions became progressively more specialized. Thus, for reconnaissance, there was the Ni.12 (slightly larger, powered with engines ranging from 110 to 130 hp). Many Ni.10s were assigned to fighter missions, compensating for the added weight of the machine gun by flying as single-seaters. On the Ni.10 the weapon had a Foster gun mount which permitted forward fire with the option of inclining the gun for upward firing and reloading.

From this first operational experience and from the pre-war design for a racing plane (the XB of 1914), Delage developed a true fighter, the Ni.11, better known, because of its smaller size, as the Nieuport *Bébé*. This model developed so fast that by the summer of 1915 a few Bébés had already appeared in the French and British squadrons on the Western front and the Dardanelles. In February 1916 the Ni.11 was active in the battle of Verdun, where it proved to be the best Allied fighter. The plane was also manufactured under license in Italy by Macchi and in Russia at the 'Dux' plant in Moscow, Shchetinin Works in Petrograd, and Anatra in Odessa.

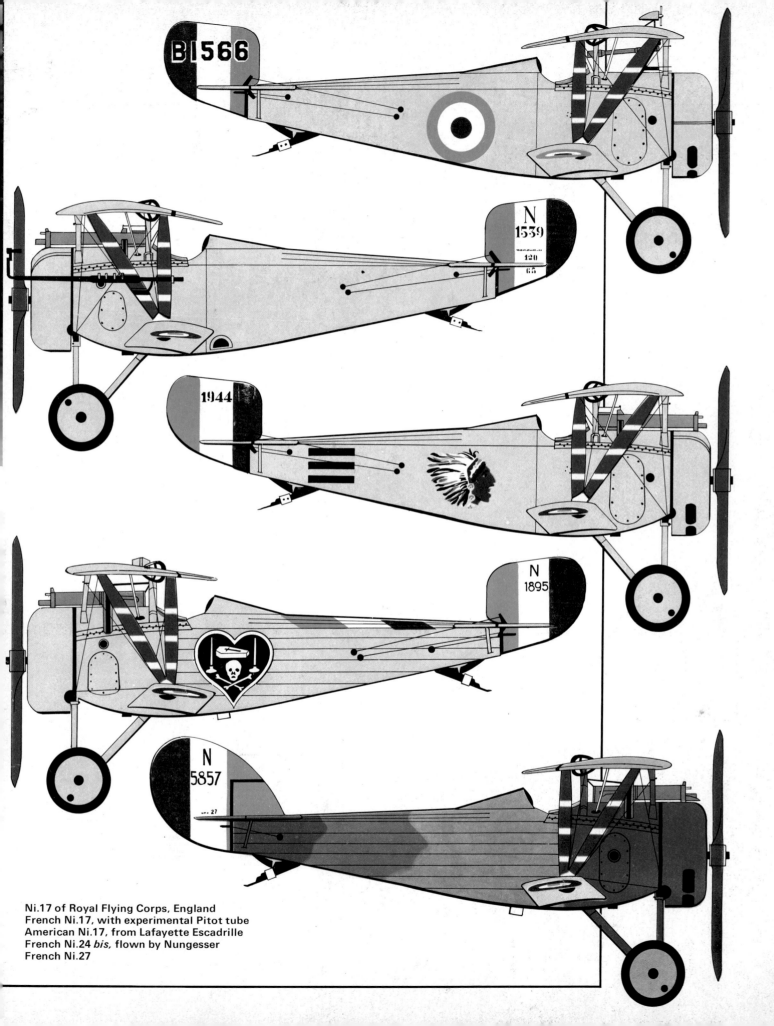

Ni.17 of Royal Flying Corps, England
French Ni.17, with experimental Pitot tube
American Ni.17, from Lafayette Escadrille
French Ni.24 *bis,* flown by Nungesser
French Ni.27

these units included André de Meulemeester, Francis Jacquet, Jean Olieslager and Edmund Thieffry.

The Ni.17 was exported to neutral countries as well: 20 were sold to Holland and, after the Armistice, two to Finland and a certain number to Switzerland.

Development of the Nieuport Series

Although the Ni.17 represented the culmination of the possibilities of the 1914 formula, Delage attempted further improvement with a few later designs, some of which were simply variants of the basic type.

The first to appear was the Ni.21, a two-seater designed basically as a training plane and also known as the Ni.80 (perhaps because it was powered by an 80-hp Le Rhône engine, sometimes replaced by the 110-hp Le Rhône). Variants 81 and 82 were forthcoming, the latter with a wing area of 23 square metres, followed by 83, with a wing area of 30 square metres, two pairs of struts and auxiliary safety wheels available for the landing gear to guard against ground looping. This two-seater was used by the Americans and Russians as well as the French.

Next came the Ni.23, a single-seat fighter identical to the Ni.17 except that it was slightly heavier, powered by a 120-hp Le Rhône (or the 80-hp model in training planes). A few units equipped with the Ni.23 served in the air arms of France, the United States, Gt. Britain, Russia and possibly Italy.

More important changes came with the Ni.24, which had a rounded fuselage. The engine was the 120-hp Le Rhône 9Jb. According to some authorities, only the *bis* variant of this new Nieuport kept the traditional form of the tail surfaces, while normally these would have been identical to those of the later Ni.27. The distinction between the latter and the Ni.24 is consequently difficult to establish and doubtful at best.

The US Army Air Service was the best customer for the Ni.27, procuring more than 100 as advanced training planes. The availability of excellent new fighter planes had reduced the importance of Nieuport sesquiplanes to second place, and British and French orders were few. A few machines, perhaps 50, were sent to Italy from October 1917 on.

With the Ni.27 the dynasty of Nieuport sesquiplanes came to an end. Delage's next model, the Ni.28, had wings of equal span, with parallel struts. The influence of the Nieuport sesquiplane series on other manufacturers continued, however, for some time. In the postwar years certain reminiscences of the typical design of the small French fighter planes were still to be seen in such fine British fighters as the Armstrong-Whitworth Siskin, the Bristol Bulldog, and the Gloster Grebe.

Top: *One of the earliest of the Ni.11 Bébés of the Italian Army air arm. These planes had a single gun mounted above the upper wing. Later the gun was mounted above the engine and synchronized with the propeller.*

Bottom: *The Macchi Corp. in Italy built 150 of these Nieuport 17s, a development based on the Bébé. The engine was a 110-hp Le Rhône. In some countries the N.11 and N.17 were active in the same period.*

On the Italian front the Ni.17 was for a long time the cutting edge of the Italian fighter force, but the heavy losses incurred in the intense winter fighting of 1917-18 and the increasing supply of the excellent Hanriot HD-1 and SPAD fighters soon led to a decrease in the number of *Superbébés* in operational service. By December 1918 none was left in front-line units.

Russia acquired a certain number of Ni.17s from France but then began to produce them under license. They were manufactured by 'Dux' Moscow, although apparently the quality was not very high. The Nieuport 17 acquitted itself with honor on the Russian front, particularly when flown by such veteran pilots as Ivan Kazakov, who continued fighting after the Armistice, still flying the Ni.17. in the White Army against the Bolsheviks from the base at Archangel (Arkhangelsk).

The US Army Air Service bought 75 *Superbébés* for the AEF in France but used them only for training. (Even before the entry of the United States into the war American volunteers in the Lafayette *Escadrille* of the French Air Force were flying the Ni.11, and an Ni.17-*bis* was shipped back to the States.)

The Belgian Air Arm consistently used the French fighter plane; their 1st and 5th Squadrons, based at Coxide, were equipped with them. Aces from

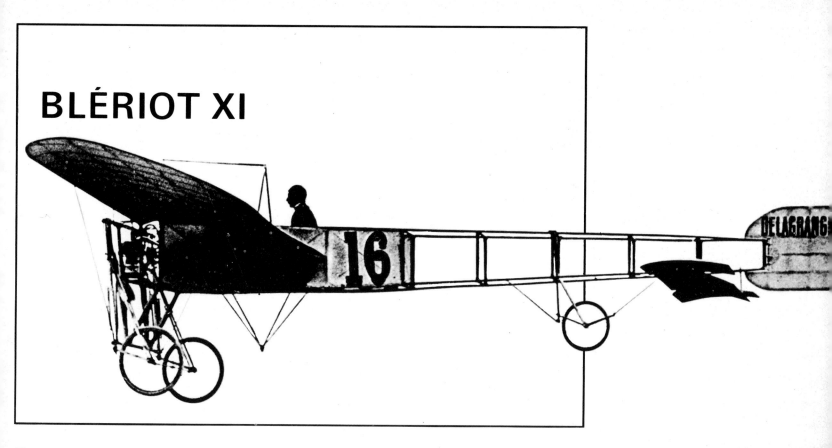

BLÉRIOT XI

From the earliest beginnings of aviation, inventors and builders of aircraft experimented with many different approaches. Stabilizers could be aft or (in the *avion canard*) forward of the main wings. Engines could either be fixed (in-line) or rotary, propellers might be of the tractor ('pulling') type or 'pushers'. Some designers preferred the covered fuselage, others the open frame. But the hottest dispute concerned the number of wings—whether an aircraft should be a monoplane, biplane, triplane, and whether even more wings might not increase efficiency. Some remained faithful to their original formula with a tenacity which was often unjustified, while others tried all solutions before adopting one more or less definitively.

Among the latter, a group obviously including the more practical designers, was a French engineer named Louis Blériot, who built aircraft of every type and from them gained as good an idea as anyone could in those early days of what each formula had to offer. When, after long experiment, he finally chose the monoplane for his most serious efforts, others had to listen to his arguments. Time proved him right—his 'definitive' monoplane, the Type XI of 1908, was accepted as one of the most efficient machines of the period, safe and with excellent flight characteristics.

In 1909 Blériot developed an improved version, and it was in this machine that he made his historic first flight across the English Channel. He covered the 40 kilometers in 36 mins. 30 secs., flying at an altitude of 100 m (328 ft).

The historic flight of July 25, 1909 was more than just a milestone in the history of a technology: it was also an unmistakable demonstration that flight had put an end to the splendid isolation of the British Isles and that the Home Fleet would no longer suffice to ensure Britain's invulnerability. The military implications of Blériot's flight were immediately evident. The General Staffs of the various powers did not, of course, share the enthusiasm and faith in the military potential of aircraft which many military experts had, but they were forced to recognize the great improvements achieved in the heavier-than-air field.

It was Blériot's Channel flight which dramatized it. Military orders for aircraft began to rise, and it was only natural that a majority of such orders went to the Blériot firm at Levallois-Perret. Several countries obtained licenses for manufacturing Blériot aircraft, among them the SIT of Turin, which began building the Blériot XI in 1912. Blériot also organized training schools at Pau and Buc in France and at Hendon in England (there was already a Blériot office in London).

The Blériot pilot above is one of the great pioneers of aviation—Léon Delagrange, photographed in 1909. Below: a modified Blériot monoplane, showing the characteristic 'dovetail' tail structure. (Musée de l'Air)

Blériot XI-2 built by **SIT** of Turin and assigned to the *3a Squadriglia*, based in Cuneo in northern Italy (1914)

0   1   2 m

marcello ralli

Technical description

The Blériot XI was a monoplane with the single wing 'at shoulder height' in all models except the 'Parapluie' — ('the Umbrella') — which had a raised wing and a tractor propeller. It was a single-seater or three-seater, depending on the model, and it could be adapted as a seaplane.

The fuselage consisted of a box girder of rectangular cross section; four longerons were joined to horizontal and vertical supports braced by wire. The structure was of wood, with only the forward section covered with either fabric or plywood.

The wing, in two easily removable sections, had two spars made of ash with poplar wing ribs. The spars were square in cross section, with lightening holes in the spaces between the wing ribs; the leading edge was rounded at the wing root. The wing tips were rounded, except in a few 'speed' models with shortened wings (and in others where the wings were shortened for experimentation in roll maneuvers). Toward the wing root they generally had either curved or straight cutouts for improved vision. Roll control was through warping of

the trailing edge of the wing tips. The wing was secured to the fuselage by bracing wires attached to the upper mounting and the landing gear axle. Warp control wires were secured to the engine bearers beneath the fuselage; upper wires were attached to the cabane pulley.

The rudder was one-piece, generally symmetrical above and below the fuselage hinge mount, and completely mobile; the stabilizer was below the fuselage and could be set for incidence (normally: 4°).

The landing gear was of split-axle design, with two vertical struts reinforced by two or more braces, all made of wood reinforced with steel cable, and two supporting posts of steel tubing on which the bushings of the spring shock absorbers ran connected to the adjustable V-legs attached to the wheels. The wheels measured 0·64 m in diameter and, in the two-seat model, were 1·60 m apart.

A bit of imaginative rhetoric, justified by the exceptional character of the scene, as printed in the Petit Journal *of August 8, 1909, showing Louis Blériot arriving at Dover after his historic flight across the English Channel.*

Development of the Blériot XI

Derived directly from the civilian model, of which Blériot's plane for the Channel crossing was the prototype, the Blériot XI-1 or 'Military Blériot XI' differed in few respects, except for the stabilizer, which was divided in the classical design with a fixed element and a movable elevator instead of being in three sections (of which the center one was fixed, the two end ones movable). Blériot had also decided to adopt the two-part, U-shaped tail skid in place of the wheel, and the engine was a radial rotary type, generally a Gnôme, in place of the stationary Anzani engine. Use of the rotary power plant involved redesigning the forward fuselage to permit rotation of the cylinders, and this problem was solved by cutting two lateral openings usually covered by convex panels. Sometimes, especially on the Blériots built under license in Turin, there were transparent panels on the sides of the cockpit to improve, to that limited extent permitted by the poor transparency of the mica then in use, the otherwise limited visibility from high-wing monoplanes. For the same purpose the trailing edge of the wing had two cutouts. Engine power ranged from 25 to 35 hp in training planes to 50 and, later, 70 or 80 hr in operational aircraft.

In France the single-seaters were designated either as 'XI *Militaire*' or 'XI *Artillerie*,' and they were powered by 50-hp engines. The latter version was distinguished by a higher stabilizer and a larger cutout in the trailing edge at the wing root.

As for the two-seater, the official classification included Types XI-2 *'Artillerie'* and XI-2 *'Genie'*. The former was a two-seater version of the artillery single-seater, using the newly designed rudder, while the latter was identical to the *'Militaire'*. Both were powered by 70-hp Gnôme engines.

There were more important changes in the two-seaters, obtained by exploiting the 'modular' concept of the basic design, which permitted lengthening of the fuselage by the addition of another bay to the normal frame, in addition to the variation in the span and wing area achieved by using longer spars and a greater number of wing ribs, the chord remaining constant. The fuselage was lengthened only forward, and balance was maintained by moving the second cockpit aft. The landing gear was moved forward and strengthened by the addition of two struts between the fuselage and the rigid axle. The tailskid was generally one-piece, inserted fairly well forward.

In the 'Parapluie' model, four struts carried, above the fuselage, a wing support of span equal to the width of the fuselage, to which the wings were attached, thus offering better visibility and a slightly increased wing area. To the raised wing (which had a negative warp, reducing the incidence of the wing tips to 0) there was added a curious detail: the rudder was made in two parts, which could on landing be opened like a book to serve as an air brake!

Column 1: *Two photographs of Blériot's epoc-making flight. Bottom: at Calais shortly before take-off; top: shortly after take-off. The flight lasted 36 minutes 30 seconds*

The two-seat model could also be converted into a seaplane by adding two floats to the wheels and a third to the tail skid; the rudder was generally extended both below and above. These modifications were also adapted in Italy, where engineer Triaca of the SIT was in charge of the seaplane conversion as well as the 'Parasol'. The attachment of the floats to the airframe was flexible.

The Blériot XI-3 was little used, in part because being a single-engined three-seater it was at too great a disadvantage in combat. The XI-3 had a longer fuselage and carried a 140-hp Gnôme engine and a considerably bigger wing. The greatest changes, however, were made in the landing gear, which was lower, stronger and equipped with double wheels. The bracing system was also strengthened, adopting the 'Channel-crossing' arrangement, while the stabilizer resumed the original three-part design with a fixed center section.

In addition to these basic models there were other, purely experimental versions and a few *ad hoc* designs, built for specific purposes. Among the former, a single-seater built in 1911-12 had the fuselage entirely covered, even aft to the newly designed tailplane assembly: the rudder was curved and set well forward of the tail end of the fuselage, and the stabilizer was identical to that used on the original German 'Taube' monoplane. There was a monocoque version of 1913-14, a two-seater with a fuselage of octagonal cross section covered completely with plywood. The Blériot XVII, which found little use, was fairly streamlined and had an improved tail design.

Column 3: *Capt. Piazza's Blériot was the first aircraft to be officially used as a warplane. Piazza took off from Tripoli in Libya and reconnoitred over the enemy lines during the Italian-Turkish War of 1912. (Aeronautica Militare Italiana)*

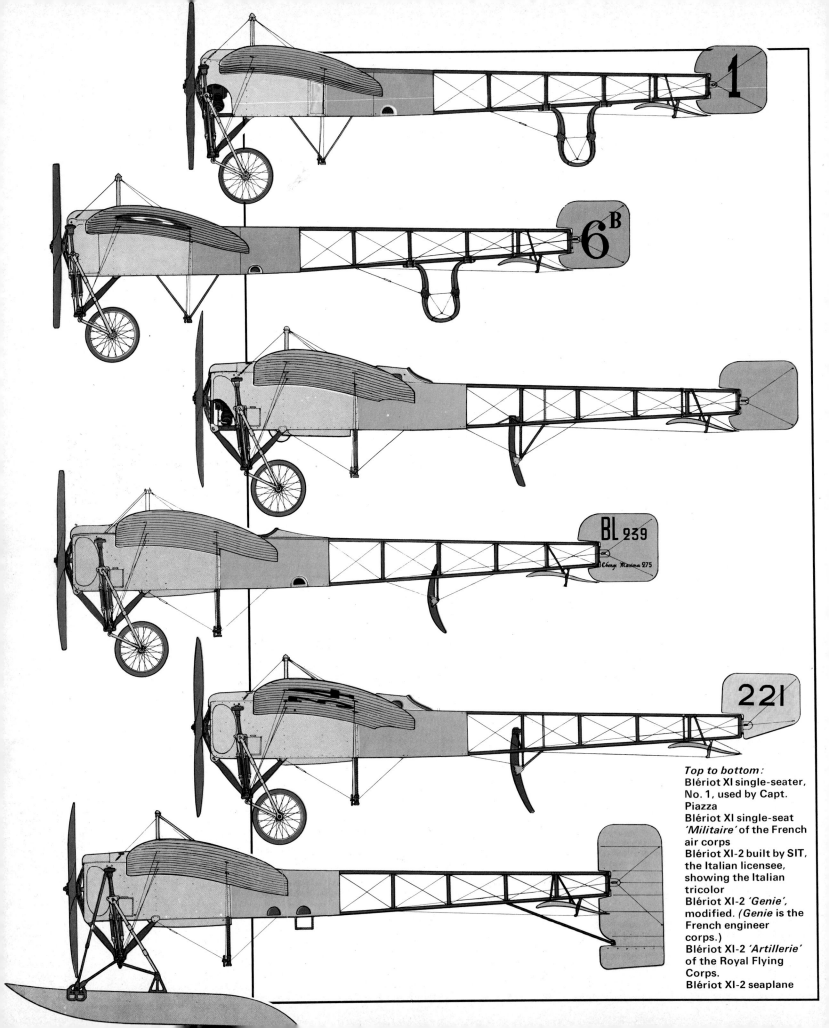

Top to bottom:
Blériot XI single-seater,
No. 1, used by Capt.
Piazza
Blériot XI single-seat
'Militaire' of the French
air corps
Blériot XI-2 built by SIT,
the Italian licensee,
showing the Italian
tricolor
Blériot XI-2 *'Genie'*,
modified. *(Genie* is the
French engineer
corps.)
Blériot XI-2 *'Artillerie'*
of the Royal Flying
Corps.
Blériot XI-2 seaplane

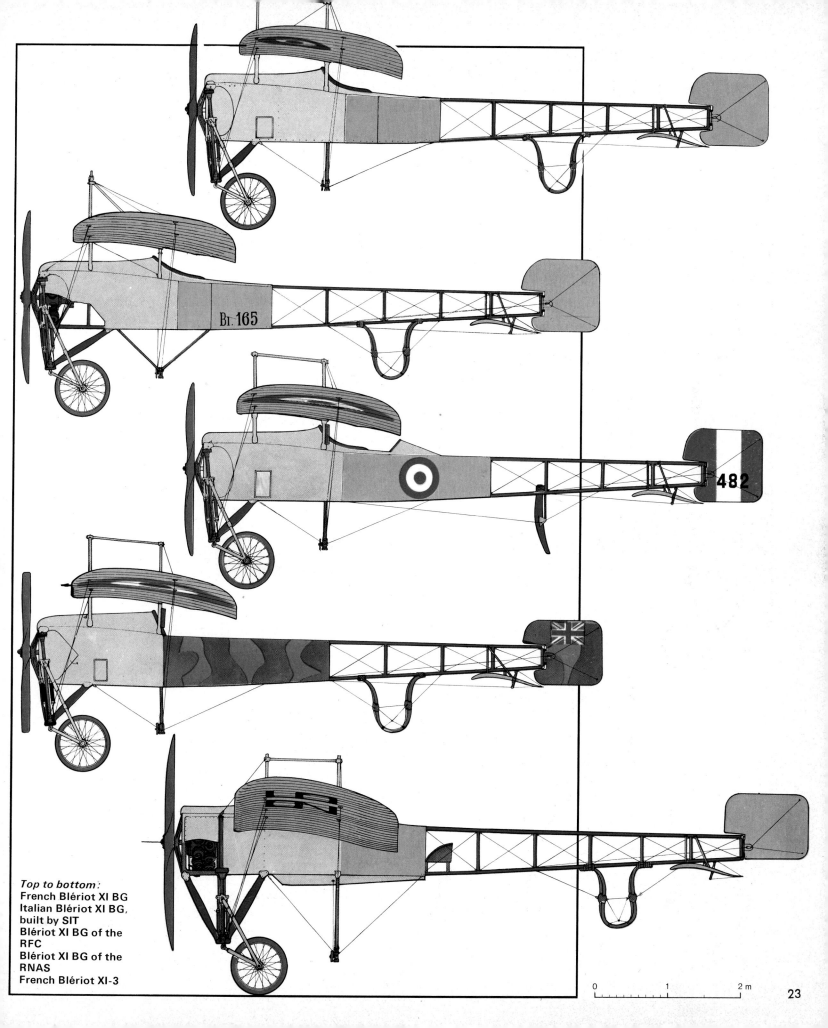

Top to bottom:
French Blériot XI BG
Italian Blériot XI BG,
built by SIT
Blériot XI BG of the
RFC
Blériot XI BG of the
RNAS
French Blériot XI-3

Bt. 165

482

0   1   2 m

How the Blériot XI was used in the War

Many war pilots, both French and those of other nationalities, earned their spurs in Blériot planes, and the French army used the monoplane version for their first experiments in photo reconnaissance and the biplane for early attempts at target spotting for the artillery. Many of the officers sent by their governments to Pau and Buc carried with them authorizations to purchase Blériot planes for their nascent air services—one of them from so far-away a place as Japan (Lieut. Reishiro Kimura).

The first to get interested in Blériot's product, however, were probably the Italians. Maj. Moris visited France in 1910, specifically to procure two Blériots for his government, and two months later the Italian government bought another three. These five aircraft were based at Centocelle and were used as monoplane trainers (biplane pilots were using Henry Farmans at the same base) in the first aviation unit activated in Italy for military service. The five machines included: (1) a two-seater with a 50-hp Gnôme engine; (2) two single-seaters with 50-hp and 35-hp Gnômes respectively; and two single-seat trainers with the 25-hp Gnôme. Later some of these planes were re-engined with 70-hp Gnômes Meanwhile other planes were being delivered, and two new military flying schools were being organized at Aviano and Cascina Malpensa. Three of these planes, piloted by Piazza, Ginocchio and Roberti, took part in the first-ever air operations in Italy and especially in the maneuvers at Monferrato in August 1911. In September of that year the same three aircraft were requisitioned as the nucleus of the first air group with an operational mission in Libya. Testimony as to the longevity of Louis Blériot's aircraft is given by the fact that several Blériots were still on active duty in Libya in 1922!

Compared with the Etrich Taube and the Nieuport, the Italian Blériots were classed as 'light monoplanes, and were assigned mainly to mountainous areas. (The 3rd *Squadriglia* in Italy specialized in mountain work.) Blériots were also used in a variety of other missions—including tests of bomb release through vertical steel tubes and the releasing of carrier pigeons. Meanwhile in France the continued use of Blériots had led to the classification of military aircraft. They were also used by the air services of all nations taking part in the Balkan Wars of 1912-13.

When World War I broke out Blériots equipped (besides the two squadrons already mentioned) the 1st, 3rd, 9th, 10th, 18th and 30th squadrons of the Italian air arm. In England they formed part of the equipment of Nos. 1, 3, 7, and 16 Squadrons of the Royal Flying Corps, and a number of Blériots were enroled in naval service with the RNAS. Belgians, Russians and Serbs all had several Blériots in their contingents.

All of these aircraft were very active in the early months of the war, but soon their limitations began to appear—especially their limited useful load, which greatly restricted their range and prohibited the carrying of any defensive armament. As soon as it became feasible to do so, the Blériots were relegated to secondary operational duties and eventually limited to use as trainers.

The same sequence of events took place a year later on the Austrian-Italian front. Because of their late entrance into the war, the Italians still had only Blériots when the more experienced Austrian forces had already been supplied with Etrich Taubes. Production of the Blériots was stepped up in the spring of 1915, and by May 24 the following units, all equipped with Blériots, were reported at the front: *Gruppo* I (with the Italian Third Army); 1, 2, 3, 13, *Squadriglie*; and the 4th Autonomous Sq. assigned to the Venetian Naval Headquarters. A total of 30 planes were assigned to the front, with 7 in reserve. Other groups were meanwhile being prepared for operational service.

Together with the Nieuport monoplanes, these Blériot aircraft had to bear the brunt of action in the early part of the war while awaiting delivery of more up-to-date machines. When the new planes arrived, the Blériots and Nieuports continued to make a valuable contribution to the Allied war effort as training aircraft.

Bengasi (Benghazi) was the home base of one of the very first squadrons of the fledgling Italian air force. This photograph shows an aircraft grounded by heavy rain in 1913. (Aeronautica Militare Italiana)

ETRICH TAUBE

The Taube ('dove') was an Austrian plane which was very successful not only in its native land but in other countries as well. The one shown here is a two-seater belonging to the British Royal Flying Corps. (Musée de l'Air)

Among the aircraft which had become established before World War I as standard types for military use, the Taube (the word means *dove* in German) was an especially fine design. It was an elegant monoplane, the wings of which were of somewhat complex structure and rather birdlike in appearance. The origin of the Taube, which eventually supplied a name for an entlre class of aircraft, goes back to 1910, when the first design was made by Igo Etrich, an Austrian inventor. Like most other engineers of the day, Etrich was convinced that stability was the most important characteristic in an aircraft, and his first practical inspiration came from the winged seed of a plant, *Zanonia macrocarpa,* which provides the most impressive example of stable flight to be found in nature. After various experiments with a glider, Etrich built his first powered Taube, which had warped wings modeled on the plant seed-carrier. The plane was successful, and for a long time aircraft designers, particularly among the Germans and Austrians, used the warping device instead of the aileron control system, which was to be universally adopted within the next few years.

Technical description

So far as military use is concerned, before describing the Etrich Taube we should recall for a moment the criteria which prevailed at the time and consider the differences in operational principles as applied to the Taube and to the other monoplane of those early days, the French Blériot XI. For single-engine, two-seater monoplanes, French standards of 1914 called for a duration of 3 hours, a useful load (not including fuel) of 150 kg, a speed of 110-120 km/hr, and a climbing capability of 1000 m in 14 minutes. German requirements for the same parameters were, respectively: duration, 6 hrs; useful load, 250 kg (i.e., 80 kg+crew); speed, 120 km/hr; climb to 1000 m, no more than 12 mins 30 secs. Take-off and landing requirements had to be less than 80 m for the French plane and no more than 120 m for the German. It should be noted that the Blériot XI satisfied French requirements for maneuverability, while the Taube lent itself more to long-range operations or operations with a sizeable offensive load (with a slight trade-off in stability), which however did not exclude respectable standards of speed, climb and ceiling.

25

ETRICH TAUBE

The Etrich Taube was piloted by Italian Lieut. Giulio Gavotti in Libya. Its racing number, 5, was painted over after its debut as a combat plane

0   1   2 m

pino dell'orco

Top: *All early air forces had a complex mix of planes and models. The Italian forces in Libya included the Taube shown here. Its pilot, Lieut. Giulio Gavotti (foreground), was the first pilot ever to drop a bomb from an aircraft in flight.* (Aeronautica Militare Italiana)

Bottom: *In the earliest air actions, carried out by Italian airmen in Libya (Tripolitania), the bomb dropped by Lieut. Gavotti was a 2-kg weapon like the one shown here; it was known as a Cipelli bomb, so named after its inventor.*

The Taube had a wooden airframe (except in the Jeannin *Stahltaube*) covered with fabric. In the initial Taubes a transverse beam in the fuselage braced the wing, constituting a truss similar to the trussed structure of biplanes and giving the Taube a far greater ruggedness than any other monoplane of the day, although at some loss in speed. The wing tips, swept back, were strongly warped, giving a wing profile which ensured qualities of stability similar to those of a flying wing; the stabilizer, then, served above all for maneuvering rather than for stabilizing the longitudinal trim. The fin was in two sections, one above and one below the stabilizer, and was thus reminiscent of the most admired monoplane of the pioneer era—the beautiful but fragile Antoinette. The Taube fin was smaller, because the directional stability of the aircraft was ensured by the wing form itself. The stabilizer was also strengthened, in the earliest versions, by a transverse brace to which various bracing wires were connected (in addition to the elevator controls); note than in these aircraft the élevator was originally a warping device, as were the wing tips. Etrich never abandoned the system of warping, but more or less conventional ailerons, sometimes obliquely hinged, were used on later versions, especially those built by Rumpler. The undercarriage was originally similar to Blériot's, with the addition of one or two skids (similar to those on the Bristol, and later the Halberstadt; these aircraft also featured raised front wheels to prevent ground looping) as well as two wheels at the tips of the lower brace which was parallel to the wing: this was abandoned on Kondor models and, shortly thereafter, on Rumpler models, and then by the other manufacturers, who very soon also simplified the landing gear.

Many types of engine were used on the Taube, but they were invariably water-cooled, in-line models. The only known exception is the 1913 type German Taube, which was powered by a 9-cylinder, 80-hp Stahlherz rotary engine. These were used on some models in place of the usual 80-to-100-hp Argus, Benz and Mercedes engines, which replaced the Austro-Daimlers of the original series. Only the Austro-Hungarian Taubes continued using Austro-Daimlers.

Development of the Etrich Taube

As mentioned above, the name 'Taube', originally the name of a single type, became the general name for a whole class of aircraft. The same thing was to happen many years later in the case of the term 'Stuka', which was not a nickname for the Ju87 but became such because the Ju87 was a *Sturzkampfflugzeug* (dive bomber) *par excellence*, and in the case of the Russian term *Shturmovik* ('assaulter'), used almost exclusively to describe the heavily armoured Ilyushin IL-2.

The Etrich factory (*Motor Luftfahrtzeuge GmbH*, originally In Vienna, later in Josefstadt in Bohemia) turned out two principal series of Taube aircraft, which were known as Etr. A I and Etr. A II. The former carried an 85-hp engine, the latter a 120-hp engine, both Austro-Daimlers. The second series was slightly modernized (1) by the adoption of a front radiator instead of the two elements applied to the structure supporting the wing control cables; (2) by the use of a tail wheel instead of a skid; and (3) with the elimination of the forward skid of the undercarriage. The system of control by warping was kept, however. In the Austro-Hungarian terminology, the letter A indicated aircraft of the older model, which were no longer assigned to combat missions; in German terminology, the letter A indicated an unarmed monoplane. This system, however, was adopted after hostilities were well under way, when Taubes marked with the black cross had already taken part in operations on the Italian front and possibly on the Balkan and Russian fronts as well.

The few existing older Taubes powered by 60-hp engines were used as training aircraft.

In Germany, besides Rumpler, other firms which built Taube airplanes included the *Albatroswerke* (Johannisthal), *Deutsche Flugzeugwerke* (Leipzig), *Goedecker* (Mainz-Gonsenheim), *Harlan, Kondor* (Essen), *Gothaer Wagonfabrik* (Gotha), *Emil Jeannin* (Johannisthal), *Halberstadt* (formerly Bristol); the Lübeck Naval Yard and *Roland (Luftfahrtzeug GmbH,* Berlin). Others which built planes very much like the Taube included Ehrler, with a seaplane version, following the example of Rumpler, and possibly the Etrich Austrian plant. All of these factories rang many variations on the basic design, including considerable changes in dimensions, to the point where some Taube aircraft were three-seaters, but without ever changing the characteristic wing design. The fuselage was, on the other hand, freely varied, sometimes with an oval cross section which provided good streamline qualities (the Albatros-Hirth, for example, of 1912-13). The Austrian Etrich Taube of 1913 had already abandoned the Blériot-type undercarriage in place of a much simpler arrangement. Many changes, some of them quite drastic, were made in the tail structure. Jeannin was the only builder to introduce a radical structural change, in his *Stahltaube* ('steel dove') of 1913.

How the Taube was used in World War I

After the development of various models, including two-seaters and three-seaters, featuring various improvements, only a rather limited production was undertaken in the Austro-Hungarian empire, and for economic reasons Etrich was forced to find a market in Germany. After several fruitless attempts at interesting the German government, Etrich turned over his rights to the Rumpler factory, and Rumpler succeeded where Etrich had failed. The Germans gave him a first order for 20 planes, and in those days that was a big order. Some time later the Austrian government set up its own company in Germany under the name *Etrich-Fliegerwerke,* at Liebau, in Silesia.

This commercial success was the natural result of the fine performance of this rather heavy but very reliable monoplane. The Taube had distinguished itself in competitions, winning the 'Prince Heinrich' race in 1912 and setting an altitude record of about 6,000 meters on July 9, 1914 (the former victory was won by a Harlan Taube, the latter by a Rumpler powered by a 100-hp Benz engine). In all of these events the Taube had demonstrated good handling qualities generally, rising to meet every challenge satisfactorily, and had also shown signs of being a useful offensive device.

In fact, a Taube was the first aircraft from which a bomb had ever been dropped. In 1911, during the Libyan campaign of the Italian-Turkish War, two Taube aircraft were assigned to the Italian squadron in Tripoli. The commanding officer, Lieut. Giulio Gavotti, had already piloted a Taube during military maneuvers in August 1911 in the Monferrato area. The planes in Tripoli were two-seaters, and a two-man crew was assigned to several reconnaissance missions; but frequently, to increase his flying range, Gavotti flew alone, since the remarkable stability of the Taube let him fly and observe with binoculars at the same time. On November 1 he replaced his second pilot with a load of 2-kg Cipelli bombs and thus became the first airman to bomb from an aircraft.

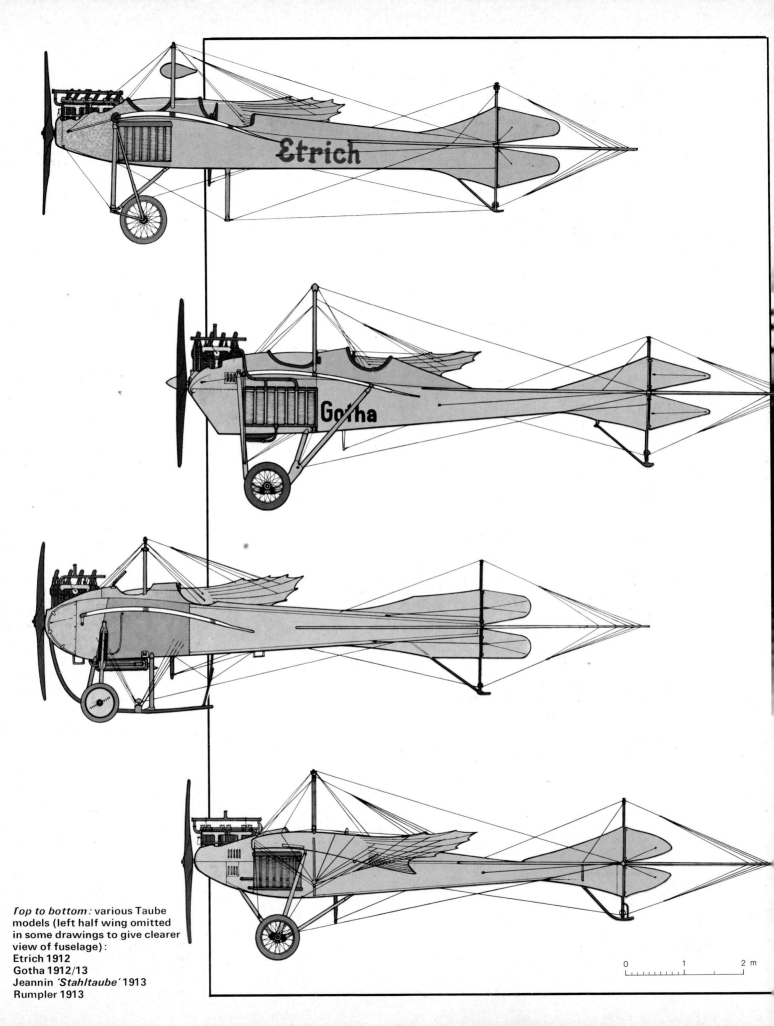

Top to bottom: various Taube
models (left half wing omitted
in some drawings to give clearer
view of fuselage):
Etrich 1912
Gotha 1912/13
Jeannin *'Stahltaube'* 1913
Rumpler 1913

0   1   2 m

30

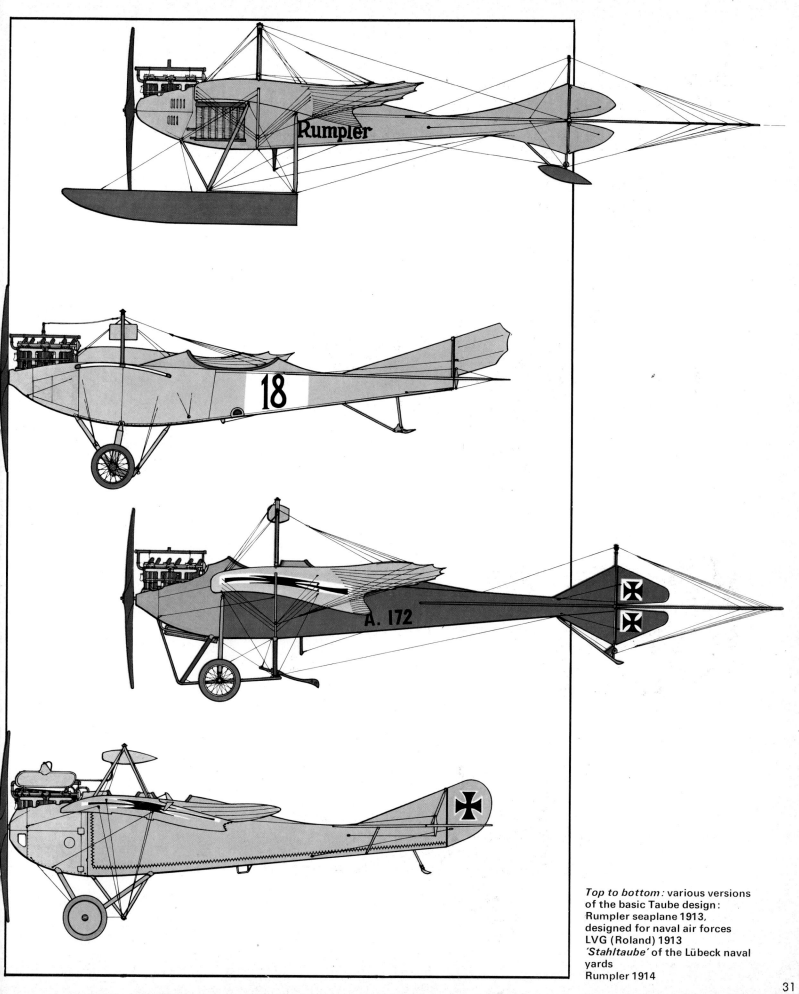

Top to bottom: various versions of the basic Taube design:
Rumpler seaplane 1913, designed for naval air forces
LVG (Roland) 1913
'Stahltaube' of the Lübeck naval yards
Rumpler 1914

31

Three photographs of a Taube being readied for take-off in an early air show. Top and center: *The complex undercarriage and tail skid are visible, as well as the wheels which served as yaw-control devices on early planes;* bottom: *A Taube being wheeled out, probably at the beginning of a race or other competition*

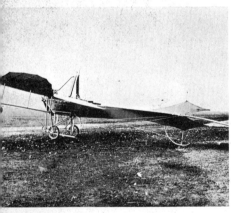

Gavotti's bombs were almost harmless, but their use made a strong impression on the general staffs of practically every nation. The aircraft had finally proved itself capable of striking directly at the enemy—of not being limited only to reconnaissance. This achievement resulted in an order for 20 aircraft from the Rumpler plant, and other orders followed, together with a number of orders for the German branch of Etrich and several other firms which were working under license or simply turning out unauthorized aircraft resembling the Taube in design.

One of the first nations to order the sturdy little monoplane was Turkey, which had learned its lesson at the hands of the Italians and thus had an air arm ready for the second Balkan war when that quarrel broke out in 1912. Although there is little definite documentation on the matter, there were doubtless a number of Taubes flown by belligerents in that brief conflict. The Turkish planes were from the Harlan factory.

The Japanese were also Rumpler customers, having bought one possibly as early as 1913 and certainly having acquired two of the planes in 1915 to use against another German Taube operating out of Tsingtao.

Military Taubes were very active in the period just before the Great War, not only in important maneuvers and training programs but also in sport flying, with many military pilots taking part in such events both for training and propaganda.

Especially noteworthy among these competitions was the 'Prince Heinrich's regularity Race', organized by the Kaiser's brother in 1911. In its last run, in 1914, it involved a competition over a 2,400 km total course (1,491 miles) in laps of 400 and 600 km, to be covered in nine days, including two rest days, with exercises in reconnaissance. Another contest was the Rally of May 5, 1914, which required seven squadrons to reach Döberitz (nr. Berlin) from various areas, some of them as much as 600 km distant, in unfavorable weather conditions. In 1912 the Kaiser ordered planes assigned to each military Zeppelin, and this program led to the Taube's being selected as the basic component of the nascent German air force.

In August, 1914, the air arm of the German Army had 246 planes assigned to 41 army units. Of these, about half were various models of the single- and two-seater Taube aircraft. However, the rigors of active military service soon showed up the age of these machines, which had remained almost as they had been in the earliest pioneer days of successful heavier-than-air flight, and the Taubes, compared with newer planes, was no longer impressive. They remained for a few months at the front, where they acquitted themselves with honor and were then withdrawn. The first bombardment of Paris, for example, was assigned to Lieut. Franz von Hiddeson, who dropped four 18-kg bombs on the Parisian suburbs on 13 August. A few days later, Lieut. Max Immelmann, who was to become a greater fighter ace, flew his Taube over Paris dropping leaflets calling on the French to surrender. These harmless bits of derring-do gave the Taube good publicity: its birdlike silhouette caught the popular fancy, and it soon acquired a reputation for martial qualities which it actually didn't possess. In fact this rather slow monoplane had made such an impression that, for quite some time, the name 'Taube' was applied by the French to every German aircraft they set their eyes on. Another element which contributed to the mystery of the Taube's 'personality' was its relative invisibility, due to the translucence of the light-colored fabric covering on its wings. Above 300 meters it practically disappeared.

Meanwhile on the other side of the earth a German naval pilot, Lieut. Günther Plütschow, was flying his Taube on reconnaissance around the German-occupied free port of Tsingtao on Kiaochow Bay, where the cruiser *Emden* was stationed. Japanese forces were besieging Tsingtao, and their facilities included Farman and Nieuport airplanes. Plütschow attacked a Japanese ship with two bombs on October 2, 1915, without making a hit, however. On October 13 three Japanese aircraft tried to intercept Plütschow's Taube, which was able to escape thanks to its higher ceiling (he climbed to 3000 meters).

After these incidents the Taube was overestimated in Japan as it had been in France, and two Rumpler Taubes belonging to the Imperial Aeronautical Association were rushed to the scene under the command of Cmdr. Isobe. Isobe took off on November 5 for his first combat flight, which ended up in a bad landing. The garrison at Tsingtao surrendered on November 7, 1915, but Plütschow escaped with his plane to Hai-Jow, where he burned it to keep it out of the enemy's hands. He then set out for Germany, where he arrived after a long and adventurous trip which he described in a book entitled *The Tsingtao Aviator.*

German and Austrian Taubes were useful at the front in noncombat roles until early in 1915, when they were retired from active duty. Second-generation Taubes, some of them biplanes, were not very successful.

SOPWITH CAMEL

Sopwith Camel F.1. More than 500 of these planes were produced during World War I. (Archivio Bignozzi)

The most famous British fighter plane of World War I, and one of the best aircraft of any type in those early years, was the Sopwith Camel, a biplane of legendary—even excessive—maneuverability, well armed and fast. It was built in considerable numbers, estimated by various authorities as between 5490 and 5695 machines or even more. The Camel achieved the record for the number of enemy aircraft downed—1294. It was also credited with the first night kill by a fighter plane when a Gotha bomber was shot down over London on January 25, 1918, and Lieut. S. D. Culley was the first pilot to destroy a German airship, the Zeppelin L.53, which he set afire on August 10 of the same year.

The Camel was designed by Herbert Smith on the basis of suggestions made by the directors of the Sopwith Corporation (T. O. M. Sopwith, Fred Sigrist, Harry Hawker). In their conception, which extended the natural lines of development of the earlier Sopwith Pup and the Sopwith Triplane, the new plane was designed to re-establish the balance of power against the new two-gun German fighters,

particularly the Albatros D.I, which had appeared on the front in September, 1916, and the D.II, which came out shortly thereafter. At the same time the Admiralty had requested development of a scout to replace the Sopwith 'Baby' seaplane, and the combination of these two requirements fathered the famous Sopwith Camel.

Technical description

The first machines were apparently an improved version of the seaplane, the F.S.1 'Improved Baby', with a 130-hp Clerget rotary engine. Following the destruction of one plane during a test flight in March 1917, a second was built as a land plane

SOPWITH CAMEL

Sopwith Camels of No. 65 Squadron, shown here with the colors of the Camel now in the RAF Museum at Hendon, near London.

m. ralli - p. dell'orco

and served as prototype for the 2F.1, which could be launched from a barge for use at sea (apparently the project of reconverting it to a seaplane for operational tests on the Belgian coast was never carried through). The two first aircraft ordered by the Admiralty were land planes, as were the three prototypes ordered by the Royal Flying Corps.

The F.1 was originally to have equal dihedral on both wings, but to speed up production it was decided to use a flat, single-piece upper wing, with the dihedral of the lower wing doubled as compensation. As it turned out, only the first prototype had a single-piece upper wing, after which the wing was built in three sections, as originally planned; no restoration of the dihedral was made, however.

The plane was extremely compact, and this quality, together with the generous dimensions of the tail and the presence of ailerons on both wings, gave the Camel outstanding agility, which was increased by the torque effect of the powerful rotary engine. The concentration of the main masses (engine, fuel, armament, pilot) in a small space made it possible for the Camel to make extremely tight turns, but the torque reaction forced the nose upward in left turns and downward in right turns. This fault, negative in so many ways, was exploited by some pilots: wanting to turn right, they would make a very tight left turn through 270°. This three-quarter circle was a strange way of turning right, but it was justified by the peculiar maneuverability of the Camel.

It took a very expert pilot, of course, and one familiar with every last quirk of the Camel, to be able to exploit even its faults, and any pilot who wasn't aware of them paid dearly for his ignorance. The Camel brought down a goodly harvest of enemy planes, but at the cost of quite a number of British pilots who hadn't fully understood the tricky instability of the new aircraft. Fearful as it was to its own pilots as well as to the enemy, the Camel owed its success in part to the fact that it was flown only by the best pilots around.

The airframe structure was wholly of wood, covered with fabric except immediately aft of the engine (where the covering was of aluminum alloy), on the sides of the cockpit and on the fuselage decking (which was of plywood). The trailing edge and the wing tips were of steel tubing. Production aircraft had longer ailerons than the prototypes. The F.1/1 had tapered wings, but this modification apparently did not offer enough advantage to offset the additional work involved, so the rectangular wings continued to be used. After tests made in 1917, the idea of producing the modified Camel in series as the 4F.1 was abandoned.

The Camel's guns were mounted close together, and the humped fairing over the gun breeches led to its exotic name (which never became official). The guns were two fixed 7·7-mm Vickers with a Constantinescu synchronizing mechanism for use with the 110-hp Le Rhône engine. In night flight the flashes from the guns tended to blind the pilot, so many of the aircraft assigned to Home Defence duties were modified by moving the cockpit aft and putting the main fuel tank forward of the cockpit and replacing the synchronized Vickers by fitting two Lewis guns on double Foster mounts (originally designed for another fighter, the S.E.5). This arrangement made it possible to incline the guns for reloading with 47-round drums.

In this solution the guns fired over the wing. Some pilots preferred a middle way (adopted in the 2F.1), with one Vickers and one Lewis gun, where the upper gun was fitted on an Admiralty mounting. It was possible to add racks for four small bombs beneath the fuselage.

An interesting development was the TF.1 'Trench Fighter'. Forerunner of the assault plane, the TF.1 was an F.1 armed with three Lewis guns, two of them downward-firing, the third mounted on the center section. The objective was to be able to fire into enemy trenches at low skimming altitudes. For protection against ground fire, the pilot and fuel tanks were protected by an 11-mm steel plate. Only one plane was modified in this way. Other solutions were proposed, such as guns firing obliquely to the rear. Preference was given to the project designated as TF.2 (which led to the development of the Salamander). The Camel was used with excellent results for close support of ground forces, sometimes with standard armament.

The engine used most often on the Camel was the French 9-cylinder 130-hp Clerget rotary (140-hp on the latest production machines). Many planes, however, carried the 110-hp Le Rhône, and all machines of the 2F.1 series had the 150-hp Bentley BR.1. At the end of the war there were 1342 Camels with 130-hp Clergets and at least 427 with the 140-hp version, while only 356 were powered by Bentleys, since the latter were never produced in sufficient quantity to satisfy all those pilots who wanted them for the reliability and power. All 181 planes flown by the Home Defence were powered by 110-hp Le Rhônes.

Among many experiments, mention should be

Sopwith Camel 2F.1. Note synchronized Vickers machine gun over the engine cowling and the Lewis gun on the upper wing center section. The small propeller on one of the cabane struts served to turn the generator. Power plant is a 130-hp Clerget rotary engine. (Archivio Bignozzi)

made of the installation of a 100-hp Gnôme Monosoupape (the power of which could be varied by using some odd number of its nine cylinders). The Gnôme was scheduled for installation in 300 planes earmarked for delivery to the US, but these aircraft ended up with 130-hp Clergets instead. In the autumn of 1918 tests were run with the 170-to-186-hp Le Rhône.

The bad reputation which the Camel had among inexperienced pilots was due in part to the idiosyncrasies of the engines, especially the Clergets, which would flood after take-off if the fine-adjustment fuel control was not used immediately to give a leaner mixture. Neophyte pilots also risked stalling at the critical phase of take-off, and a good number of crashes did in fact occur.

Development of the Sopwith Camel

The 2F.1, the so-called 'Ship Camel', was derived from the standard model. It differed by a reduction in the wing span, which resulted from a variation in manufacturing technique as applied to the center section of the upper wing, and by the two-piece fuselage, which could be taken apart. Both of these modifications facilitated stowing of the aircraft for seagoing use. From January 1918 on, modifications were made in the elevator and rudder controls: the cables were run entirely outside the fuselage so that they would not be in the way of the four inflatable bags designed to keep the plane afloat in case of forced landing at sea—a fairly frequent emergency.

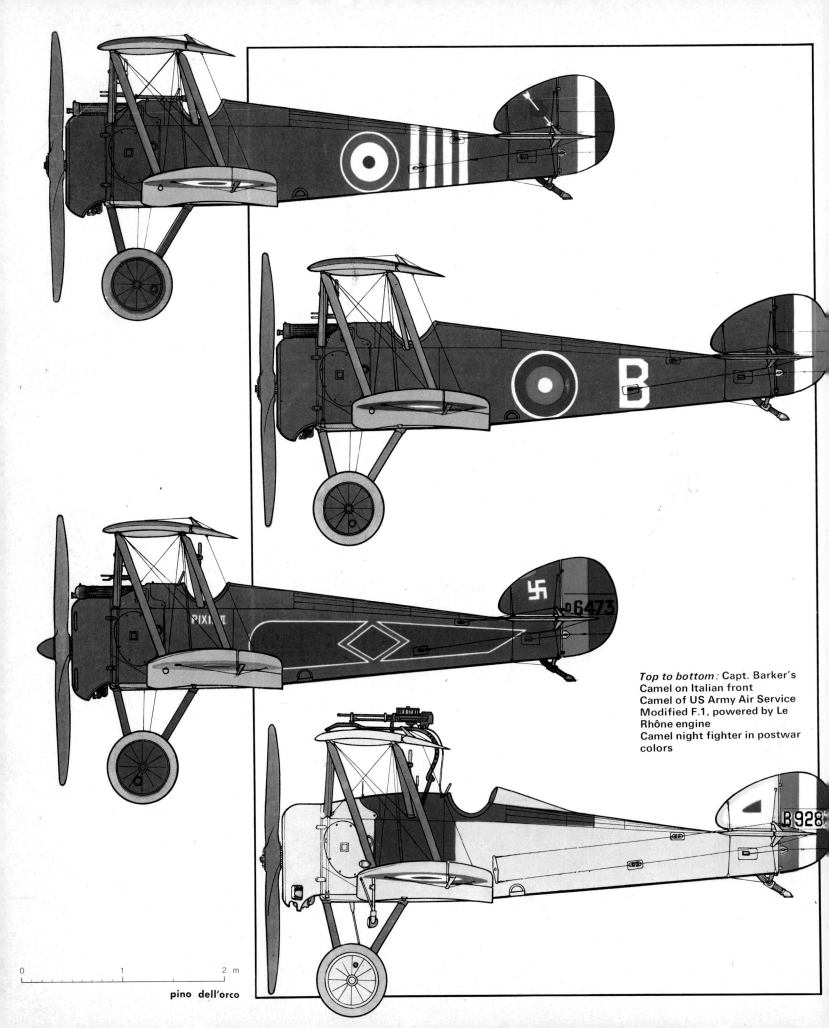

Top to bottom: Capt. Barker's Camel on Italian front
Camel of US Army Air Service
Modified F.1, powered by Le Rhône engine
Camel night fighter in postwar colors

0   1   2 m

pino dell'orco

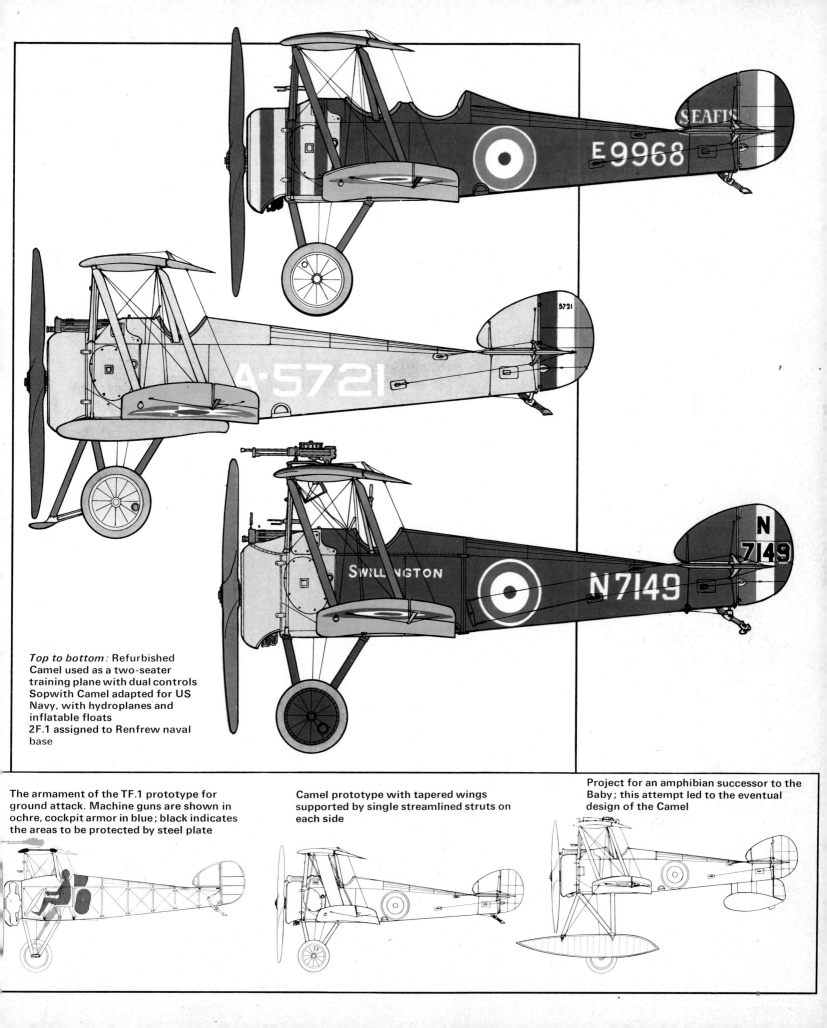

Top to bottom: Refurbished Camel used as a two-seater training plane with dual controls
Sopwith Camel adapted for US Navy, with hydroplanes and inflatable floats
2F.1 assigned to Renfrew naval base

The armament of the TF.1 prototype for ground attack. Machine guns are shown in ochre, cockpit armor in blue; black indicates the areas to be protected by steel plate

Camel prototype with tapered wings supported by single streamlined struts on each side

Project for an amphibian successor to the Baby; this attempt led to the eventual design of the Camel

Because of a shortage of suitable vessels for naval aviation uses, the British carried out a series of experiments to test the feasibility of launching aircraft from lighters towed at high speed by destroyers. Above, a Sopwith 2F.1 Camel takes off from a lighter with Lieut. S. D. Culley at the controls. Culley later brought down a Zeppelin, and his Sopwith Camel is now in the Imperial War Museum, London. (Hawker Siddeley Review)

There were other minor differences in the landing gear and tail skid. Experiments were also made on the feasibility of attaching floats to the landing gear and skid for use at sea, as well as external inflatable bags.

How the Sopwith Camel was used in World War I

No fewer than 1379 out of the 4188 Camels on active duty were used by fighter training schools. From the autumn of 1918 on, some were converted into two-seater training planes by reducing the dimensions of the main fuel tank, eliminating armament and adding a second cockpit.

The Camel became operational as a fighter in July 1917.

The first squadron to be equipped with the new plane was No. 70, RFC, on the French front. Other units flying Camels followed in England, France and Italy.

In Italy the first Camels arrived, with British pilots, after the retreat from Caporetto. The first planes landed in Milan on November 12,1917, and it was on the Italian front that a British pilot, Alan Jerrard, won the only Victoria Cross (the highest British decoration for valor) ever awarded to a Camel pilot. Other groups of Camels flew in the Aegean, the Balkans and, from 1918 to 1920, in Russia.

The naval version of the Camel was used at sea, being launched from battleships, cruisers and the flight decks of the first make-shift aircraft carriers, *Campania* and *Manxman,* as well as from barges towed by destroyers. About 130 aircraft were used in this way in the North Sea, chiefly in operations against Zeppelins but also to a limited extent on

special bombing missions against German airship bases.

In countries outside Great Britain Camels were used by American and Belgian airmen. The Americans also used some of the 2F.1s. Several F.1s were assigned to the combined Russian-British units in the civil war between White and Red Russians after the October Revolution. Polish pilots also flew Camels in Russia. Earlier a number of Greek pilots had also flown Camels in the Aegean.

The 2F.1 model was also operational abroad. In 1924 several of these aircraft were sent to Canada (where the last one was still flying in 1929), and after the war Camels were also used by the new air forces of Estonia, Latvia, and Lithuania. It also had a great influence on the development of Japanese fighter planes assigned to aircraft carriers. (Shortly after the war Herbert Smith went to work in Japan, where he designed the first aircraft to be built by the Mitsubishi Co.)

In the summer of 1918 there was also an experiment carried out aimed at providing fighter escort to airships. A 2F.1 was released in flight from the British dirigible R.23, using a support for the plane attached to the belly of the airship. The experiment was successful but was not followed up at that time because it was an excessively complicated procedure.

Capt. J. L. Trollope of No. 43 Sqn., RAF, was one of the outstanding Camel pilots of the first air war. He once shot down six enemy aircraft in a single day, one of them another fighter. This record was later tied by Capt. H. W. Wollett of No. 209 Squadron. Another fighter ace whose fame is associated with that of the Camel was the Canadian pilot Maj. William George Barker, who chalked up the majority of his 53 victories with the Camel. Barker was active for an extended tour on the Italian front. Another ace was Lieut. S. D. Culley. Taking off from a towed barge to intercept a German dirigible, he succeeded in downing the airship by firing from below, although the altitude of the dirigible was greater than the Camel's effective ceiling.

The most famous, but at the same time most controversial, victory attributed to a Sopwith Camel was the downing of Manfred von Richthofen, the Red Baron, by the Canadian ace, Capt. A. R. Brown of No. 209 Squadron. His feat, however, has been disputed by some historians, and the controversy continues to this day.

FARMAN 1914

Specifications

	Maurice Farman 1914	Henry Farman 1914
Power Plant	Renault 70-hp	Gnôme 60-hp
Wing span, *m*	16·13	15·58
Length, *m*	9·48	8·86
Height, *m*	3·20	3·20
Wing area, *m²*	54	46
Empty weight, *kg*	510	385
Total weight, *kg*	810	710
Maximum speed, *km/h*	100	100
Climb to 2000 *m*	22·0 min	22·0 min
Flight endurance	approx. 3 hrs	approx. 3·5 hrs

Henry and Maurice Farman, two brothers of British origin, were among the prime movers in the development of aviation in France in the second decade of the century. Henry's career as a builder of aircraft began when he bought one of the earliest Voisin planes, which he modified greatly by eliminating the lateral surfaces between the upper and lower wings, adding a small forward stabilizer and introducing ailerons to improve maneuverability. With this plane he soon set a number of records—on January 13, 1908, he made the first 1-km circular flight in Europe, and in October of the same year the first cross-country flight, from Châlons to Rheims, a distance of 26·4 km. He designed his first

Top: *the second Henry Farman aircraft built in Italy by the Aviation Works of the Specialists' Battalion in Rome*
Center: *one of the earliest Farmans*
Bottom: *a Henry Farman 1910 rounding a pylon at low level during an early air race*

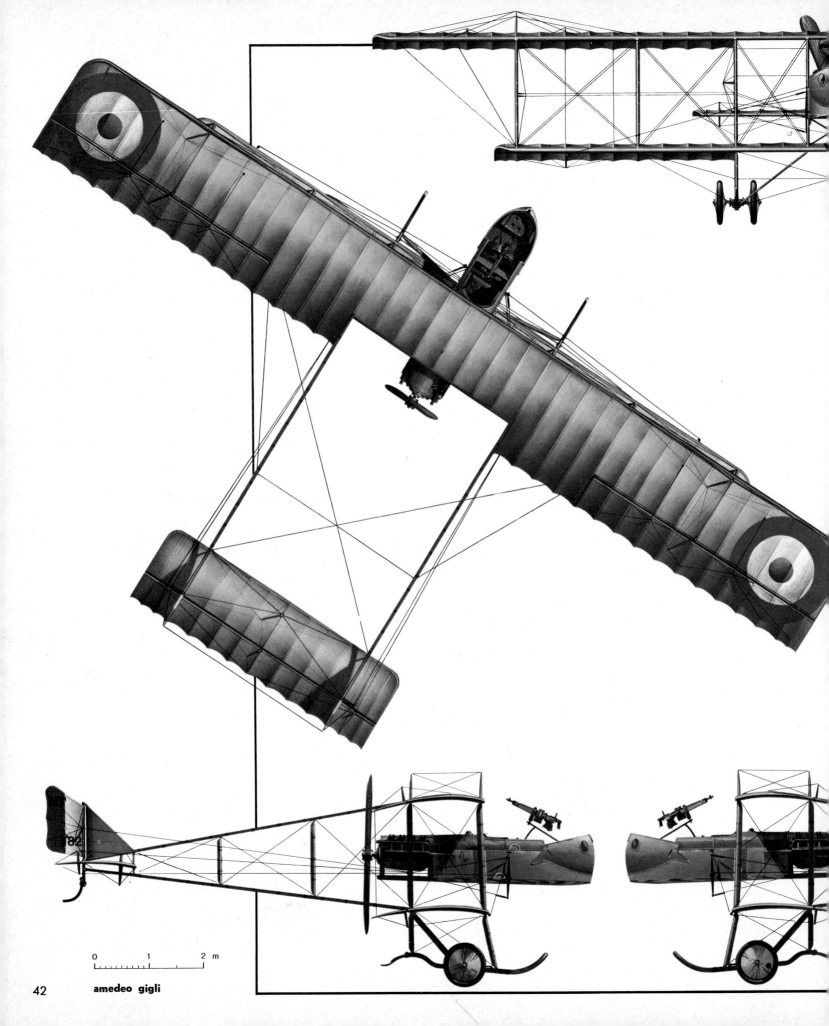

amedeo gigli

0   1   2 m

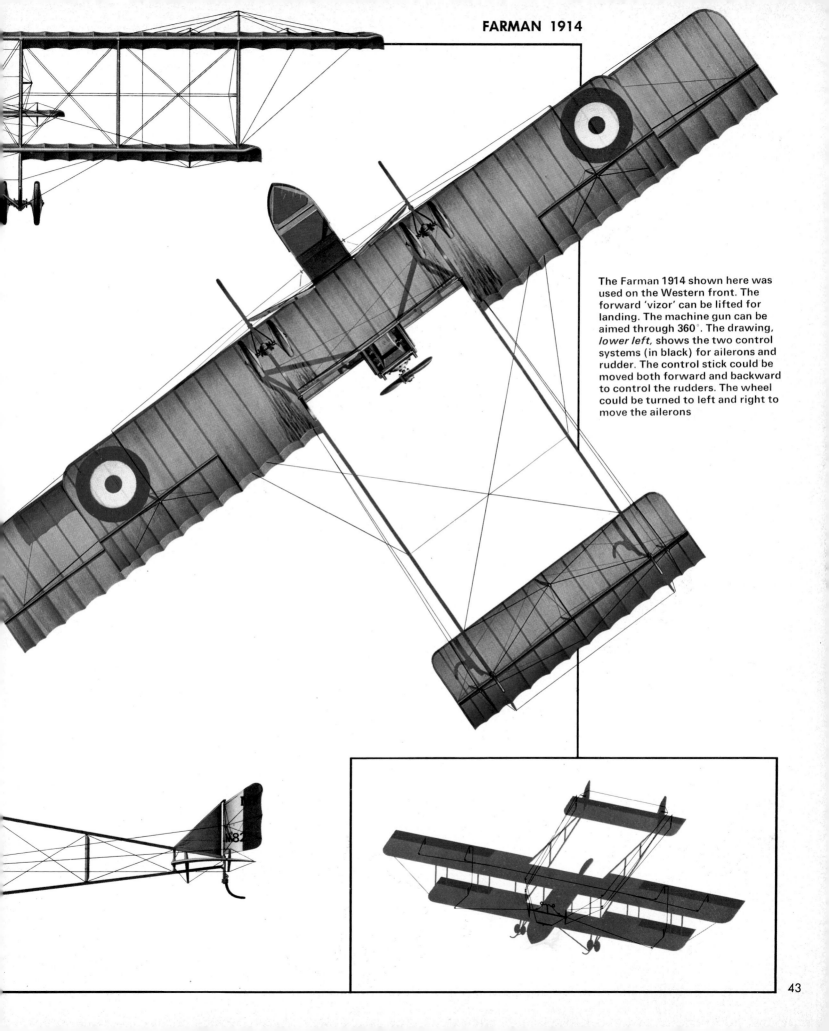

FARMAN 1914

The Farman 1914 shown here was used on the Western front. The forward 'vizor' can be lifted for landing. The machine gun can be aimed through 360°. The drawing, *lower left,* shows the two control systems (in black) for ailerons and rudder. The control stick could be moved both forward and backward to control the rudders. The wheel could be turned to left and right to move the ailerons

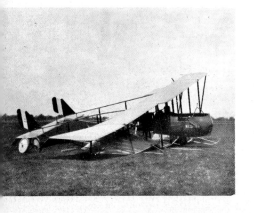

A squadron of Italian-built Maurice Farman MF.11s. These planes usually had the earliest wartime markings — rudders and undersurface of lower wing marked with the red, white and green Italian tricolor. Opposite page, in oval: Pilot and observer in the characteristic cockpit of an MF.11. The weapon is a Fiat machine gun. (Archivio Falessi)

A Savoia-built Farman F.11 damaged in a ground-loop while landing. (Museo Caproni, Taliedo)

commercially successful airplane in 1910. It was used widely by the French and, as a trainer, by the British and the Italians. Licensing agreements led to the manufacture of the plane abroad, notably by the German Albatros firm.

In the summer of 1910 one of Henry Farman's planes landed at the Italian military school at Centocelle, near Rome. It had been bought by a private citizen, not by the government — Lieut. Vivaldi-Pasqua, who had been in training at the Mourmelon Le Grand school in France. The machine was powered by a 65-hp Renault engine; its maximum speed was not much above 50 km/hr. Vivaldi-Pasqua started flying his new Farman on August 11. On August 15 he set a record of almost 5 hours in the air in a number of flights, and on August 16 he made another ten flights to add 4 hours to his record. On August 20 he crashed while making a turn and was killed. He was the first Italian military airman to die in a flying accident. Later the army's Specialists' Brigade built three copies of the airplane.

Other Farmans were purchased in France or built under license by Italian firms. In a short time the Farman was better represented in Italy than almost any other type of aircraft.

In 1912 Maurice Farman joined his brother who, until that time, had been an independent builder of aircraft. The two brothers had been designing different types of aircraft until then, but when they joined forces they started to unify their production, and soon all their planes were known simply as Farman aircraft. The firm, known as the *Société Henry et Maurice Farman,* was located at Billancourt.

Technical description

There are so many types and subtypes of these early Farmans that it is hard to list them all. They differed in many details, such as the number of rudders, and in the wing configurations — either with both wings of equal span or with the lower shortened and the upper lengthened. The cockpit could be covered or open, and power plants varied from the

50- or 60-hp Gnômes to 70-hp Renaults and the Dion-Bouton engines. The Henry Farman 1912 was powered by a 60-hp Gnôme; it had a span of 14·40 m and was 13·80 m long. The Maurice Farman 1912, with a span of 15·00 m, was 12 m long and was powered by a 70-hp Renault engine.

Three models are generally labeled Farman 1914. Except for a few minor differences, the basic structure was fairly simple: The 1914 was a biplane, with the upper wing generally longer than the lower. The lower wing, made up of three hinged sections, was joined by a split-pin system. The wings were supported by wooden struts, usually of ash, braced with steel wire. The tail elements were of similar structure. The framework fuselage was composed of four main longerons joined to the wings and braced with wire. The longerons also gave support to the tail elements. The tail itself was fitted, on the underside, with a steel spring *(béquille)* to assist in braking on landing.

The wings were equipped with ailerons. The stabilizer consisted of two surfaces (only the upper had an elevator) on the Henry Farman models up to 1912 and on the Maurice Farman models through the MF.7. Later models were monoplanes.

Only the earliest models had forward stabilizers. Two rubber-tired bicycle wheels sprung by an elastic system made up the landing gear. Skids, present on earlier models, were sometimes used on the 1914 versions, especially on the Maurice Farman 1914. They were entirely absent from the Horace Farman model. (Horace=*H*enry+*M*aurice; explained below.)

The cockpit was of the cabin type, mounted between the wings in a slightly forward position; it could accommodate two or, in exceptional cases, three crew. The engine, a 'pusher' type, was mounted aft of the cabin. It drove a walnut propeller with the leading edges sheathed in brass.

As in all aircraft of the period, instrumentation was minimal: an altimeter, a clock and a manometer. An air pump was available to increase fuel tank pressure when necessary. The sole control was the stick, which was used for both ailerons and elevators. A few British-built Farmans were powered by 135-to-140-hp engines, far more powerful than the standard Gnôme, Renault or Dion-Bouton engines.

vertically. Bombs were released through a long vertical tube, similar to that which the earliest bombardiers had used on Blériot planes in Libya. Basic specifications of the Farman were: wing span, 10·61 m; length, 11·58 m; weight, empty, 235 kg.

The definitive versions of the new planes designed by the Farmans came out just before the beginning of World War I and shortly thereafter they joined forces in producing a unified Farman which they called 'the Horace Farman', *Horace* being not a third brother but a kind of corporate compromise created from *Henry* and *Maurice*. There were eventually several models of the Horace design, the last of which was the F.27, with a metal frame, equal span wings, and a new type of undercarriage similar to that used on the Voisin planes. The engines were, on the whole, more powerful, up to the 140-hp Salmson.

In the early days when there were two distinct lines of Farmans, Maurice had followed up his MF.7 with an MF.11, which was accepted by the French as an operational warplane in May 1915. In England the same plane, but without the forward stabilizer and its mount, was nicknamed the 'Shorthorn'. The aft stabilizer was monoplanar, with two rudders. The cockpit was slung between the wings.

The Italians had purchased a few of the new Farmans from France but were soon turning them out under licensing agreement at the SIA plant at Mirafiori. The Italian version of the MF.7 was called the F5B. The Savoia plant built the MF.11, Henry's HF.22 and the Horace at Turro Milanese and Bovisio. The MF.11 was designed to accept many types of engine; as a rule it was equipped with a 70-to-80-hp Renault, often with the Italian Fiat A.10 and occasionally the Rolls-Royce Hawk or the Curtiss OX-5. Most Italian Farmans had the 100-hp Fiat A.10 or the 100-hp Colombo engine, although some, particularly those assigned to the training schools, were powered by the 100-hp Gnôme.

As in the case of the MF.7, there were both land and sea versions of the MF 1914. The latter, of which there were two types, were used chiefly by the British.

The Horace Farmans were of several generations —including the F.30, 40, 41, 56, 60 and 61. The basic design was quite similar to the late Henry Farmans, with structural elements joined at the rudder post to support the single plane of the stabilizer. The cockpit was mounted between the wings, as in the Maurice Farman designs. The F.41 had wings of reduced span; the cockpit was identical to that of the MF.11-*bis*. The F.56 was identical to the F.41, but with large side radiators and long exhausts for the 170-hp Renault. The F.60 and 61 versions were identical to the F.40 and 41 except for the engine, which was a 190-hp Renault.

The British designation for the Horace Farman was F.40; it was essentially a synthesis of two versions of the 1914 model as designed by the two brothers. Guided by their experience with other Farmans, the British equipped it with a 135-hp engine built for them by Renault.

Development of the Farman 1914

A version of the Henry Farman plane which was popular among Italian aviators in Libya was the 'reduced' model, that is, with a noticeably shortened lower wing. This machine is representative of the Farman production of that period. It had a double undercarriage and skids, the forward stabilizer was supported on convergent beams, and the aft stabilizer was of biplane design. The rudder was usually double (but not always), and set at the center. The cockpit, wholly open, could accommodate a second crew member if needed. The frame was of wood. Roll control was handled by ailerons which were kept in the level position in flight by the air flow; on the ground the ailerons hung down

Take-off of a Maurice Farman MF.11 equipped with rocket launcher, visible between the wing struts (below). Rockets were used to set fire to enemy observation balloons. The machine on the ground is an SIA 5B, which was the Italian version of the Maurice Farman 1914, powered by a Fiat A 10 engine. (Aeronautica Militare Italiana)

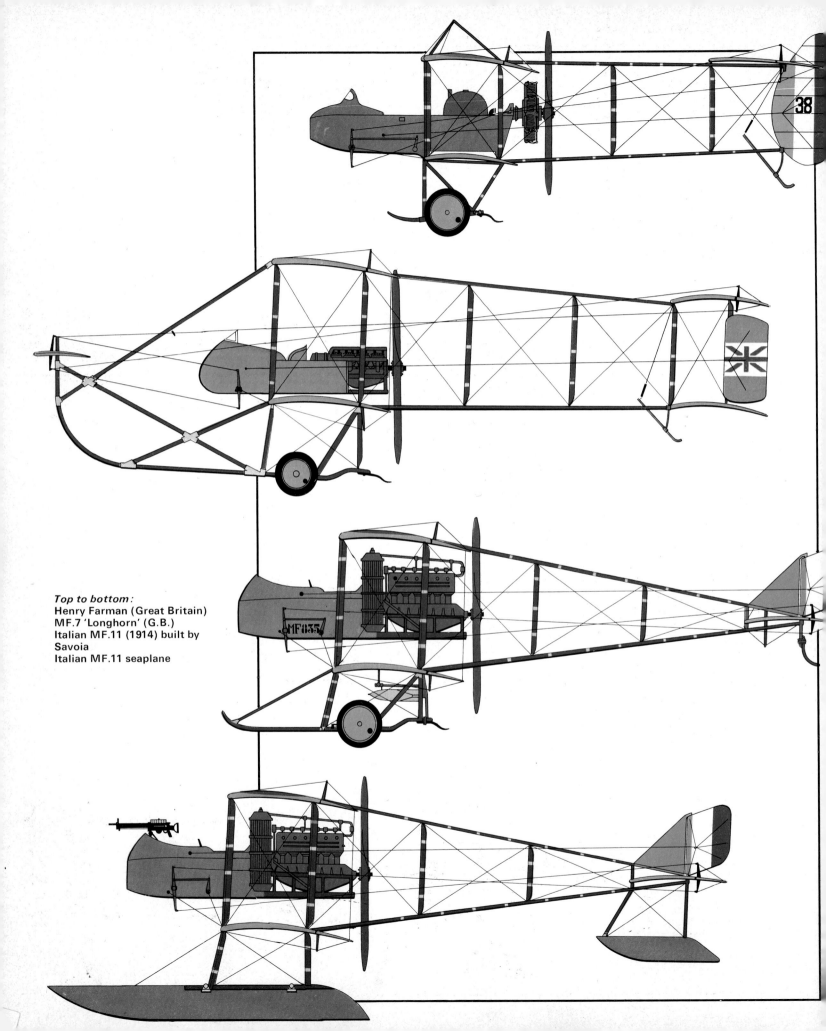

38

Top to bottom:
Henry Farman (Great Britain)
MF.7 'Longhorn' (G.B.)
Italian MF.11 (1914) built by
Savoia
Italian MF.11 seaplane

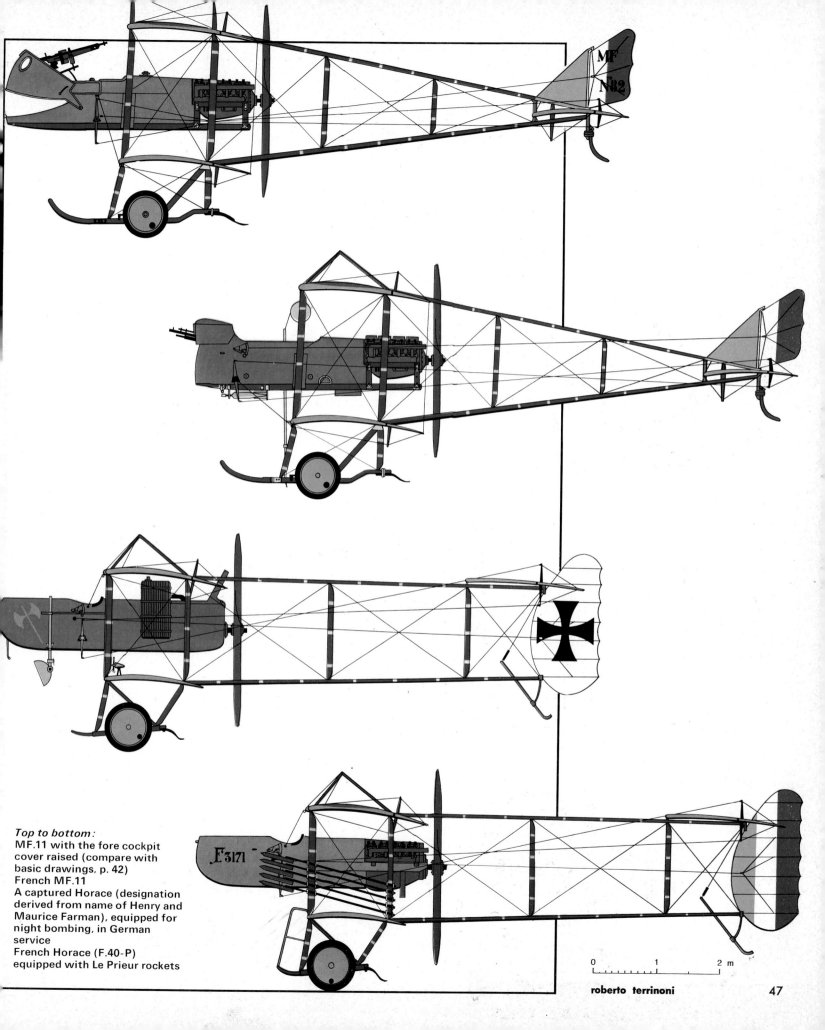

Top to bottom:
MF.11 with the fore cockpit
cover raised (compare with
basic drawings, p. 42)
French MF.11
A captured Horace (designation
derived from name of Henry and
Maurice Farman), equipped for
night bombing, in German
service
French Horace (F.40-P)
equipped with Le Prieur rockets

roberto terrinoni

47

How the Farmans were used in World War I

Farman aircraft were among the first used in active warfare, since the Italians chose the Farman 1912 as their weapon in the Libyan War after their use in maneuvers and training schools had demonstrated the safety, load capacity and visibility of these machines. Two Henry Farmans, powered by 50-hp Gnômes, were assigned to the 1st *Squadriglia* in Tripoli, and two more were soon added to the roster. With one of these planes Lieut. Gavotti performed the first night flight in a combat area; he was accompanied by Piazza, who was flying a Blériot. Another 50-hp Farman joined the *Squadriglia Bengasi,* and three others went to the Tobruk Civilian Aviators' Fleet *(Flottiglia Aviatori Civili).* One of the planes of the latter group, piloted by Capt. Montù, was hit by enemy fire during a reconnaissance flight on January 31, 1912, and Montù thus became the first aviator to be wounded by enemy fire in the air in the history of aviation. The French and Spanish air arms also used Farman aircraft in their colonial operations in North Africa.

The Maurice Farman MF.7s were used by the French, Italians and British; the British assigned them to the Royal Naval Air Service. At the end of 1913 the Italians had five squadrons of MF.7s. They were also used in various countries for interesting experimental activities, including investigation of the potential of machine-gun operation and photographic reconnaissance. In 1912 an experimenter from the Italian Navy, Alessandro Guidoni, carried out tests on the launching of weights from aircraft, providing valuable background for the development of aerial torpedoes to be used against ships.

The British gave the nickname 'Longhorn' to the MF.7 when they started to build it under license at the Aircraft Manufacturing Co. Ltd. Later the Longhorns were also manufactured by Brush, Robey and the Phoenix Dynamo Co. At first they used 70- and 80-hp Renault engines, Sunbeams and Rolls-Royce 75-hp Hawks. After the war started, more powerful engines were mounted on successive models, and on some aircraft sent over from France the British mounted 100- or even 130-hp engines, including the Lorraine. The MF.7, like the Henry Farman, was used by the French and Spaniards in the suppression of Arab revolts from 1912 to 1914.

The Japanese Farmans made an important operational contribution in their siege of Tsingtao. MF.7s were used in the first pursuit attempts against the Taube of Lieut. G. Plütschow (see p. 32, Etrich

Taube). In the same campaign the Japanese Navy used two MF.7 seaplanes.

In the Balkan War of 1913, an MF.7 seaplane of the Greek air arm attacked Turkish ships with grenades and carried out reconnaissance flights together with three land planes of the same type.

We have seen how the Italians used Farmans in Libya. They also assigned Farman 1912s to an Artillery Assault squadron, training schools, and a Seaplane Section organized in December 1913. Aircraft built by both Farman brothers were used in cavalry maneuvers in 1913, and at the end of the year they were replaced, in some squadrons, by 1914 models.

The British used Farman 1914s in the Dardanelles, in Africa, and in Mesopotamia; 80 of them were assigned to the Royal Navy. Cmdr. Sampson set a new bombing record on December 18, 1915, when he dropped a 250-kg monster bomb on Turkish encampments. The French used several versions of the MF.11 on the eastern front and in Macedonia. The Royal Naval Air Service used their Farman 1914s not only in the Dardanelles but also in their Macedonian campaigns. The 1914s assigned to Belgian bases flew operations against German submarines and Zeppelin bases. A Farman of 1 Wing was credited with the destruction of a Zeppelin L.Z.38, which was attacked at the Évère base with four 10-kg bombs. The Farmans of 2 Wing sank two German submarines, using 30-kg bombs. A 'Shorthorn' of No. 3 Squadron, powered by a 130-hp engine which had been mounted in place of the standard 70- to 100-hp jobs, rang up a first on December 21, 1914, when it made the first night combat flight, dropping a dozen and a half 8-kg bombs.

In December 1915 the Farman F.30 came out. It was used mostly in Russia, where it was manufactured under license, with 130- and 160-hp Salmson engines, by 'Dux' in Moscow and a Lyebedev Works in Petrograd.

But the most important Farman in the First World War was the F.40, which the French used a great deal in all its various versions. The Belgian used it up to 1917, as did the British Navy.

The wartime service of Farman aircraft was intense but not long, especially in the front lines where they were soon surpassed by newer planes. Only in Libya did their usefulness continue, and as late as 1922 the Italians were still using them against rebellious tribesmen, but eventually they were replaced, first by Savoia-Pomilio (SP) planes which were in a sense modifications of the basic Farman designs worked out by the SIA.

Above: *Three Horace Farman F.40 sesquiplanes at a French air base.* Below: *A Maurice Farman 1914 during its first flight to Eritrea in 1920. Even after they had been withdrawn from front-line service, Farmans were still active in colonial operations and training schools.* (Musée de l'Air, Aeronautica Militare Italiana)

CAUDRON G.3

Specifications

	G.3	G.4
Power plant	Le Rhône, 90-hp	Anzani, 100-hp
Wing span, *m*	13·40	16·88
Total length, *m*	6·40	7·20
Height, *m*	2·50	2·60
Wing area, *m*	27·00	36·80
Weight, empty, *kg*	420	500
Total weight, *kg*	710	1320
Maximum speed, *km/hr*	108	130
Climb to 3000 *m*	32·0 min	19·0 min
Ceiling, *m*	4000	4000
Flight endurance	4 hrs	4 hrs

Another pair of brothers, like the Farmans, made a name for themselves in the early years of aviation. They were the French engineers, Gaston and René Caudron. Their first factory was at Rue, in the Somme, where they built a number of biplanes in the years just before the outbreak of the war. Successful both technically and commercially, their planes acquitted themselves honorably at various flying meets—and in those days such performance was a prerequisite to commercial success. Sales to private persons and military groups followed, and the Caudrons, like many another aircraft manu-

facturer, followed a wise policy of offering instruction to would-be pilots. They set up a training school at Le Crétoy *(Aérodrome de la Baie de la Somme)*. Their corporate offices were at Issay-les-Moulineaux.

Technical description

The most popular plane built by the Caudrons was the single-engine two-seater sesquiplane G.3, the definitive version of a formula which had been de-

Above: *A typical G.3 of the French military air service.* Below: *An Italian G.3. The underpart of the upper wing had the national tricolor painted as a roundel.* (Archivio Bignozzi and Aeronautica Militare Italiana)

49

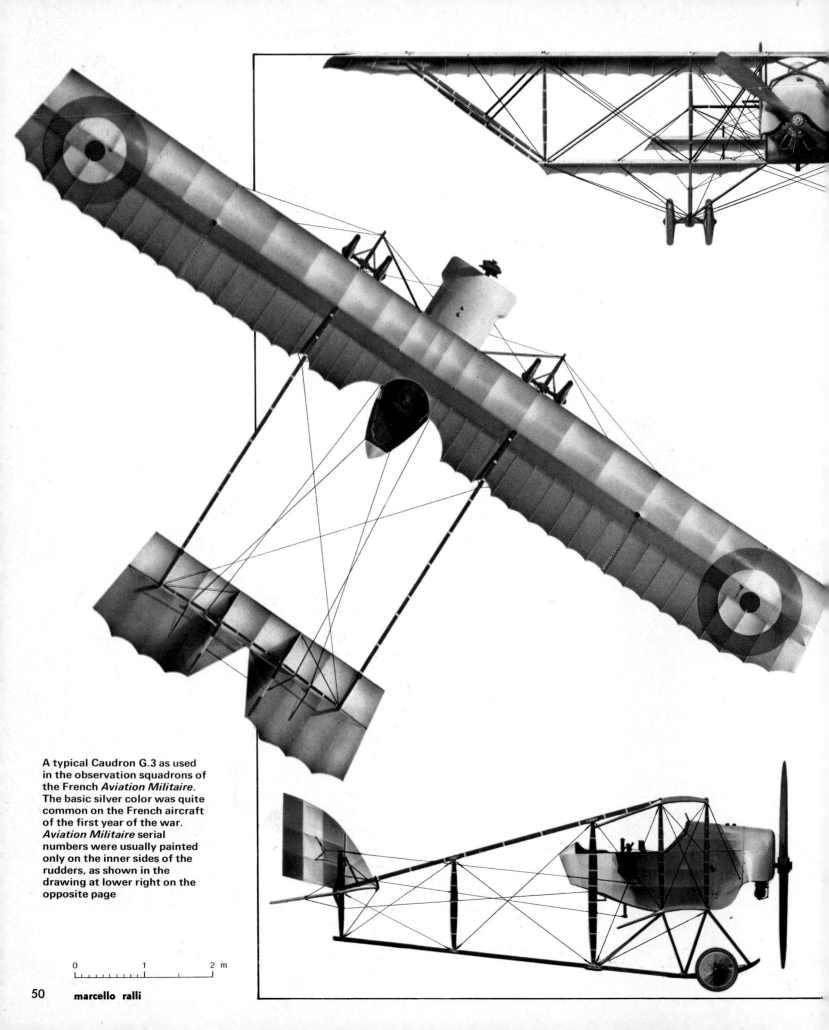

A typical Caudron G.3 as used in the observation squadrons of the French *Aviation Militaire*. The basic silver color was quite common on the French aircraft of the first year of the war. *Aviation Militaire* serial numbers were usually painted only on the inner sides of the rudders, as shown in the drawing at lower right on the opposite page

0   1   2 m

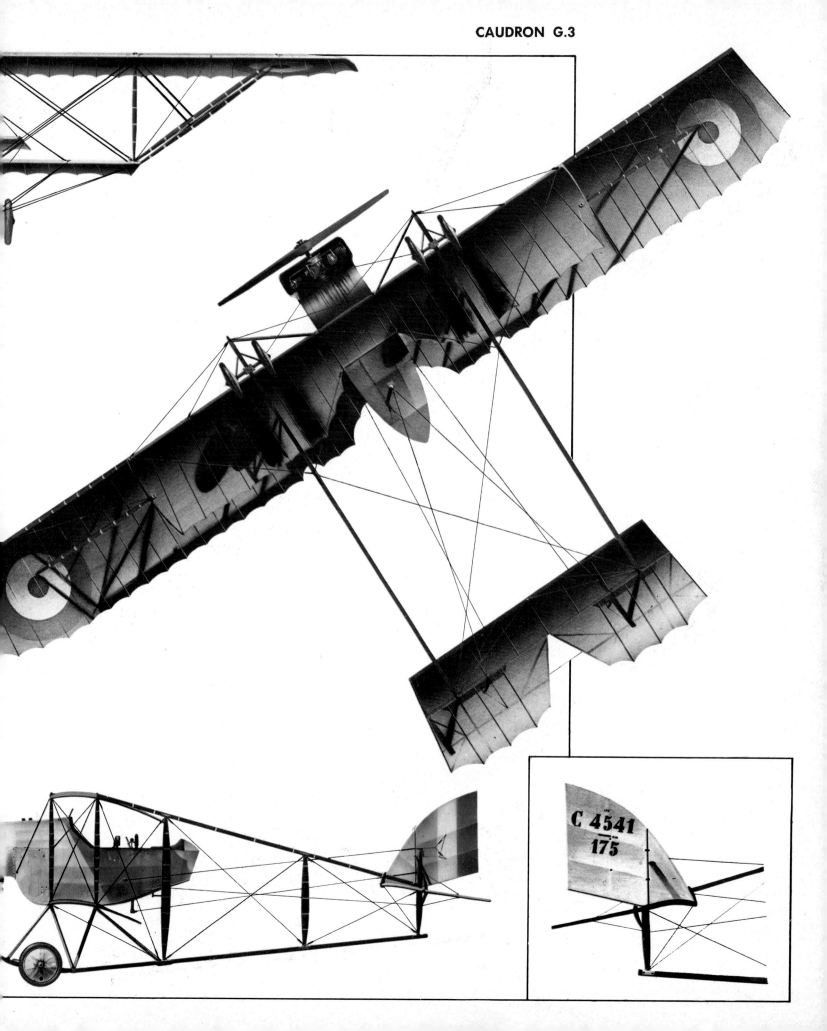

C 4541
175

Top left: *Tail structure of an Italian Caudron G.3 damaged by enemy machine-gun fire.* (Museo Caproni, Taliedo)
Center: *A Belgian Caudron G.3 in flight.* (Aeronautica Militare Italiana)
Bottom: *Caudron G.3 as restored in 1955 and still in flying condition.* (Archivio Bignozzi)
Below: *Caudron G.4, with left engine uncovered.* (Archivio Bignozzi)

veloped for the production of the small prewar racing planes, of which the first essentially successful example was labeled Type C. The typical structural formula of the firm was developed through Types E and F and reached its definitive stage with Type G (1913). The first model to see military action was Type F, but Type G was subjected to more extended military service, even in its earliest version (Type G.2, single-seater).

The most widely used of these machines was the G.3. A two-seater, it was far better suited than the others for use as a trainer or as an operational aircraft for reconnaissance and light bombing (its modest performance and the lack of armament prescribed any broader military use). The G.3 was a favorite with pilots, who liked its stability and ease of control.

Characteristic of these aircraft was the unusual combination of their particular tail structure and the traction propeller. Caudron planes, moreover, were unmistakable in their head-on profile, with the long top wing, flexible ribs, and short lower wing, and in their long landing skids, which constituted the underpart of the tail structure. The tail assembly consisted of a single stabilizer with two rudders.

The wing structure included double strongly ribbed spars, with no dihedral. The upper wing tip beyond the slanting struts could be folded back for easier transport and storage. Roll control was handled by warping the trailing edge of the upper wing tips. The great stability of the aircraft came from the flexibility of the wing ribs, which, according to a manual of the day, permitted the wings 'to flatten out at high speeds, thus automatically correcting for changes in center of pressure'. Generous cutouts in the trailing edge of both wings near the center section increased visibility from the cockpit.

The cockpit was made of ash covered with fabric; the engine, mounted forward, was either open or protected by an aluminum cowling. The fuel and oil tanks and the observer's cockpit separated the engine from the pilot's cockpit. This arrangement necessarily obviated any possibility of defense of the aft sector, which the use of a traction propeller would have permitted—at least to some extent.

(The complex of struts supporting the tail would have made it safe to fire only upwards and downwards.)

The stabilizer on the earliest models was in a single piece, that is, not divided into stabilizer and elevator. The entire aft section of the upper wing tips was flexible and could be raised or lowered for zooming or diving by moving the control stick. Both rudders, hinged to small fins, were controlled by pedals. In the later models a hinged stabilizer was introduced, and sometimes ailerons were used instead of the standard wing warping system. As on the wings, at the center of the rudder there was a cutout, different in size and shape from model to model. On some planes the trailing edge of the stabilizer might have quite a different outline.

The landing gear consisted of wheels and skids, essentially similar to those used by the Farmans. The struts were of steel tubing, and the wheels were arranged in pairs, each pair connected elastically to a skid. In the seaplane version the wheels were replaced by two rather short floats, with a third compensating at the tail. Apparently such a conversion was used on only a few planes, chiefly single-seater G.2s, usually by modifying the tail structure and empennage. It was also possible to mount skis in place of the wheels.

The engine was invariably of the radial type, either fixed (Anzani) or rotary (Gnôme, Le Rhône); the Anzani was open, the Gnôme and Le Rhône cowled, with power ranging from 50 to 100 hp, depending on the engine. Aircraft for military purposes were usually powered by 80-hp engines.

The Caudron G.3 was used by a number of nations; it was built on license in England by the British Caudron Co. and in Italy by the AER, which turned out 170 of them, and others. Eventually the two-engined version came out, and it was also built in England and Italy by the same firms.

Development of the Caudron G.3

The Caudron G.2 was a single-seater, essentially identical to the prewar Type F. Other single-engined Caudrons differed only in the relatively small details diversifying the various production series of G.3s, chiefly in the engines used. The engine could be either the fixed 6-cylinder 45-hp Anzani radial or the 10-cylinder, 100- to 110-hp radial, which was often installed in the planes ordered by the British and Americans. The smaller Anzani was for training machines, the larger for operational versions of the later series. In the majority of cases, however, the G.3 had a Gnôme or Le Rhône engine, both of 80 hp, and occasionally a Clerget engine, also of 80 hp.

In a few planes the 45-hp engine was fitted on a longer mount to compensate for the lower engine weight.

The seaplane had a different airframe, with the lower elements of it originating at the base of the rear wing struts rather than at the skids, while the upper elements were parallel to the line of flight. The two pairs of beams joined at the fin-rudder hinge (the seaplane version had a single rudder), while the upper elements supported the stabilizer. The general effect of these changes was to make the Caudron seaplane resemble the Voisin more closely than it did its land brethren. The earliest seaplane version made by the Caudrons, however, dating from 1913, kept the box airframe structure and the typical Caudron tail.

The twin-engined version marked a greater departure from previous structures. The G.4, which made its debut in the spring of 1915, was designed to increase appreciably the operational capabilities of the G.3, since the good flying characteristics of the G.3 were not sufficient to counter-

balance its shortcomings in performance. The G.4 had sufficient power and lifting capability to guarantee a good useful load. Its rate of climb was extraordinary, much higher than the already respectable rate of the G.3, and thus it was singularly suitable for use in mountainous territory. The G.4 could carry an offensive load of about 100 kg (220 lb) and, at last, defensive weapons; it could also be equipped with a radio, as the G.3 had been. One feature of the G.4 was the closeness of the two engines, a desirable feature making it easier to control the aircraft if one engine should fail; this was paid for, however, by a severe limitation of the field of fire of the forward gun. Soon the designers added another gun to cover the aft sector; it was mounted on the upper wing, in a precarious position which did little to improve the defensive potential of the Caudron in comparison with the classical single-engined planes with tail beams and pusher propellers. Another distinctive feature of the Caudron twin-engined version was the number of rudders (four). Initially the engines were 80- to 90-hp Le Rhônes, later replaced by the 100-hp Anzanis.

The Caudron factory turned out a kind of transition plane, probably in very limited numbers; this was the G.6 (summer 1916). It was a twin-engined descendant of the G.4, in which an authentic fuselage replaced the tail beam assemblies used previously. The fuselage ended in a polygonal tail assembly, with cruciform empennage, wholly covered. Changes in the cockpit put the pilot in front, the observer-gunner behind. This interim model, powered by 80-, 110- and 120-hp engines, led to the new generation of Caudron aircraft which bore the designations R.4 and R.11.

How the Caudron G.3 and G.4 were used in World War I

The French had equipped one of their squadrons—the C.11—with Caudron aircraft before the outbreak of war. The C.11 had six G.3s with 80-hp Gnômes. The French Navy experimented with Caudron G.2 and G.3 seaplanes, especially as on-board equipment. In the same period Caudrons were exported chiefly to England and Russia, but also to other nations, including China, which was a good customer for both land and sea versions.

Once the war had got under way, G.2s were used to form the C.25 *Escadrille*, but these slow single-seaters couldn't cut the mustard and were soon relegated to training; meanwhile the G.3s had been put into service, and the French used them for reconnaissance, and especially artillery target spotting.

Center spread: *Caudron G.4 at an Italian air base, together with a SAML with unusual markings. Note defensive machine gun mounted on upper wing of the bimotor* (Archivio Bignozzi)
Below: *Nose of an Italian Caudron G.4, with a windscreen protecting the unarmed forward cockpit; this was probably a training plane.* (Museo Caproni, Taliedo)
Center: *Base of the Italian 48th Squadriglia after a snowfall in February 1917.* (Museo Caproni, Taliedo)
Below: *An Italian Caudron G.4 taking off with full bomb load.* (Museo Caproni, Taliedo)

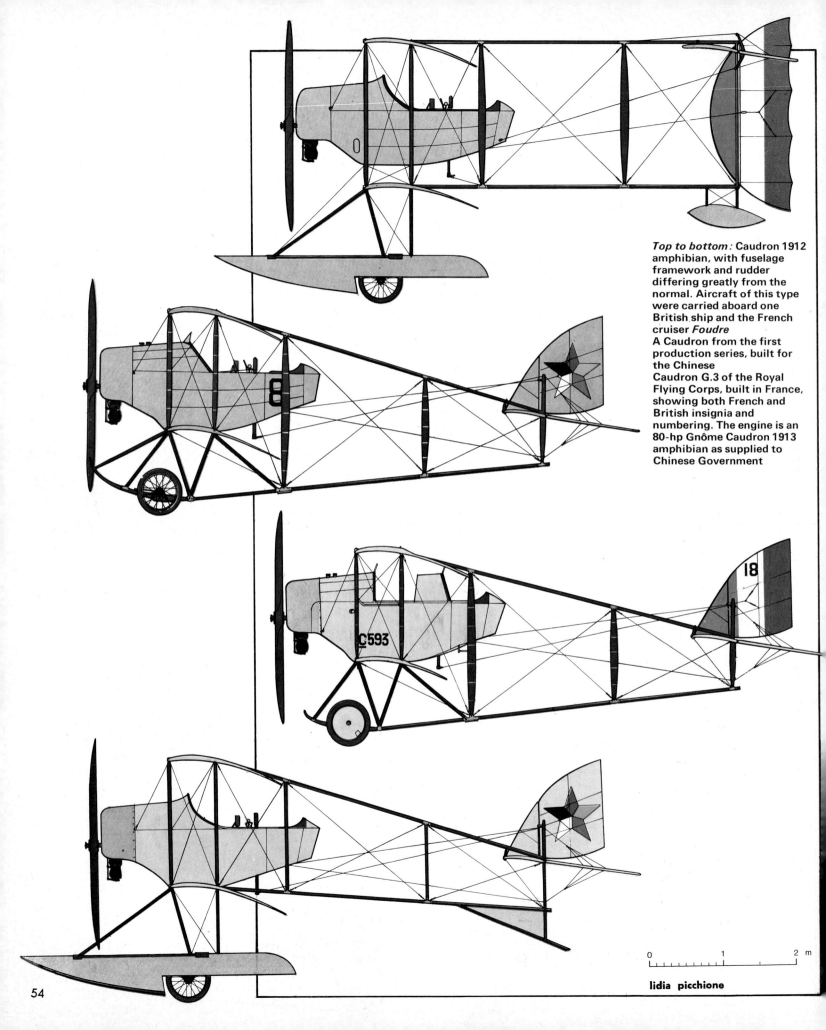

Top to bottom: Caudron 1912 amphibian, with fuselage framework and rudder differing greatly from the normal. Aircraft of this type were carried aboard one British ship and the French cruiser *Foudre*
A Caudron from the first production series, built for the Chinese
Caudron G.3 of the Royal Flying Corps, built in France, showing both French and British insignia and numbering. The engine is an 80-hp Gnôme Caudron 1913 amphibian as supplied to Chinese Government

0   1   2 m

lidia picchione

54

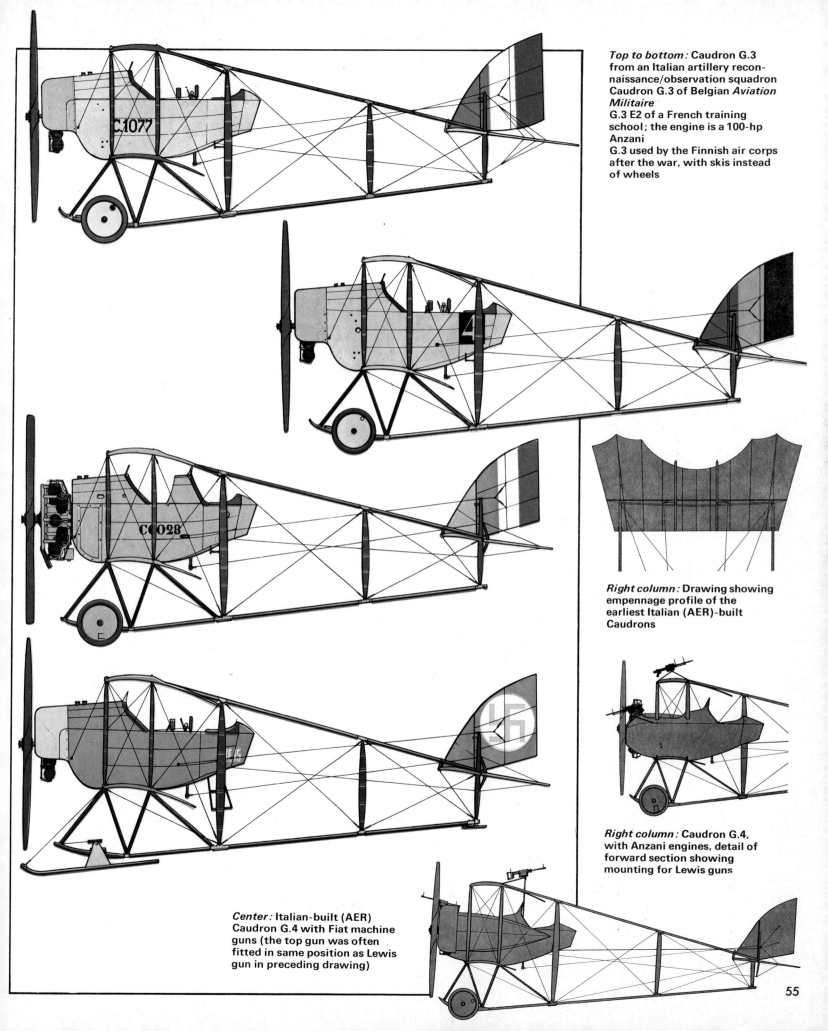

Top to bottom: Caudron G.3 from an Italian artillery reconnaissance/observation squadron
Caudron G.3 of Belgian *Aviation Militaire*
G.3 E2 of a French training school; the engine is a 100-hp Anzani
G.3 used by the Finnish air corps after the war, with skis instead of wheels

Right column: Drawing showing empennage profile of the earliest Italian (AER)-built Caudrons

Right column: Caudron G.4, with Anzani engines, detail of forward section showing mounting for Lewis guns

Center: Italian-built (AER) Caudron G.4 with Fiat machine guns (the top gun was often fitted in same position as Lewis gun in preceding drawing)

Apparently the French Navy did not like the Caudron type of seaplane, and the British, who had at least four G.2 and G.3 seaplanes, made only limited use of them (we have already mentioned one shipped out on the *Hermes*). The situation was probably not much different in the Russian Navy.

Caudron land planes, however, were present in force in the French air arm, which also used them on the Balkan front. The Royal Flying Corps in England had 109 Caudrons and the Royal Naval Air Service had 124 of them, although they were used chiefly for training except for a few operational missions, including some in Macedonia. Belgium and Russia also had a good number of Caudrons.

After the first year of the war the G.3's career as an operational plane began to end in France and England, just at the point when it was beginning for Italy, which entered the war in 1915.

Shortly before Italy joined the Allies the AER company of Orbassano, near Turin, had opened its doors; AER's operations involved the manufacture under license of the Caudron biplane. In May and June it supplied enough planes to equip the *1a Squadriglia* of artillery reconnaissance flyers.

As mentioned above, owing to its exceptional climbing ability the Caudron was most suitable for use in mountainous country and therefore an ideal aircraft for the Italians. Six more Italian squadrons were equipped with Caudrons, all of them powered by 90-hp Le Rhône engines. The Italian pilots were obliged to go through all of 1916 still flying the slow, unarmed G.3s, and this situation continued into 1917, when all the Caudrons were retired to training units. The Americans, however, used the Caudron G.3s only for training when they bought 192 of them in 1918, as by that time these machines were long past their operational usefulness.

Two variants of the G.4 were used—the A2 and the B2, for bombing and reconnaissance respectively. At the start the G.4 was greatly admired, and it was the first twin-engined aircraft to be supplied in quantity to operational units. It proved to be even more reliable than its single-engined predecessor, in spite of the more complex demands it set upon the pilot. It was well spoken of by the legendary René Fonck, who flew it early in his career, before he became the highest-scoring French fighter ace. In other countries, some of the earliest recognized fighter aces, such as Silvio Scaroni in Italy, also flew G.4s.

Many G.4s were assigned to the 38 *Escadrilles* which constituted the young French air force, and they continued to be active throughout the war. In November 1915 the commanders started to assign them to daytime bombing missions, and the Caudrons pressed on to targets beyond the Rhine. Unfortunately, even when flying in formation for mutual protection, these underarmed, slow biplanes were an easy prey for the speedy German fighters, and so they were gradually relegated to less challenging assignments, and by autumn 1916 their days as combat planes were over.

The British used G.4s almost solely in their naval air groups. These machines included 43 imported from France and a dozen built at the British Caudron plant. No. 4 and 5 Wings used them in important raids on German Zeppelin, submarine and seaplane bases along the Belgian coast. One of the last actions involving Caudrons was the strike of the G.4s of No. 7 Squadron against the port of Bruges in February 1917. In the autumn of 1917 the French bimotors were replaced by Handley-Page 0/100s.

In Italy the AER began production of G.4s in the summer of 1915. The G.4 was particularly effective in mountainous territory, and the *1a Squadriglia* soon learned how to exploit the fine climbing capability of the G.4—No. 48—operated in the mountainous region between Carnia and Valsugana in the Austrian-Italian Alps, where it gave a very good account of itself in the winter of 1916-17. The AER delivered 51 aircraft, of which six were in the bombing group made up of 124 aircraft organized on May 27, 1917 to support the Carso offensive. G.4s set up two Italian altitude records in 1916, and on May 24, 1917 a pilot named Natale Palli flew from Belluno to Castenedolo, the first flight across the Trentino region. Italian squadrons flying the G.4 included the 48th, 49th and 50th.

In 1918 the Army Air Service of the American Expeditionary Force acquired 10 G.4s, which were used as training planes in France.

After the war Caudron G.3s and G.4s continued to be useful at training fields, and many of them were sold as war surplus to civilians. They continued to figure among the record-setting exploits of the postwar period, piloted by some of the best airmen of the day. Among them was a woman, Adrienne Bolland, who flew a G.3 in the first-ever flight over the Andes in 1919.

Top: *Detail of an Italian-built Caudron G.4 armed with a Fiat machine gun.*
Bottom: *Forward section of a G.4 of the Italian 48th* Squadriglia *at the Bellun air base. Note the bomb rack beneath the cockpit.* (Museo Caproni, Taliedo)

FOKKER Dr.1

Technical Data

Power plant	Le Rhône 110 hp	Landing gear panel area, m^2	1·18
Span, upper wing, m	7·19	Weight, empty, kg	406
Span, center wing, m	6·225	Useful load, kg	180
Span, lower wing, m	5·725	Total weight, kg	586
Total length, m	5·77	Maximum wing loading at take-off, kg/m^2	31·3
Height, m	2·95	Maximum speed at 4000 m	165 km/hr
Upper wing area, m^2	7·58	Climb to 1000 m	6 min 5 sec
Center wing area, m^2	5·04	Climb to 4000 m	15 min 15 sec
Lower wing area, m^2	4·86	Ceiling, m	6100

The most famous of all World War I German fighter planes was the small triplane known as the Fokker Dr.1. *Rittmeister* Manfred von Richthofen, the famous 'Red Baron', won his last 21 victories with a Fokker Dr.1, and he was flying one when he was shot down while trying to claim (and almost succeeding) his 81st victim.

The Dr.1 was designed and built in record time by Reinhold Platz, the brilliant, self-educated aircraft designer, on the basis of a few vague instructions given to him by Anthony Fokker, who also flight-tested the early prototypes V3 and V4.

Reinhold Platz, born at Cottbus in 1886, had joined Fokker's shaky firm in 1913 as a welding engineer. In a few years he had amassed a lot of experience as sheetmetal worker, welder, designer, structural tester, chief of production and chief of research. His scientific education was minimal, but he was a born engineer with great technical talent and more than the average amount of good sense. His ideals in aircraft design were simplicity and reliability, which he believed to be inseparable qualities, never one without the other.

Anthony Hermann Gerard Fokker was born in

FOKKER DR.I

amedeo gigli

58

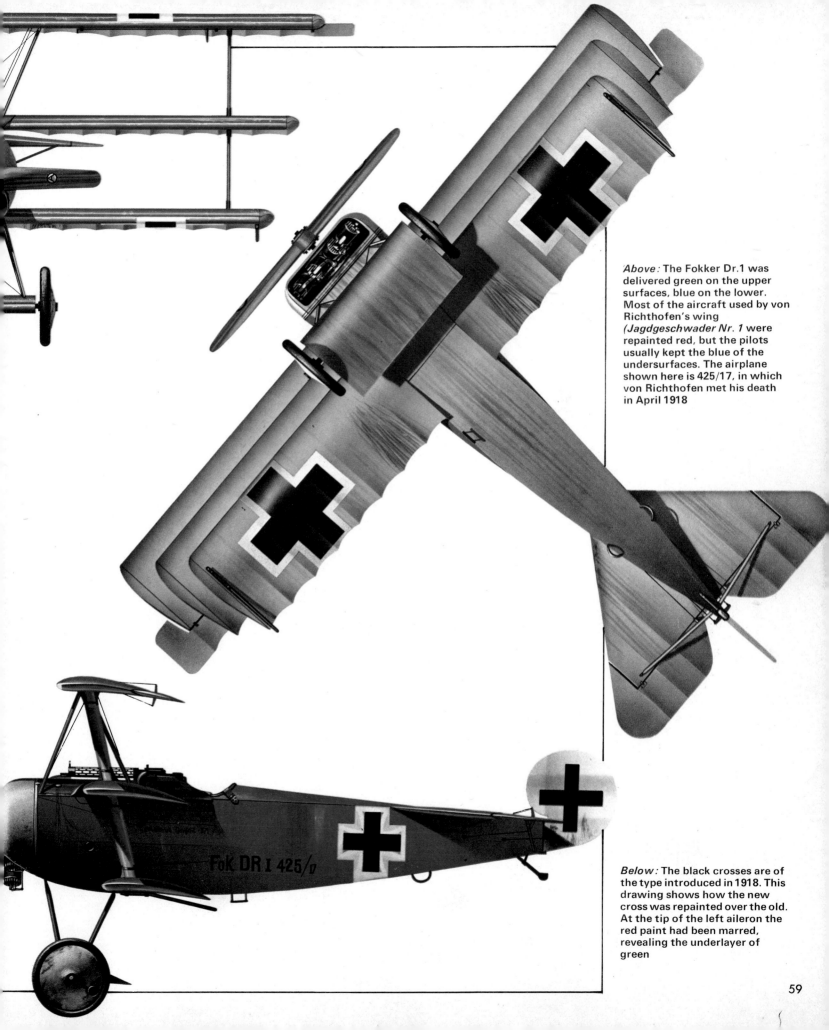

Above: The Fokker Dr.1 was delivered green on the upper surfaces, blue on the lower. Most of the aircraft used by von Richthofen's wing *(Jagdgeschwader Nr. 1* were repainted red, but the pilots usually kept the blue of the undersurfaces. The airplane shown here is 425/17, in which von Richthofen met his death in April 1918

Below: The black crosses are of the type introduced in 1918. This drawing shows how the new cross was repainted over the old. At the tip of the left aileron the red paint had been marred, revealing the underlayer of green

A common sight behind the German lines during World War I was a Fokker Dr.1 being towed to the airfield by a horse

In the hands of Fokker and Platz, the triplane formula inspired a light, compact aircraft of great maneuverability. The choice of engine proved particularly wise: The Dr.1 was powered by a 9-cylinder, 110-hp rotary engine built in Sweden by Thulin under license from the French engine firm of Le Rhône. It was light and reliable, although a great consumer of gasoline and even more so of oil. Since it was really a French engine, Fokker conscientiously garnished each engine with a plaque identifying it as *Beute*, that is, captured equipment, thus protecting the 'neutral' Swedish licensee.

Incorporating the technology common to all Fokkers, the Dr.1 had a fuselage made of welded steel tubing braced with transverse cables, forming a rigid box-girder structure covered with fabric. Each of the three wings was in a single piece and without dihedral, and was a sturdy, wooden-sparred structure covered with fabric. The undercarriage struts were of faired tubing, with an additional aerofoil surface which increased the already considerable lift characteristics of the aircraft. The propeller measured 2.62 m and gave exceptional climbing rate to low and medium altitudes. Both ailerons (only on the upper wing), the rudder and the stabilizer were all faired, making it possible for the pilot to control the Dr.1 literally with his fingertips. All in all, the aerodynamics of the new triplane were far in advance of anything the Allies were then able to put in the air and gave the plane that unrivaled maneuverability which made it so fearful an adversary in dogfights. Such praise, however, should lead no one to forget that Fokker's shoddy manufacturing procedures resulted in a number of cases of structural failures in the air.

The Dr.1's armament inspired the enemy's respect: twin synchronized LMG 08/15 7·92-mm guns (the famous Spandau guns, named after the district of Berlin where the German Royal Arms Factory was located), each carrying 500 rounds. Speed performance of the Dr.1 was not brilliant, however, and many an Allied plane could outrun the German fighter with its maximum speed of only 165 km/hr at 4000 m. The limited power of the engine, moreover, kept the plane from operating at altitudes above that level. This low power was also the cause of the Dr.1's short operational life—going into service at the end of August, 1917, it was retired the following May by squadrons on the western front after unsuccessful attempts to beef up its performance at altitude.

The cockpit was small and uncomfortable for any husky pilot. The breechblocks of the machine guns were ready to hand so that they could be operated directly whenever jammed, but this was dangerous in an emergency landing, where the pilot's head could easily be rammed into the butts by inertia.

Cockpit equipment was minimal: a control stick, rudder pedals, throttle and ignition lock switch. The grip of the control stick was designed for two-handed operation; it incorporated the trigger and a remote-control throttle connected to the main throttle by a flex cable. Thus the pilot could control the plane, engine and armament with both hands on the stick, with obvious advantages in combat. The

Haarlem in the Netherlands in 1890. At the age of 20 he went to Bingen, Germany, to study at the technical institute, but in a few months he was devoting his energies entirely to the fledgling science of aeronautics. He became a pilot with little instruction from anyone, almost entirely by self-training. He began to build aircraft, but although he tried his hand at several types, none was particularly successful. His natural talents as an airman, however, soon earned him an outstanding reputation as a test pilot, and this ability, combined with a sharp business sense and a certain lack of excessive scruples, made up for his shortcomings as an engineer.

After rather uncertain beginnings, the success of his Series E armed scout monoplanes (the first to synchronize machine-gun fire with the propeller and therefore the first fighter-aircraft in the world) made him the most famous of all warplane manufacturers. Once started, he soon built up a highly profitable aeronautical industry. His product was often almost criminally shabby from the safety point of view, but his fighter scouts were planes capable of extraordinary performance, and they met with the approval of the daredevil aces of the day.

Technical description

The Dr.1 was built to specifications issued by the *Inspektion der Fliegertruppen* for a triplane fighter scout capable of regaining supremacy in the air to the German *Jagdstaffeln* (fighter squadrons). Such supremacy had been won by the early Fokker monoplanes and the Albatros biplanes, but it had definitely passed to the British when the first Sopwith triplanes roared into action.

meagre instrumentation included a compass, tachometer, fuel gauge, oil gauge (fuel and oil were stored in a divided tank in the fuselage between cockpit and engine); there was also an ammunition counter on the guns.

In spite of the immediate successes of Richthofen and other German aces, the debut of the Dr.1 was not a happy one, since two aircraft broke up in flight on October 28 and 31, and at least one of the pilots was killed. The Dr.1 was immediately grounded, and an investigating commission determined that the causes of the accidents lay in structural defects in the wings and in the poor quality of the materials used. The manufacturer had to accept new quality standards and more careful inspection and replace all wings on aircraft then in service. But the Dr.1 never did become entirely safe, and on February 3, March 15 and May 9, 1918, other planes broke up in flight, fortunately without fatalities.

Development of the Dr.1

The short operational life of the Dr.1, the small number of machines built (about 320), the limited size and weight which proscribed the development of a two-seat assault version, and especially the lack of suitable more powerful engines, prevented the appearance of other models, except for a few experimental aircraft built in an effort to improve performance at altitude.

An attempt to replace the Thulin Le Rhône engines with the 110-hp rotary Oberursel UP II was not successful, in spite of the insistence of Fokker, who had meanwhile become the owner of the

Above: A Fokker Dr.1 triplane of Jagdstaffel 27 in May 1918. The pilot standing next to it is Lieut. Klimke, who brought down 16 enemy aircraft and survived the war. Below: Rittmeister Manfred von Richthofen's red Dr.1 being prepared for take-off. The mechanic is helping the celebrated pilot into the cockpit. Note the two synchronized Spandau machine guns

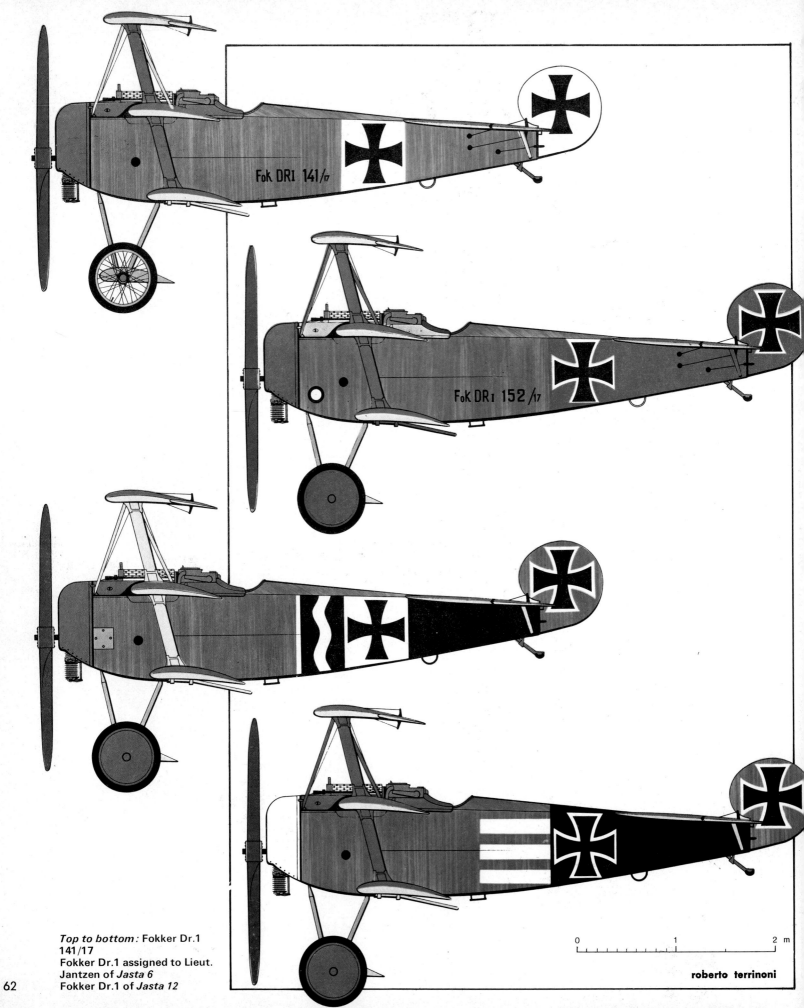

Top to bottom: Fokker Dr.1
141/17
Fokker Dr.1 assigned to Lieut.
Jantzen of *Jasta 6*
Fokker Dr.1 of *Jasta 12*

62

roberto terrinoni

0   1   2 m

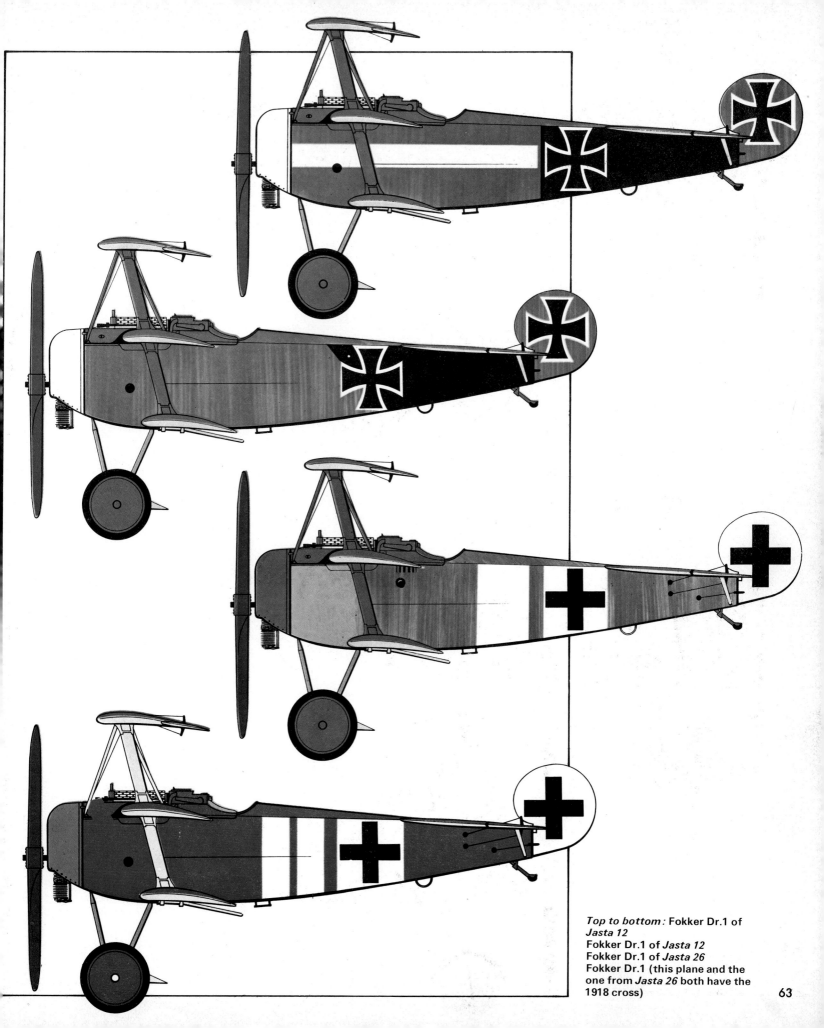

Top to bottom: Fokker Dr.1 of
Jasta 12
Fokker Dr.1 of *Jasta 12*
Fokker Dr.1 of *Jasta 26*
Fokker Dr.1 (this plane and the
one from *Jasta 26* both have the
1918 cross)

Oberursel plant. As quickly as they could, fighter pilots removed the German engine and replaced it with the Swedish model, which had better materials and was assembled with far greater care. A test with the 145-hp, 11-cylinder Oberursel III rotary failed for lack of proper tuning, and for similar reasons the Goebel Goe III rotary engine was also a flop. The latter, although it had adequate power (170 hp) at take-off and altitude and could be boosted up to 200 hp, was used in the autumn of 1918 on only some 30 Dr.1s assigned to Home Defense; they were never deployed at the front. Several Fokker triplanes were equipped with captured Clerget engines (130 hp), but the difficulty of getting spare parts soon dried up the delivery of this version to operational units. The end of the war obviated design of high-altitude models of the Dr.1, which, powered by high-compression engines, should have been able to climb to 9000 meters or even higher.

Such altitudes were achieved by an experimental model of the Dr.1 called the V7, powered by an 11-cylinder, 160-hp counter-rotary Siemens-Halske Sh.3 engine. This radial, driving the propeller at low revs (about 900 rpm as compared to the 1200 rpm of the Thulin Le Rhône), required a four-bladed propeller of larger diameter, and this in turn necessitated raising the landing gear so the propeller tips could clear the ground with sufficient margin. Such heightening of the landing gear also involved lengthening the fuselage by about 50 cm to ensure good visibility when taxi-ing. Eventually the V7 reached 9000 meters, but only at the trade-off of its legendary maneuverability.

Even less satisfactory was the V8 version, very slightly larger than the Dr.1 and with a 120-hp water-cooled Mercedes D II engine.

How the Dr.1 was used in the War

The first two Dr.1s were delivered on August 21, 1917, to *Jagdgeschwader I*, based at Courtrai and commanded by *Rittmeister* Manfred von Richthofen. Within a very few days, after some flights to ac-

quaint themselves with the new machine, both the 'Red Baron' and the youthful ace Werner Voss chalked up a number of victories piloting the new aircraft. The Dr.1 was used by numerous German *Jagdstaffeln* (usually abbreviated to 'Jasta'), among them the Second (better known as the *'Jasta Boelcke'* after its legendary first commander, who had lost his life in a mid-air collision with a squadron comrade) and *Jastas* 4, 5, 6, 10, 11, 12, 15, 17, 26, 27, 32 and 36.

Several German Home Defense units were also equipped with the Fokker triplane when it was retired from operations on the Western front. In the same period several Dr.1s were assigned to training schools, often after removal of the armament and substitution of the 7-cylinder, 110-hp Goebel Goe II engine for the Thulin le Rhône.

The only use of the Dr.1 in combat was on the Western front, where this fighter was highly appreciated by its pilots in spite of its limitations. Indeed, when the plane was grounded after the October crashes, several pilots insisted on permission to use it anyway, although by then it was clear that the plane was far from safe.

The Dr.1 Aces

The most famous, of course, was *Rittmeister* (Cav. Captain) Manfred von Richthofen, who at one point rotated three planes so he could be sure of having one finely tuned up at all times. The most exceptional Dr.1 pilot, however, was probably Lieut. Werner Voss, who achieved his last 21 victories (out of a total of 48) in 25 days, always flying Dr.1 103/17. He was shot down by Lieut. A. P. F. Rhys-Davids of the British Royal Flying Corps, after having accepted combat with a patrol of British SE 5as. Only his excellent qualities as a pilot, marksmanship and the superb maneuverability of the Fokker triplane gave him a chance to duel alone for 10 minutes against the seven planes of No. 56 Squadron, succeeding in shooting holes into each of them before the inevitable end.

The Red Baron's brother, Lothar von Richthofen, the winner of 40 dogfights, made numerous kills in his Dr.1, as did Lieut. Ernst Udet, victor in 62 fights and the second-highest scoring German fighter ace of World War I.

A Fokker Dr.1, August 1917. Efficient only within certain limits of altitude, this fighter was, however, highly maneuverable because of the configuration of its three wings, finger-light controls, and the quality of its rotary engine. It could surprise the enemy with unexpected maneuvers. Certain structural defects persisted, however, and, like other planes of its day, the Dr.1 was a quality aircraft only when flown by a quality pilot. (Jarrett Collection)

VOISIN L

Gabriel Voisin was one of the most talented of the early aircraft builders and one of the first to put his output on an industrial footing. As early as 1902 he had started to build flying apparatus on commission (for Ernest Archdeacon's Aviation Syndicate), and he built many others to his own designs or to the designs of others in the workshop which he had set up at Billancourt in association with his brother Charles. His first real success, the 1907 biplane in its various versions, was flown by such pioneers as Delagrange, Paulhan and Henry Farman. His 'canard' model of 1910 was also converted

A Voisin Type 3 LA fresh from the SIT aircraft factory of Turin. This side view shows details of the machine with great clarity. Voisin aircraft, manufactured under license in Great Britain, Italy and Russia, were among the most active early planes in the First World War

Specifications

		Type 1	Type 3	Type 3	Type 5	Type 8	Type 10
Type	L 1913	L 1914	LA	seapl.	LA	LAP	LBR
Span, *m*	13·80	13·50	14·74	15·00	14·74	18·00	17·90
Total length, *m*	10·00	10·50	9·50	8·00	9·50	10·35	10·35
Height, *m*	2·90	2·90	2·95	—	3·80	3·95	3·95
Wing area, m^2	37	42	54	50	45	63	61
Weight empty, *kg*	500	825	800	—	970	1310	1450
Total weight, *kg*	860	1100	1200	—	1370	1860	2000
Maximum speed, *km/hr*	100	95	115	110	112	118	130

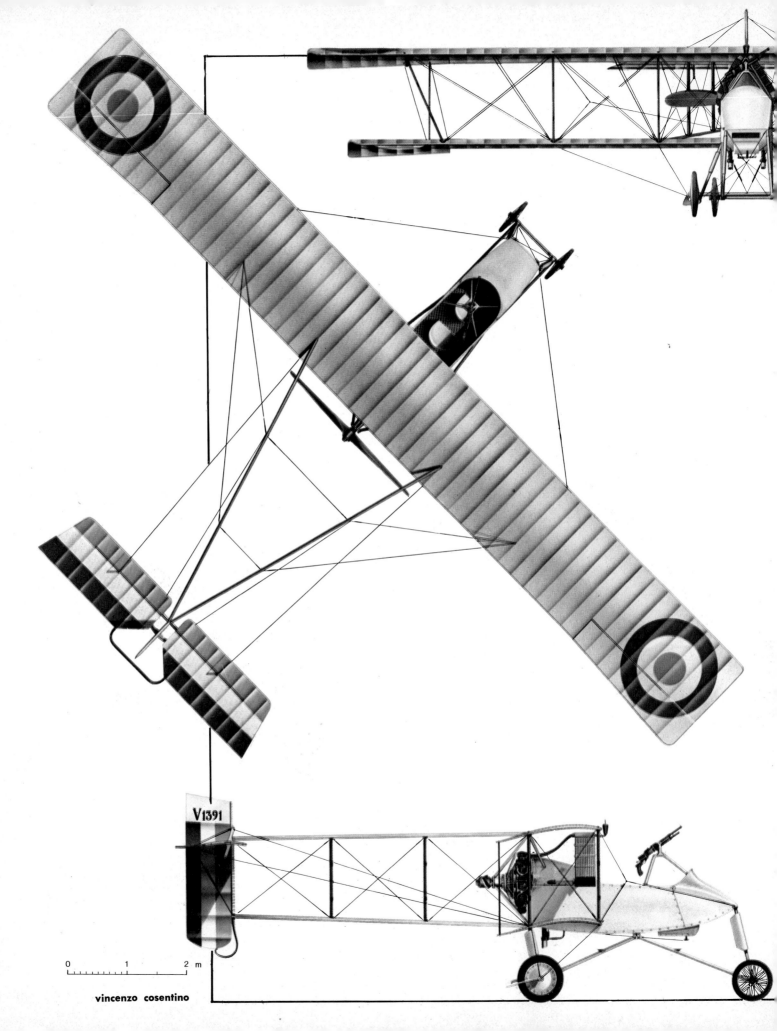

V1391

0   1   2 m

vincenzo cosentino

66

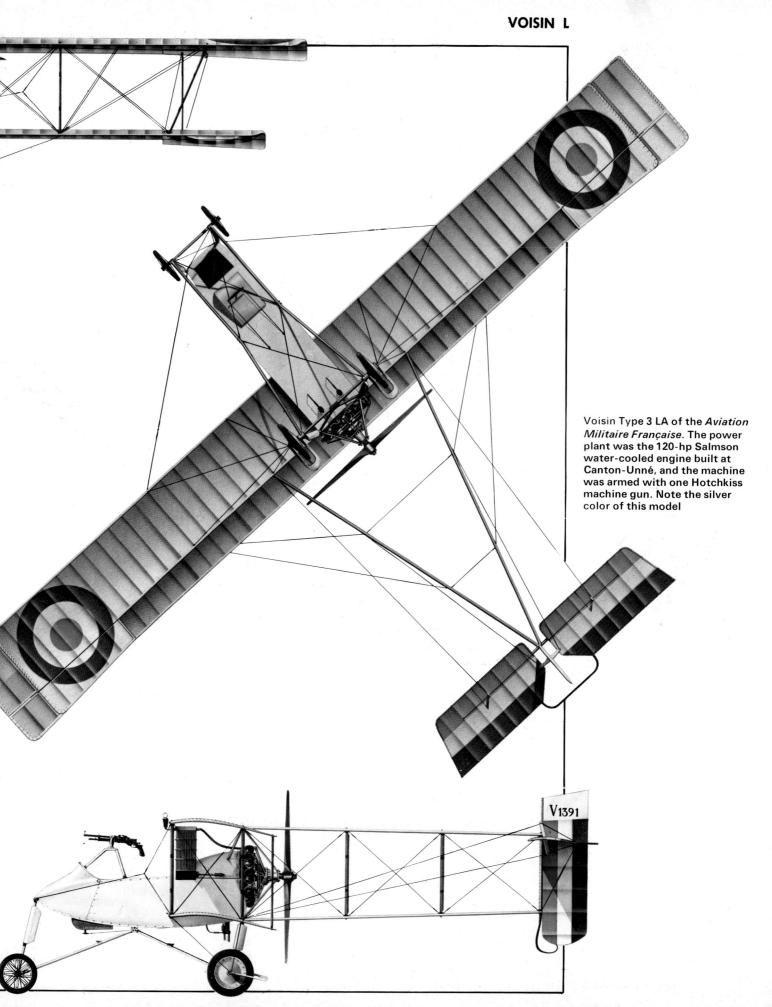

Voisin Type 3 LA of the *Aviation Militaire Française*. The power plant was the 120-hp Salmson water-cooled engine built at Canton-Unné, and the machine was armed with one Hotchkiss machine gun. Note the silver color of this model

V 1391

Above: *Voisin Type 5 LB armed with 47-mm quick-firing cannon. These machines, often armed with weapons which were unusual in their day, was used chiefly against ground targets.* (Archivio Bignozzi)

Above, right: *Voisin Type 3 LA with an Isotta-Fraschini in-line power plant, probably assigned to the Italian 5th Squadriglia.* (Aeronautica Militare Italiana)

Right: *This photograph shows details of the forward Hotchkiss 8-mm machine gun with drum magazine, operated by the flight observer. In the Voisin the observer's cockpit was behind the pilot's rather than in front of it, as was usually the case. The first aircraft ever to be shot down in the air was downed by a Voisin observer.* (Archivio Bignozzi)

into a seaplane, one of the first such aircraft to perform satisfactorily; this was followed in 1913 by the *'Icare'* (Icarus), an enormous seaplane with 200-hp engines. For a while he was associated with Sanchez-Besa, the South American aviation pioneer, and together they built the 1914 military model, called the Voisin L, which was eventually to be one of the planes most used in the war. Conceived as an armed aircraft, and in some cases produced as an *armored* aircraft, it was designed in two versions, the A (with a single flexible machine gun in the nose) and B (with a small quick-firing cannon in the nose instead).

Technical description

The principal characteristic of the Voisin L series was the metal structure, rare for its time. It gave the airframe exceptional toughness—the Voisin L could endure long exposure to the elements. Extremely spartan in design, the plane was relatively light considering its power, and could thus carry a good load. This factor together with its good flying characteristics and great general reliability, made up for its modest performance.

The biplane wing configuration varied from model to model. There were machines with equal span wings or with the upper wing of greater span; and the wing struts, generally parallel, were sometimes (as in Type 4) slanted to stagger the wings. The cockpit rested directly on the lower wing center section or else, as in Type 7, slightly raised, with the pusher engine aft. The engine was sometimes mounted at a slight downward angle to reduce drag and ensure greater traction in flight.

The tail was supported by four lengths of metal tubing joined in pairs to the vertical shaft on which the rudder was hinged. The stabilizer, mounted on a level with the upper pair of tubing sections, was fully movable.

The undercarriage was another peculiarity of the Voisin: it had four wheels with shock absorbers, with brakes on the rear pair. The aircraft stood on the ground like on a tricycle landing gear.

At first the engine was an 80-hp Gnôme or Le Rhône rotary; later versions were powered by an air-cooled stationary engine, the radial Salmson (Canton Unné) or the water-cooled Isotta-Fraschini vertical V.4 (on only a few Italian models) or the Peugeot or Renault V-type engines. The radiator was in two sections mounted on the slanting struts between the cockpit and the upper wing, but occasionally (on Types 7-10) it was a single piece fitted frontally, or a three-piece radiator, with one mounted frontally and two obliquely.

Armament on the Voisin LA was limited to a single flexible machine gun on a rotating mount, generally of a type that made at least a limited upward defense possible. Sometimes there was a second defensive gun in the upper sector (on Italian planes it was a double-barreled 9-mm Rivelli machine pistol). On the Voisin LBs, however, there was a small quick-firing 37-mm or 47-mm cannon, with limited field of fire, in the extreme nose. The bomb load was racked horizontally under the fuselage or, vertically, along the sides. It was also possible to install cameras and radio equipment. The crew could be two or three, but were generally limited to two, thus permitting heavier loads of armament or fuel. In machines from Type 7 onwards, two auxiliary fuel tanks, well streamlined, were carried beneath the upper wing.

Development of the Voisin L

The immediate ancestor of the Voisin L was the 1913 military biplane, with its 80-hp engine and empty weight of 500 kg (1102 lb), most of it due to the weight of the fuselage. The single stabilizer was carried by two thick, round longerons, and supported in turn the double rudder. The 1914 model, in part simplified, was the Voisin L described above, powered by a 70-hp Gnôme; this model was retroactively designated as Type 1.

In the same year Types 2 and 3 were introduced, together with at least the prototype of the machine which was later to be designated as Type 7. Type 2 was identical to Type 1 except for the engine, an 80-hp Le Rhône, while Type 3, which made up the bulk of Voisins produced (at least 800 for the French air force), had not only a more powerful engine (the Canton Unné 9M, 120 hp) but also an upper wing of greater span. This version was manufactured in Italy as well, by the *Società Italiana Transaerea*, which built 112 machines some with the 190-hp Isotta-Fraschini V.4 engine, some with the Fiat 100-hp A.10, and at least one with an experimental installation of the 120-hp Le Rhône with external reduction gear. In England Savages Ltd. built another 50 aircraft of this type.

Type 7 was a large three-seat, heavily armored (comparatively speaking) aircraft. It was the first to carry a small quick-firing cannon and to have the cockpit set slightly above the lower wing.

Type 4 existed in the LA version (with machine gun) and the LB (with light cannon); the wings were slightly staggered (upper wing slightly forward of lower). A total of 200 aircraft of both versions were built.

In 1915 Types 5 and 6 made their debut. The former (total production: 350 machines) was characterized by wings with gradually increasing chord from roots to wing tips, and it differed from Type 3 in having a considerably more robust undercarriage. Type 5 was powered by a 150-hp Salmson radial engine. Type 6 had a 155-hp Salmson featuring new type of valves. In both of these Voisins the engine was mounted slightly oblique, and both models were designated LAS (or LBS if they had a light cannon in place of the machine gun).

The generation stemming from Type 7 (1914) entered into active service only in 1916. These machines were larger, heavier, and had a slightly raised cockpit. Production finally got under way when more powerful engines became available returning a better weight/power ratio than anything the Salmsons could show. The first of these new models to go into production was Type 8, of which 1123 machines were built, some of them armed with cannon. Type 8, powered by the new 220-hp Peugeot 8Aa, was given the designation LAP (or LBP), but it was popularly known as the *'Voisin Peugeot'*. A lighter version designed for reconnaissance was designated Type 9.

In spite of the increased engine power, overall performance of the Voisins did not improve a great deal, since there had been no essential improvement in the basic aerodynamics of the aircraft (and thus drag was notably increased), but load carrying capacity did increase from 60 kg of bombs in Types 1 and 2 to 180 kg in Type 8. The Peugeot engine, however, was not free of bugs, especially in carburetor gas feed at altitude. For this reason the next version, Type 10, was fitted with the more reliable—and more powerful—300-hp Renault 12 Fe. This made it possible for the Type 10 to take not less than 300 kg of bombs, the maximum which any single-engined plane of the day could carry. Such a load of bombs, of course, reduced the range, but the Type 10 could still give an incredible punch, as is proved by the production figure of 900 aircraft, almost all of the LAR (R for Renault) bomber version, and very few of the LBR attack version, which were armed with a Hotchkiss 37-mm cannon.

Types 8 through 10 had an increased rudder area, which was sometimes enhanced by a forward extension which succeeded, aerodynamically, in easing the strain on the pilot.

How the Voisin L Planes were used in the War

Among Voisin's first customers were the Portuguese, who bought a single plane in 1913. By August 1914 two French squadrons (V.14 and V.21) were fully equipped with Type 1 and 2 Voisins, and two more were ready to receive similar machines on the outbreak of hostilities, since the French government had tentatively requisitioned a number of Type 3 Voisins ordered by the Russians. These aircraft were unarmed, but Gabriel Voisin had bought six Hotchkiss machine guns with his own

Above: *Voisin powered by a Salmson engine. This Italian aircraft is armed with a Fiat machine gun operated by the observer and a 9-mm Revelli machine pistol fired by the pilot.* (Archivio Bignozzi)

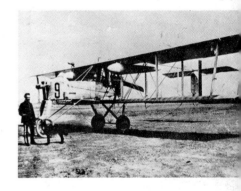

Center: *The most advanced Voisin model was the Type 10, usually powered by a 300-hp Renault engine. Note the battery of directional searchlights mounted on the forward section of fuselage for use in night bombing.* (Musée de l'Air)

Below: *Voisin Type 3 LA of the Italian 7th Squadriglia, with squadron personnel. Early type of bomb rack is visible beneath the cockpit; French airmen of the day preferred to carry their bomb loads attached to the sides of the fuselage.* (Aeronautica Militare Italiana)

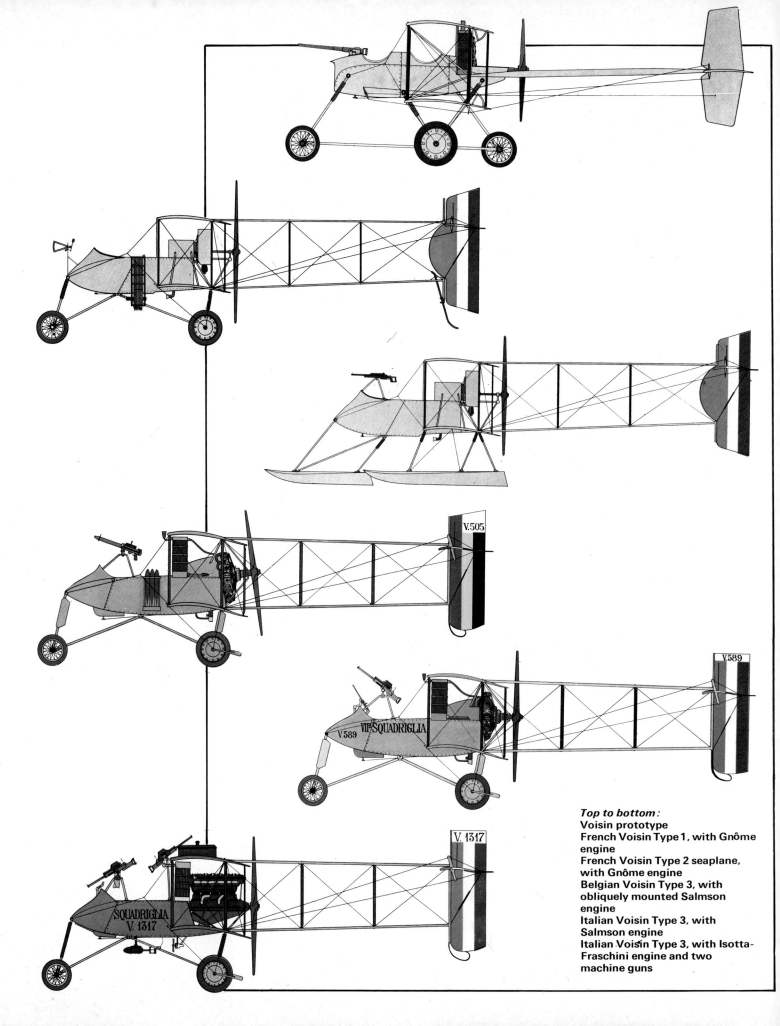

Top to bottom:
Voisin prototype
French Voisin Type 1, with Gnôme
engine
French Voisin Type 2 seaplane,
with Gnôme engine
Belgian Voisin Type 3, with
obliquely mounted Salmson
engine
Italian Voisin Type 3, with
Salmson engine
Italian Voisin Type 3, with Isotta-
Fraschini engine and two
machine guns

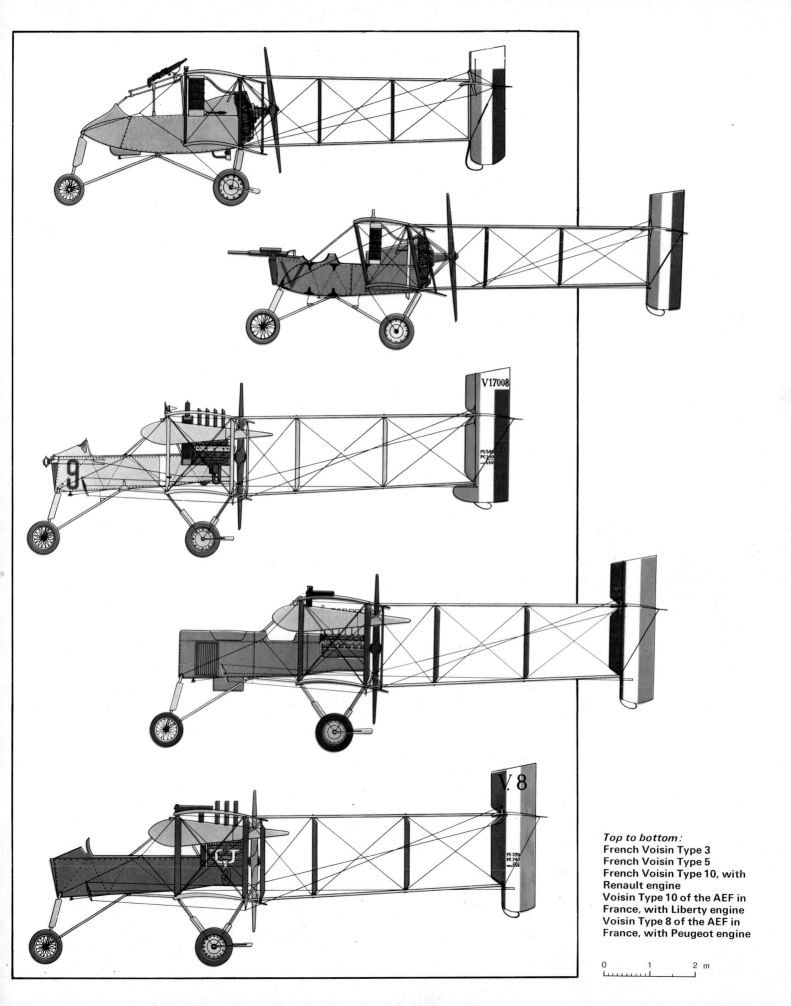

Top to bottom:
French Voisin Type 3
French Voisin Type 5
French Voisin Type 10, with
Renault engine
Voisin Type 10 of the AEF in
France, with Liberty engine
Voisin Type 8 of the AEF in
France, with Peugeot engine

The United States Army Air Service also used Voisin aircraft, almost exclusively for training. Above: *One of two Type 10s in US markings experimentally equipped with a 400-hp Liberty engine.* (Smithsonian Institution) Right: *Voisin Type 3 LA captured by the Germans in the early months of the war. Note the markings on the rudder.* (Archivio Bignozzi)

Detail showing installation of the huge Salmson engine on an Italian-built Voisin Type 3 LA Below: *The kernel of the Voisin: the semifuselage, with engine, propeller, armament and undercarriage.* (Archivio Bignozzi)

money, planning to use them eventually, and, in the event, it was one of the 'Russian' planes, armed with Voisin's personal weapon, which achieved the first aerial victory of the war on October 5, 1914.

At first Voisins were used mostly on reconnaissance, and especially as artillery observers. Soon this quiet task was taken over by the Farmans and Caudrons, and Voisin's husky mules were assigned to bombing missions, escorted by other Voisins armed with light cannon. It wasn't long before it became obvious that these cannon-armed machines were not suited for escort duties, and they were assigned to ground targets. Sorties were flown in daylight during 1914 and 1915, carrying out the directives of the French general staff, which aimed at striking at strategic targets fairly deep into enemy rear. In November 1914 the first *Groupe de bombardement* was formed, known as GB.1, consisting of *Escadrilles* VB.1, 2 and 3. The first important action was a raid on May 26, 1915, led by Capt. De Goys, on the Ludwigshafen factories manufacturing toxic gases. Groups GB.2, 3 and 4 followed, but meanwhile daylight sorties had proved to be too costly. At the same time there were essential changes in strategic and tactical planning, and so, starting in September 1915, Voisins were almost invariably used on night missions.

Several Type 3 planes were in service with the French Navy, but their actions were chiefly land

missions. In 1914 a Type 1 floatplane had been procured, but the navy's preference for seaplanes with central hulls soon brought an end to Voisin activity in this sector.

Two Voisin seaplanes, carried on the French scout cruiser *Foudre,* were active in the Adriatic before Italy entered the war, particularly in reconnaissance in the Kotor sector along the Balkan coast.

Some 30 Type 3s were in service with the British Royal Naval Air Service (three armed with light cannon, of which two were powered by 200-hp Hispano-Suiza engines). These machines operated in Africa, Mesopotamia (now Iraq) and in the Aegean. The equipment of Nos. 4, 5, 6, 7 and 16 Squadrons included at least 23 French Voisins and 50 British-built machines.

An entire Belgian squadron was equipped with Type 3s. A consistent production was also coming out of Russia where Types 3, 4 and 5 were license-built by 'Dux' in Moscow and elsewhere. Part of this production was handled by Anatra, and their planes were designated VI (Voisin Ivanov, named after the Russian aeronautical engineer who had modified the original French design). Anatra, incidentally, was named after its Italian founder, the banker A. A. Anatra.

Italian production by SIT got under way only after the outbreak of hostilities and deliveries began in 1915. These SIT-manufactured machines formed the equipment of *Squadriglie* 5, 7, 25, 26 and 35. In Italy the Voisins were assigned to special missions, such as the infiltration and recovery of intelligence agents and saboteurs in enemy-occupied territory. The trusty Voisin acquitted itself well in this highly specialized but very useful activity.

Voisins were also used extensively by France, Great Britain and the United States for training, and many planes were converted to the variants designated D or E *(Double Commande* and *École).* Aircraft of the second generation found similar use; eight Type 8s were produced by the US Army Air Service in France for this purpose in 1918.

However, almost the entire production of Type 8 was absorbed by the French *Aviation Militaire,* which used them in vital night missions (the primary target was still the toxics plants, as in 1915). The French Navy acquired only 20 machines of this type. One French squadron, the V.293, specialized in night reconnaissance, probably using Type 9 exclusively. Gradually the Voisins armed with light cannon disappeared from operational units but towards the end of the war, as late as August 1918, there were still 50 Voisin Type 8 aircraft in active service.

Type 10 was introduced early in 1918 and was flown only by the *Aviation Militaire,* almost always in the LAR-Bn2 version, specializing in night bombardment.

The Voisin aircraft were phased out as soon as the war was over. New design concepts had established themselves, the basic Voisin design was outdated and too primitive to merit further development. But it was a great and useful aircraft, fruit of the unquestionable Voisin talents, and it had pioneered a number of interesting design concepts.

ROYAL AIRCRAFT FACTORY B.E.2

The original design of the B.E.2: the fuselage was completely open between the engine and the observer's seat and so was the pilot's cockpit. Roll control was performed through warping of the wing tips. The engine exhaust was well muffled. Note the four-bladed propeller

Specifications

	B.E.2a	B.E.2c	B.E.2e
Power plant	Renault, 70 hp	RAF 1a, 90 hp	RAF 1a, 90 hp
Wing span, *m*	10·68	11·28	12·42
Length, *m*	9·00	8·31	8·31
Height, *m*	3·10	3·40	3·66
Wing area, *m²*	32·41	34·20	—
Weight, empty, *kg*	587	610	—
Weight, total, *kg*	726	972	953
Maximum speed, *km/hr*	112·7	—	—
Maximum speed at 1980 *m*	—	116	132
Climb to 1000 *m*	9·0 min	—	1 min 36 sec
Climb to 3000 *m*	—	45·0 min	—
Ceiling, *m*	3048	3048	3048
Flight endurance	3·0 hrs	3 hrs 25 min	4·0 hrs

A few years before World War I Mervyn O'Gorman, one of the greatest British designers, checked into the Royal Aircraft Factory at Farnborough and reported for work as an aeronautical research designer. The Factory, which is still in operation, was concerned with trying out new inventions in the aeronautical field, setting up new projects and evaluating prototypes submitted for possible procurement by the British armed forces. It was not licensed to build planes or to submit its proposals

73

2560

marcello ralli

0   1   2 m

The machine shown here is a
B.E.2f of the British No. 2
Squadron. The BE.2f was simply
a BE.2e with a few last-minute
changes made in response to
demands from operational units

to military competitions. O'Gorman got around these prohibitions by interpreting the Royal Aircraft Factory's authority to repair damaged aircraft in the broadest possible sense: his technical office, directed by Frederick Green, and especially its general director, Geoffrey de Havilland, took on the job of converting these crippled vehicles into totally new aircraft, sometimes using no more than the engine of the damaged plane. The Duke of Westminster donated a damaged Voisin to the government; the Royal Aircraft Factory took its Wolseley engine and around it de Havilland designed an extraordinarily up-to-date (for 1911) biplane which received the designation B.E. through a bit of bureaucratic sharpstering. The B stood for Blériot, implying that the reconstituted plane would be of the general class of which the Blériot was the ancestor, and the E meant 'Experimental.' Similarly the Royal Aircraft Factory gave birth and berth to the F.E. (Farman Experimental) and the S.E.1 (Santos Experimental), which had absolutely nothing in common with the Farmans and the Santos after which they were named.

In 1909, de Havilland built an airplane of his own design. It was not particularly successful, but it did show signs of original and basically sound ideas. His work with the Royal Aircraft Factory quickly proved his extraordinary talents as he began to turn out designs for aircraft which were far ahead of their day and capable of outstanding performance. The B.E.2 was a special case, however: a fine aircraft for its time, it was soon outdated as a warplane, yet it remained in production beyond any reasonable limit, until 1916, the total production amounting to at least 3535 machines.

Technical description

The B.E.2 was one of the first successful attempts at building a fuselage biplane with a tractor engine driving a four-bladed propeller. The wings were of two-spar structure supported by two pairs of struts on each side. The fuselage had harmonious lines, rectangular in cross section with curved

Above: *A B.E.2b, with skids in addition to the regular undercarriage. This was one of the first B.E.2s to arrive in France with the British Expeditionary Forces. The photograph was taken at Bailleul in 1914* Below: *A B.E.2C of the Royal Flying Corps (US Air Force)* Upper right: *A curious accident involving a B.E.2 of the Royal Flying Corps. Note the markings on the stabilizer. (US Air Force)*

top decking. The pilot and observer were seated in tandem. The elevator and rudder were of metal construction with fabric covering. The engine was invariably an in-line and the landing gear was of the bogie type, with single wheels.

Development of the B.E.2

The B.E.1 made its first flight on January 1, 1912, with de Havilland at the controls. Since it was equipped with special mufflers which reduced engine noise radically, it was soon dubbed 'Army Silent Plane Aeroplane'. The wings were without dihedral, roll control was by warping, and the tandem cockpit was without a bulkhead between the pilot's (rear) and passenger's seats. The B.E.1 was powered by a 60-hp Wolseley V-8, water-cooled by an enormous vertical radiator just forward of the cockpit. Assigned the serial number 201 by the Royal Flying Corps, this prototype was widely used for experiments of all kinds and modified many times over.

The second prototype, designated B.E.2, was completed in 1912 and featured various modifications which were retroactively applied to the B.E.1, such as the 70-hp air-cooled Renault engine and a slight dihedral in the equal-span wings (the B.E.1 had a slightly longer upper wing). The 202, as it was designated, also had a busy experimental career and took part, as an outsider, in the Military Aviation meet of 1912 so that the Royal Aircraft Factory could see how it stood up against the 31 other machines shown by 20 manufacturers. Four B.E.2s were ordered by Vickers, and the Royal Aircraft Factory was authorized to build another five of them. This was followed by other orders for the B.E.2 which apart from a new type of fuel feed also had a division between the two tandem seats.

Important modifications were made in the design as experiments continued with the B.E.2. A series of tests were made in an effort to improve stability to a maximum, and Edward T. Busk devised a system of vertical surfaces to be applied to the upper wing; he also experimented with an undercarriage with pneumatic shock absorbers (one of the first such designs for shock-absorber struts which were later used on the F.E.2 and the R.E.7), and with various armament fittings.

A B.E.2b was built in 1914 and provided added protection for the cockpits, especially the forward one. In all 164 B.E.2s were built by nine firms until the late autumn of 1916.

The B.E.2c, which came out in the spring of 1914, differed radically from its predecessors. Its wings had greater stagger and dihedral, but the principal innovation was the addition of ailerons to all four wing sections. These changes, resulting from Busk's researches, improved the intrinsic stability of the plane, helped still more by the greatly increased rudder area. The undercarriage was also of a new design and much simpler, without skids. The wing tips were also of new shape and less rounded, and neat cutouts at the trailing edge of the lower wing roots greatly enhanced downward visibility. The stabilizer was also radically changed, lengthened and squared off. The engine was basically the same, but baptized anew: it was now known as the RAF-1a, a British version of the 70-hp Renault stepped up to 90 hp, thus improving the load-lifting capability. One or more machine guns were often mounted, although the observer (now in the rear cockpit) could use them only to a limited extent. The potential bomb load was virtually doubled [from 50 kg (110 lb) in the B.E.2b to almost 100 kg (220 lb) in the B.E.2c], although when carrying a full load of bombs the B.E.2c had to be flown as a single-seater.

Several B.E.2cs and ds were used as Home Defense fighters against German dirigibles. Flown as single-seaters, they were armed with a Lewis machine gun mounted on the upper wing, carried incendiary bombs, and sometimes Le Prieur rockets. The total production of these two B.E.2 variants amounted to at least 1300.

The B.E.2d appeared in the spring of 1916. It incorporated great improvements from the operational point of view. For one thing, with the observer in the second cockpit it was possible to defend the rear sector efficiently. Planes supplied to the Belgians had a 150-hp Hispano-Suiza engine, and this increased power permitted installation of a fixed weapon for fighter missions.
The next series, the B.E.2e, ran to 1800 machines,

the first of which became operational in the summer of 1916. The B.E.2e had only a single pair of struts each side, since the lower wing had been greatly shortened while the upper had been lengthened. The wing and stabilizer tips were completely different, the former tapering outward rather than inward, while the latter were parallel to the fuselage axis. Powered by the same engine as its predecessor, the B.E.2e was slightly faster than the B.E.2d, but its rate of climb (like that of the B.E.2d) was less than that of the B.E.2c which was already fairly modest. Possibly the worst feature was the re-introduction of the forward position for the observer, thus compromising the efficiency of the armament. Several machines intended for training were powered by the 75-hp Rolls-Royce Hawk engines.

How the B.E.2 was used in the War

When the B.E.1 was designed, no one had very precise ideas about what a military aircraft should be, and there was even less understanding about the functions of aviation in a future war. It is not

surprising, therefore, that the characteristic most sought after was stability, since designers thought in terms of reconnaissance for which a steady and stable plane was ideal. Only then came considerations of performance, ease of maintenance and handling over difficult terrain.

At first the activities of the B.E.1 and the first B.E.2s and B.E.2as were purely experimental. Radio apparatus, brakes, bomb racks, machine guns were all tested extensively. Meanwhile the B.E.2 was gaining a good reputation in the air: on August 12, 1912, it set up a British altitude record of more than 3200 meters (10500 ft), and its future looked good. Before the outbreak of war, B.E.2s had been assigned to Nos. 2, 4 and 6 Squadrons, RFC, which

Above: *The only existing photograph of a B.E.2 rigged as a seaplane. Note the two short floats forward, with a third under the tail. On the seaplane the rudder surface was increased and the rudder was hinged to a fin. This version was never built in series.* (Archivio Bignozzi)

Below: *Armament was always one of the weak points of the B.E.2. Among many proposed solutions to this problem was the one shown here, with two machine guns mounted obliquely*

7

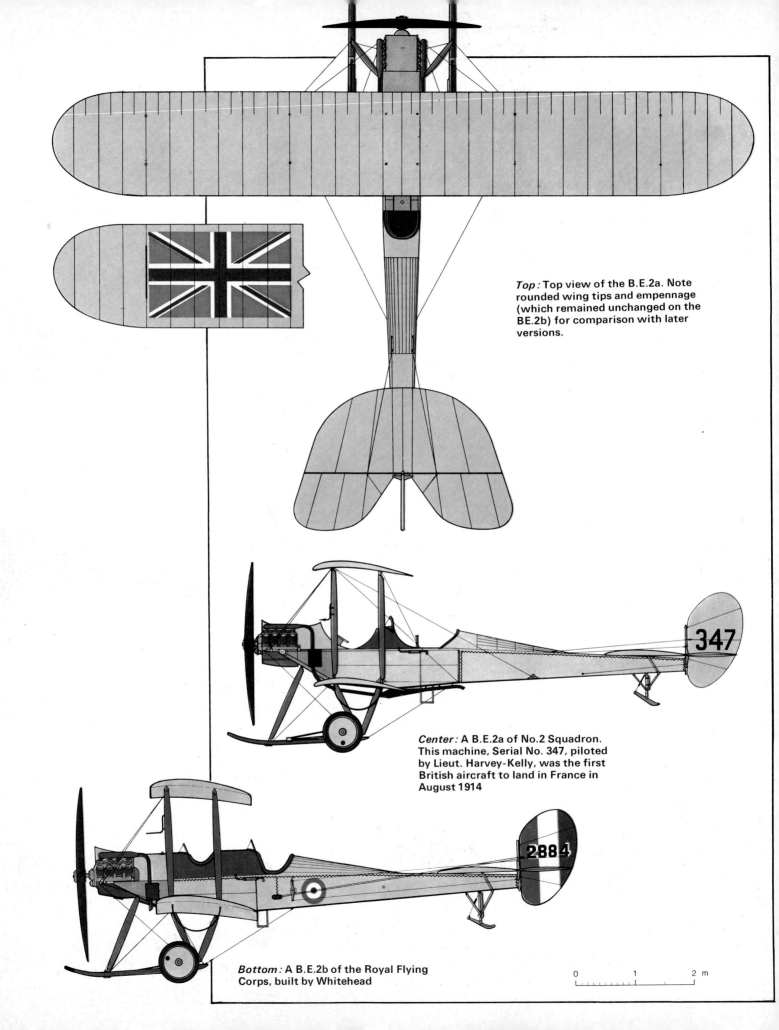

Top: Top view of the B.E.2a. Note rounded wing tips and empennage (which remained unchanged on the BE.2b) for comparison with later versions.

Center: A B.E.2a of No.2 Squadron. This machine, Serial No. 347, piloted by Lieut. Harvey-Kelly, was the first British aircraft to land in France in August 1914

Bottom: A B.E.2b of the Royal Flying Corps, built by Whitehead

0 1 2 m

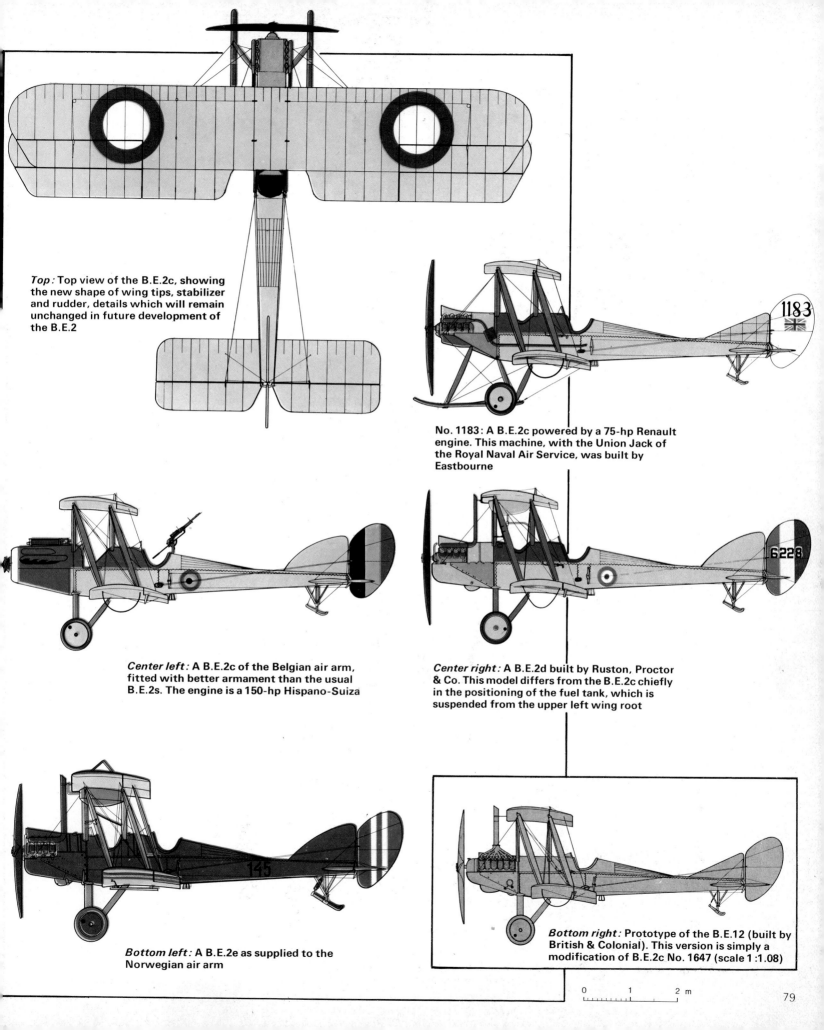

Top: Top view of the B.E.2c, showing the new shape of wing tips, stabilizer and rudder, details which will remain unchanged in future development of the B.E.2

No. 1183: A B.E.2c powered by a 75-hp Renault engine. This machine, with the Union Jack of the Royal Naval Air Service, was built by Eastbourne

Center left: A B.E.2c of the Belgian air arm, fitted with better armament than the usual B.E.2s. The engine is a 150-hp Hispano-Suiza

Center right: A B.E.2d built by Ruston, Proctor & Co. This model differs from the B.E.2c chiefly in the positioning of the fuel tank, which is suspended from the upper left wing root

Bottom left: A B.E.2e as supplied to the Norwegian air arm

Bottom right: Prototype of the B.E.12 (built by British & Colonial). This version is simply a modification of B.E.2c No. 1647 (scale 1:1.08)

0   1   2 m

Top: *The last model of the Royal Aircraft Factory's B.E.2 — the single-bay 2e. The machine shown here carried Lewis machine guns in the observer's seat for rear defense*

Bottom: *After the Armistice B.E.2s found good use in civilian aviation. This particular B.E.2e was the first plane operated by the fledgling Australian airline Qantas (Queensland and N. T. Aerial Service). (Qantas)*

bines). But in the early days of the war dogfights were rare and the enemy planes were no more fear-inspiring than the B.E.2s. However, already in this early period the B.E.2s revealed the defect of the design philosophy which held stability as the prime requisite, since their sluggish maneuvering exposed them to enemy counteraction and the German planes were substantially more maneuverable than the British.

This weakness became fully apparent in the late summer of 1915, when the Germans started to use the first fighter planes armed with synchronized machine-guns. This crisis was reported from the front and even debated in the House of Commons, but it had little noticeable effect on the men responsible for supplying military aircraft. All the modifications introduced from time to time in the B.Es were not aimed at improving maneuverability and they had little effect on overall performance. Symptomatic of this unrealistic attitude was the instruction that, when coming into land, the pilot should remain seated since if he stood up his body would add sufficient drag to stall the aircraft! With hindsight it is obvious that the potential of the design had reached its limit, yet the last consignment of B.Es did not leave the factory until the end of 1916. Meanwhile their role had been downgraded to training (including at the bases of Sitapur in India and Point Cook in Australia), but these final deliveries were received with ever-decreasing enthusiasm by the airmen.

The B.E.2c and 2d equipped 14 squadrons of the RFC in France and one of the RNAS, some of them flying these machines even up to April 1917. Moreover they were sent to the 6th *Escadrille* of the Belgian air arm, while still others were used in the Aegean, the Middle East, and Africa. Several units equipped with B.E.2s served in the Home Defense, especially at night, and in these missions the reliable old biplane gave its best, downing five dirigibles (Zeppelins L.21, 31, 32 and 34 and a Schütte-Lanz SL.11).

Great hopes had unexplainably been placed in the B.E.2e and many contracts for its predecessors had been revised to call for B.E.2es with certain revisions to which the designations B.E.2f and B.E.2g were allocated. All the old B.Es had already been recalled from the front when the first B.E.2es reached No. 21 Squadron on the eve of the Battle of the Somme (July 1, 1916). Two weeks later No. 34 Squadron arrived in France, completely equipped with B.E.2es, and subsequently 18 squadrons on the Western front were flying this machine. Other units used them in Gt. Britain, the Middle East, India and Macedonia. Several B.E.2es were turned over to the Russians, and in 1918 the Americans acquired a dozen B.E.2es for the training school which they had set up at Ford, in Sussex.

had found them admirable for long-range flights. On August 13, 1914, Nos. 2 and 4 Squadrons flew to France, the first British flying formations to show that in case of war they could operate on the Continent at a short notice.

Several B.E.2as were turned over to the Royal Naval Air Service, which up until the beginning of the war had only one machine. These B.E.2s were flown by the Squadron based at Eastchurch and on TDY at Dunquerque and later took in raids on the Zeppelin hangars at Düsseldorf and Cologne as well as bombing enemy installations at Ostende, Zeebrugge and Mittelkerke. When the unit was sent to the Aegean, it took part in action over the Dardenelles. Meanwhile B.E.2bs had been assigned to Nos. 8, 9 (radio) and 16 Squadrons of the Royal Flying Corps on the Western front and in Egypt. Among the principal actions was the bombing of the Courtrfi railway station (April 26, 1915), which merited the first (posthumous) award of a Victoria Cross to a British airman — Lieut. W. B. Rhodes-Moorhouse. These machines were unarmed except for the pilots' sidearms (pistols and car-

SPAD XIII

The SPAD is genera[...] plane represented in [...] aviation during Worl[...] can even be said to h[...] tion of 'traditional' ae[...] veloped during the co[...] only when the enemy [...] that the building of co[...]

The SPAD was de[...] the creator of the fa[...] The Deperdussin fac[...] financial reasons, but the pioneer Blériot had re-organized it as the *Société pour l'Aviation et ses Dérivés* (which made it possible for him to retain the acronym SPAD, which had originally stood for the *Société Provisoire des Aéroplanes Deperdussin),* and Béchéreau had stayed on as head of the engineering department, assisted by Mons. Herbémont, who was eventually to be his successor in the postwar period.

The first fighter plane produced by the SPAD was the two-seat A.2, an original design which was characterized by a special cabin for the machine

in front of the engine. This air-[...] certain missions by the French [...] and (much more extensively) by [...] it was too complicated and not [...] liant in performance. When the [...] dvanced to the point where it was [...] chronize permanently mounted [...] fighting aircraft, Béchéreau re-[...] as a single-seater with a fixed [...] engine. From this design, known [...] one of the first to use the fine [...] iza engine, came an entire generation of first-rate fighter planes.

Technical description

In their general structure, SPAD aircraft were a fairly conventional design for their day. The sole exception was the tie-struts at the midpoint of the wing span, so positioned as to prevent the flying and landing brace wires from whipping in flight.

A group of SPAD VIIs of the French air arm. The entry into action of the SPAD re-established a balance between German and Allied fighter aviation. The greyhound painted on the fuselage of the SPAD in the foreground was the emblem of the 81st Squadron. (Museo Caproni, Taliedo)

amedeo gigli

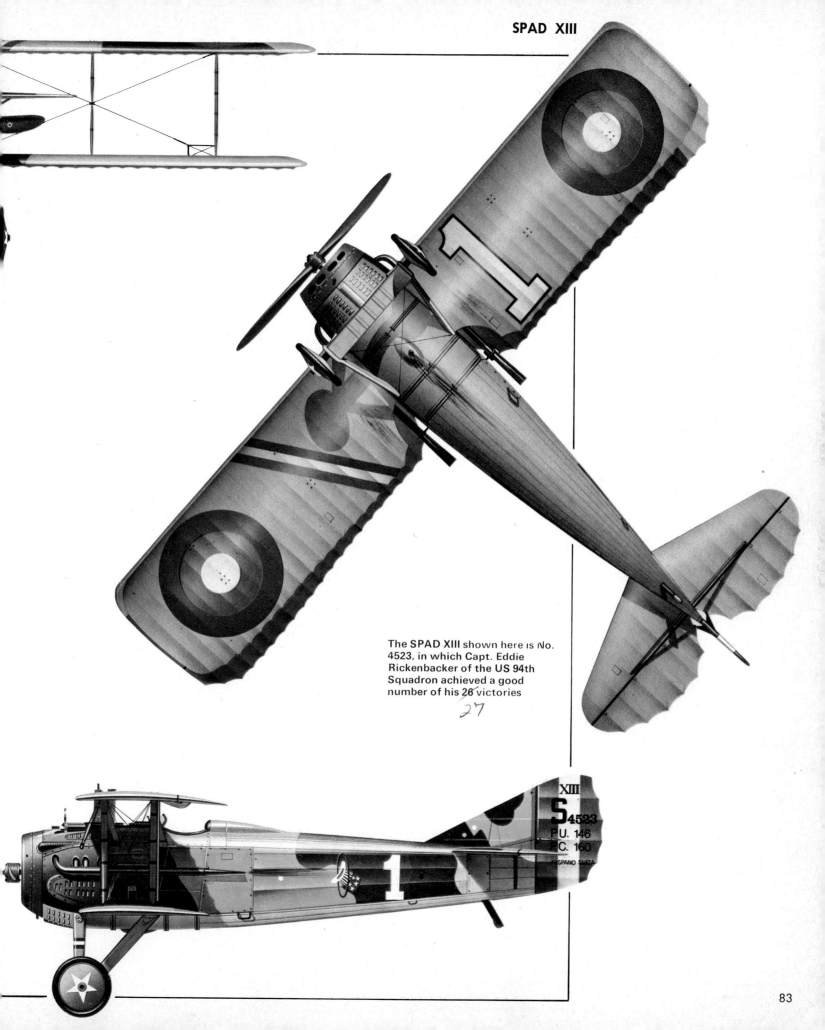

The **SPAD XIII** shown here is No. 4523, in which Capt. Eddie Rickenbacker of the US 94th Squadron achieved a good number of his 26 victories

27

XIII
S 4523
P.U. 146
P.C. 160
HISPANO SUIZA

This innovation gave the SPAD the appearance of a two-bay biplane, although it was actually a single-bay job.

This solution, unusual but not rare in aircraft technology at the beginning of the war, gave the plane its proverbial ruggedness, which was also enhanced by other structural characteristics, such as the wing construction featuring close-set ribs, the size of the engine bearers, which extended aft to support the pilot's seat, and the strong fuselage structure. These were acquired, however, only with the trade-off of a rather high empty weight.

Aerodynamically the SPAD showed good general lines, with its almost conical fuselage and the neat rounded radiator. The machine had remarkable climbing qualities, better than those of the best British and German planes of the day, although this advantage was offset to some extent by the reduced maneuverability. The SPAD was not, basically, an 'easy' aircraft to fly, especially at reduced speed, and was apt to stall suddenly owing to its rather thin wings. But its extraordinary ruggedness permitted sudden extended dives, which could be repeated with complete confidence. Thus it could maneuver vertically in a way that the Germans could not attempt until the appearance of the Fokker D.VII.

All things considered, the SPAD could give a very good account of itself, even in dogfights. Another advantage was that it provided a stable firing platform.

The upper wing was a one-piece structure, with a slightly longer span and chord than the lower, two-section wing. The spars, which formed a box structure, were built up of a number of sections joined by linen-wrapped scarfing, probably because of the difficulty of obtaining sufficiently long spruce sections in France. The leading edges were wholly of spruce, and the trailing edges were cable, tightened and doped to give a slightly scalloped effect. Both wings were without dihedral.

The fuselage was of wood, with transverse bulkheads of heavy-gauge sheet steel with lightening holes. There were four longerons joined by transverse elements, the whole structure braced diagonally with piano wire. Top and bottom deckings were rounded.

The undercarriage legs were formed in a single piece built up from laminated poplar. The axle was articulated at the center. The function of shock

absorbers was performed by elastic cord—'bungee' —between the wheels and on the steel-bound wooden tail skid. If necessary, the wheels could be replaced by skis or floats.

All variants of the SPAD were powered by 8-cylinder 90° V-type Hispano-Suiza engines, ranging in various models from 140 to 300 hp, and cooled by a nearly circular radiator with vertical shutters for temperature control. The main fuel tank was fitted beneath the main fuselage structure and connected to a fuel feed well suspended from the upper wing center section; the smaller secondary tank was fed by a pump run by the engine, which also drove the oil and water pumps.

Armament was either one or two 7·65-mm Vickers machine guns, which were mounted above the engine and synchronized to fire through the propeller. The SPAD XII and XIV also carried a 37-mm Hotchkiss cannon between the two cylinder banks, firing through the propeller hub. Le Prieur rockets could be mounted between the interwing struts.

Development of the SPAD XIII

It was the SPAD V, built towards the end of 1915, that served as the prototype for the first production machine, the SPAD VII, which was first flown in the spring of 1916 by Mons, Béquet at Villacoublay. The VII still had the 140-hp engine without supercharger and a Galia or Bloch propeller. It could reach 196 km/hr at sea level and could climb to 3000 m in 15 minutes. It was armed with a Vickers machine gun mounted above and slightly to the right of the engine which had a Birkigt synchronizer, invented by the Swiss engineer, Mark Birkigt, who had also designed the engine.

The SPAD VII was put into production at once with an initial order calling for 268 aircraft ear-

Top: Servicing the SPAD VII biplane on a French airfield.
Bottom: SPAD VIIs were imported by the Italians and did much to beef up the fledgling Italian air arm. Most of the time the new aircraft flew in company with seasoned planes.
(Museo Caproni, Taliedo, Aeronautica Militare Italiana)

marked for the French *Escadrilles*. Other orders flowed in from abroad, while in Great Britain two firms, British Blériot and Mann & Egerton, tooled up to build the VII under a licensing agreement. Deliveries began on September 2, 1916, but the new fighter had its baptism of fire a month before when one SPAD VII had been sent to the front for evaluation under operational conditions where, piloted by Lieut. Pinsard, it had taken part in actions on the Somme.

The first production series were powered by the 150-hp Hispano-Suiza 8Aa. By August 1917, 495 of these new fighters had come from the factories, enough to replace the Nieuport sesquiplanes in the 'élite' squadrons.

The second series of the SPAD VII had the 175- to 180-hp Hispano-Suiza 8Ac engine. These aircraft had a slightly larger span (by about 25 cm) and rudder. This was the SPAD series with the largest number of planes registered—about 6000, and the VII remained in production even after its successor, the SPAD XIII, had joined it in the assembly shops. There were not less than eight French factories busy turning out the SPAD VII (total production: 5600 machines), besides the two British firms mentioned above. The British Blériot & SPAD produced 100 SPAD VIIs for the Royal Flying Corps, and Mann & Egerton built 120 aircraft for the Royal Naval Air Service. The RFC also had a good supply from French sources. This enormous output sufficed to equip, in addition to the French and British units, five Italian, one Belgian and several Russian squadrons. In December 1917 the United States procured 189 SPAD VIIs and used them to equip seven squadrons, sending the surplus back to America for training purposes. The Russians also built a number of SPAD VIIs under license at the 'Dux' factory in Moscow.

The final VIIs were powered by a 200-hp engine, and in 1917 two machines were completed fitted with Renault 12D engines of the same power (but slightly larger dimensions) equipped with a Hispano 8Bc *moteur-canon*. The first of these machines remained in the experimental stage, but the second, numbered S382, flew for the first time on July 17 and served as prototype for the SPAD XII. Three hundred XIIs were manufactured by the Blériot,

Janoir and Levasseur factories. The SPAD XII was designed at the behest of the French fighter ace Georges Guynemer, who requested a highly destructive plane capable of operating over long distances. His personal aircraft was armed with a 37-mm cannon firing through the propeller hub and a Vickers machine gun. Guynemer was thus made into a highly dangerous combatant, but an uncomfortable one. His cannon had a slow rate of fire and spewed cordite fumes into the cockpit at every shot.

Eventually the SPAD XII was fitted with the 220-hp Hispano-Suiza 8Bec, and was followed by a seaplane version dubbed the SPAD XIV, of which 40 were manufactured—mainly for the Royal Naval Air Service but also for the Channel-based French *Forces Aériennes de la Mer*. A parallel conversion of the SPAD VII to seaplane configuration, built in 1916 and designated SPAD X, remained in the experimental stage.

In April 1917 the prototype of the SPAD XIII, bearing the serial number S392, flew for the first time; the test pilot was Sous-lieutenant R. Dorme. This new version of the French fighter plane had the larger dimensions of the SPAD XII and featured more rounded wing and stabilizer tips, together with a curved rudder trailing edge and an increased aileron chord. The engine was a 220-hp Hispano-Suiza 8Ba with reduction gear, which was eventually replaced by the 8Be developing 235 hp. The armament consisted of two synchronized Vickers machine guns. Beginning in May 1917 this new fighter gradually replaced the SPAD VII in the French squadrons, although the initial deliveries were slowed down owing to certain troubles with the engine. It was not until the spring of 1918 that production got into full swing and sufficient aircraft became available to equip new units formed specifically for this new fighter. Eventually there were 81 squadrons flying the SPAD XIIIs. Before the war was over 8440 machines of this type had been built by the Blériot, Bernard, De Marçay, Kellner and Levasseur factories, and a further 10000 were canceled when the war ended. A number of SPAD XIIIs were also made available to France's allies: Two units of the Royal Flying Corps (Nos. 19 and 23 Squadrons) and at least two Italian units (*Squadriglie* 77 and 91) were equipped with

Top, left: *Testing the synchronized firing of machine guns on a SPAD VII at an Italian airfield*
Top, right: *A famous Italian fighter ace, Lieut. Ferruccio Ranza, with his SPAD VII, decorated with a curious ladderlike device. This picture was taken at the Santa Caterina (Udine) air base, home of the 91st Squadron, in 1918. 1918. (Museo Caproni, Taliedo Aeronautica Militare Italiana)*

Center: *The celebrated French ace, Georges Guynemer, in his SPAD 'Vieux Charles' (Old Charles). Guynemer was the commander of the 3rd Escadrille of the group known as 'Les Cigognes' (The Storks) and flew various types of SPADs, especially the XII, which was armed with a 37-mm cannon. One of Guynemer's SPADs is still to be seen at the Musée des Invalides in Paris*
Bottom: *A SPAD of the US Army Air Service with a brilliant checkerboard insignia adopted just after the end of the war. (Jarrett Collection, US Air Force)*

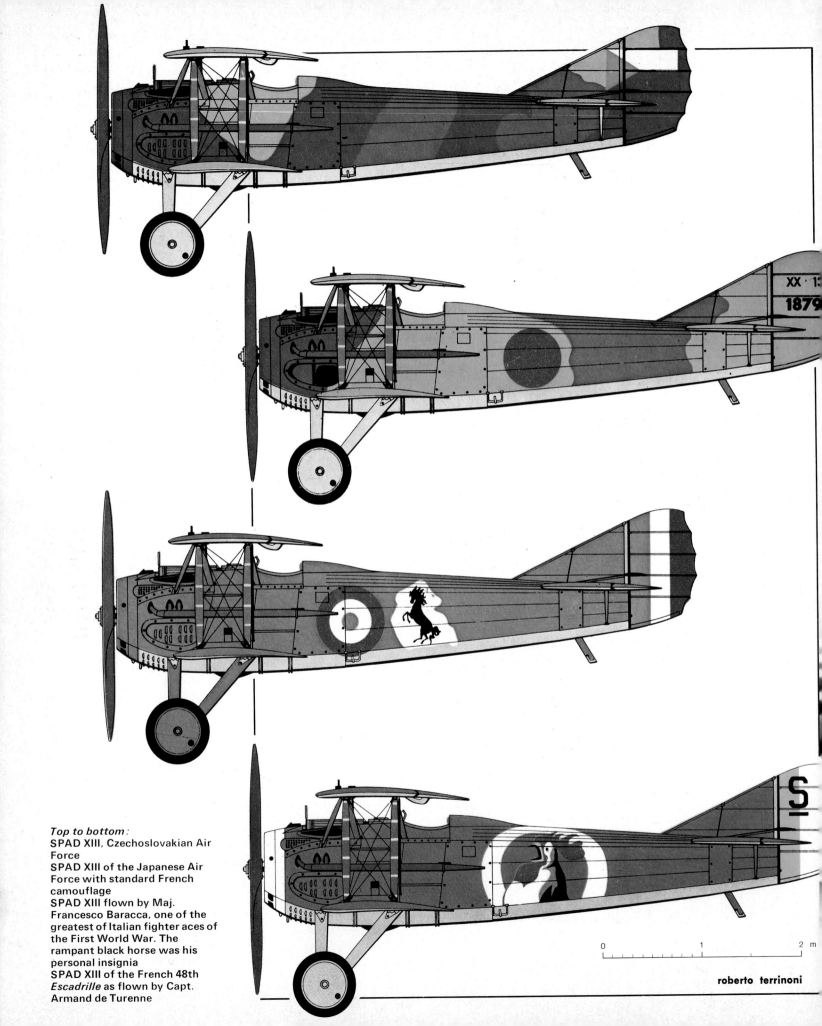

Top to bottom:
SPAD XIII, Czechoslovakian Air
Force
SPAD XIII of the Japanese Air
Force with standard French
camouflage
SPAD XIII flown by Maj.
Francesco Baracca, one of the
greatest of Italian fighter aces of
the First World War. The
rampant black horse was his
personal insignia
SPAD XIII of the French 48th
Escadrille as flown by Capt.
Armand de Turenne

roberto terrinoni

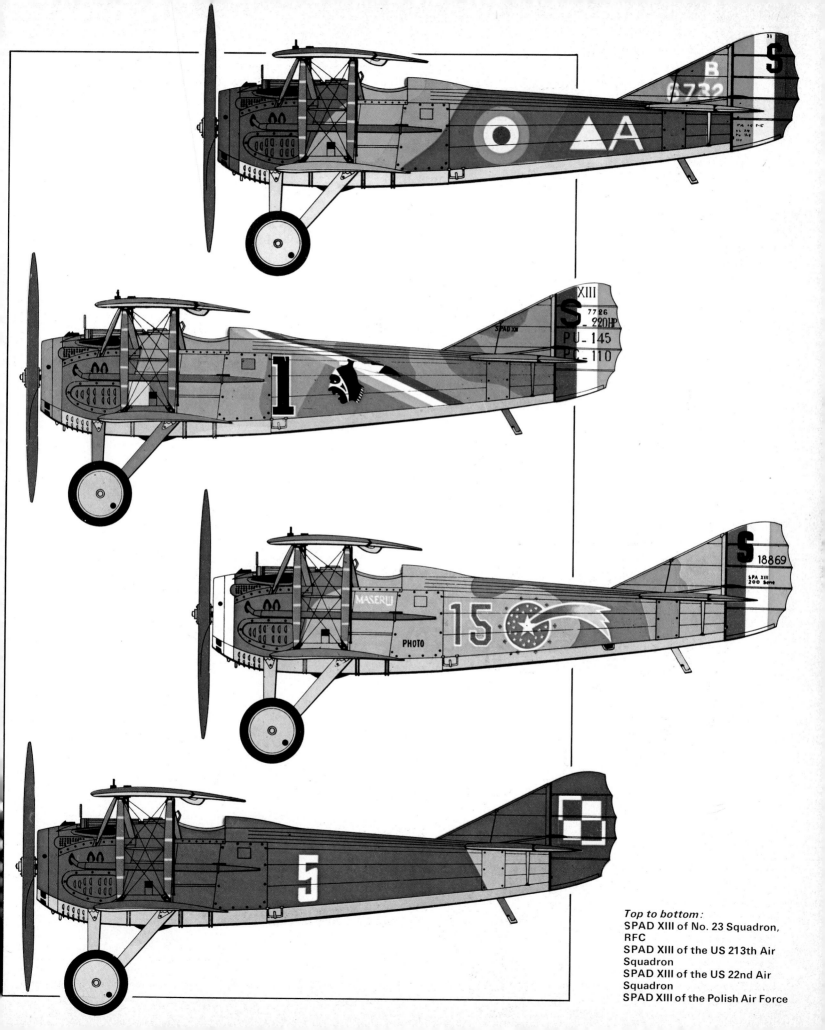

Top to bottom:
SPAD XIII of No. 23 Squadron, RFC
SPAD XIII of the US 213th Air Squadron
SPAD XIII of the US 22nd Air Squadron
SPAD XIII of the Polish Air Force

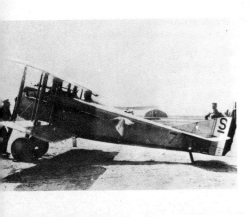

Top: *A group of SPAD XIIIs of the 1st Fighter Group of the Italian Air Force at the Malpensa airfield in northern Italy in the early 1920s. In the background are two Caproni trimotors*
Center: *When the Italian* Regia Aeronautica Italiana *(Royal Italian Air Force) was formed after the war, SPAD XIIIs were the backbone of this new air arm*
Bottom: *A SPAD VII bearing the emblem of the* Cigognes. (Archivio Bignozzi *and* Musée de l'Air)

SPAD XIIIs, while 37 aircraft went to the Belgians and not less than 893 to the Americans.

A single SPAD XXVI, a land version of the SPAD XIV intended for use on an aircraft carrier, was built and test-flown on November 5, 1918, a week before the Armistice. An updated and strengthened version of previous SPAD fighters was the SPAD XVII, designed by Herbemont who had succeeded Béchéreau in the works.

This new machine flew for the first time in June 1918 and was powered by a 300-hp Hispano-Suiza 8Fb. The XVII was a fighter-photo-reconnaissance plane and carried a single synchronized Vickers machine gun and two cameras.

Later versions of the basic SPAD included the XXI, which remained on the drawing board, the number being re-allocated to a SPAD seaplane entered in the 1919 Schneider Cup race; and a two-seat fighter designated SPAD XXIII C2 which appeared in April 1918 and served as prototype for the SPAD XX, which was basically the same aircraft except for the *moteur-canon*; 120 SPAD XXs were built. Towards the end of the war there was also a SPAD XXII derived from the XVII with a slightly swept-back upper wing (which was to become a Herbemont trade-mark) and two pairs of struts on each side.

The long list of SPAD models would not be complete without mentioning the SPAD 62 and 72 training aircraft of two-resp. single-seat layout, derived from the SPAD VII.

How the SPADs were used in the War

War pilots, accustomed to the agility of the Nieuports, were reluctant to accept the SPAD VII; but as soon as the new aircraft had a chance to demonstrate its performance and reliability, airmen understood that here they had a plane which might enable them to achieve once again a balance with the Germans, whose new machines had outstripped theirs. This happened during the critical period of the Battle of the Somme. French squadrons which received the new SPADs included the SPA.3 of the group known as *Les Cigognes* ('The Storks') which featured such aces as Georges Guynemer and René Fonck, and the SPA. 8, 12, 23 and 124. By October 1916 Nos. 19 and 23 Squadrons of the RFC on the Western front were similarly equipped, as were other British units operating in

Mesopotamia. The latter received 19 SPADs, some with an additional Lewis machine gun mounted on the upper wing. The Belgian 5th Squadron received 15 SPADs. The British Admiralty had also ordered some SPAD VIIs but turned them over to the Royal Flying Corps in 1917 in exchange for Sopwith Triplanes.

The first deliveries of SPADs to the Italian air arm began in March 1917, and some aircraft of the first series, powered by 150-hp engines, were assigned to the 77th and 91st *Squadriglie*. These were used chiefly for training and photo reconnaissance on the Isonzo front, but as other aircraft were delivered it became possible to equip—at least in part—the 71st, 75th and 76th *Squadriglie*. Shortly before the battles which flared on the Italian-Austrian front from the Isonzo to the Piave Rivers in October and November 1917, the 78th and 80th *Squadriglie* received several SPAD VIIs and the 72nd and 73rd were also supplied in part shortly thereafter. The first victory with this fighter was achieved by Maj. Francesco Baracca, one of the greatest of Italian aces, on May 13, 1917. Other Italian pilots who distinguished themselves with the SPAD included Ranza, Ruffo, Ferreri, Parvis, Olivari and Oliva; the last two also performed notable feats of photoreconnaissance.

The SPAD VII was not built under license in Italy, although the engines were manufactured by the SCAT and Itala firms. A total of 214 SPADs were used operationally by the Italians, together with 26 SPAD XIIIs, which began arriving early in 1918. Some XIIIs were not uncrated and assembled until after the war had ended, and these were supplied the new *Regia Aeronautica*.

In France the SPAD XIII became the backbone of the French fighter aviation, where it continued in active duty until 1923. Even the SPAD XII, although smaller in numbers, won honors for itself, especially in the capable hands of Georges Guynemer and René Fonck.

Almost all of the few SPAD XVIIs built were assigned to the SPA.3 of the *Cigognes* group.

On the Western front the SPAD XIIIs were also the mainstay of the United States Army Air Service fighter force: 16 Squadrons were equipped with them, including the glorious 94th, whose hero was Capt. Eddie Rickenbacker, and the 27th, with another great American ace, Frank Luke. Apparently the British did not use this aircraft in combat, although their Nos. 19 and 35 Squadrons were equipped with it. The Belgians delivered it to a single squadron, the 10th, before the war ended.

After the war 37 SPAD XIIIs were sent to Belgium (for the Belgian 3rd, 4th and 10th Squadrons); 40 went to Poland and others were shipped to Czechoslovakia, Japan (which had already secured a license for manufacturing the SPAD XX), Persia, Portugal, Spain and Thailand. A few SPAD VIIs were also exported to Brazil, Greece, Poland, Portugal, Rumania and Thailand.

After the Armistice 893 SPAD XIIIs belonging to the US Army Air Service in France were shipped back to the United States. These machines were re-engined with 180-hp Wright-Hispano Es and used as trainers.

SIKORSKY I.M.

Specifications

	Bol'shoi Bal'tisky B	Russky Vityaz	I.M. Type A	I.M. Type B	I.M. Type V	I.M. Type G	I.M. Type D	I.M. Type Ye
Total *hp*	400	400	400	530-600	528-640	580-760	640	880
Wing span, *m*	27·50	28·20	34·50	34·50	34·50	34·50	30·87	38·00
Length, *m*	20·20	20·20	20·50	19·00	17·10	17·00	17·10	17·50
Wing area, *m²*	120	125	150	150	125	159·60	—	182·50
Weight, empty, *kg*	—	2700	3300	3050	3100-3150	3800-3600	—	3850
Bomb load, *kg*	—	—	—	500	—	450-700	—	800
Total weight, *kg*	3550	4200	4800	4550	4650-4900	5200-5500	4600	7000
Maximum speed, *km/hr*	85	95	105	110	100-110	120-125	130	136·7
Range, *km*	—	—	490	380-400	400-450	630	450	750
Rate of climb, *m in min*	—	—	—	2500 in 45:00	—	—	—	3000 in 43:00
Ceiling, *m*	—	830	1800	2500	3100-3500	4000-4300	3000	4000

Igor Ivanovich Sikorsky eventually became, of course, world-famous for his helicopters, but another equally valid claim to fame lay in his large multi-engined aircraft. Something that very few people realize is that the first of these giants were designed and built already in 1912-13, when most aerodynamicists were convinced that heavier-than-air machines could never be built above rather modest dimensions.

At 23, Sikorsky was already the chief aeronautical designer of one of the biggest Russian industries, the RBVZ *(Russko-Bal'tisky Vagonny Zavod—Russo-Baltic Waggon Factory)* at St. Petersburg. Sikorsky got the approval of the firm and, with a fine group of collaborators which included G. I. Lavrov and the British engineer Kennedy, he started

work on the design of a giant, multi-engined aircraft capable of accommodating six persons in a closed, well furnished cabin.

The aircraft was given the unofficial name of *Bol'shoi Bal'tisky* (The Great Baltic). Apparently the first model was unsuccessfully flight-tested with only two engines early in May 1913, although Sikorsky in his autobiography gives May 13, 1913, as the date of its maiden flight and mentions that it was powered by four engines (100-hp Argus) mounted in tandem pairs. According to some historians, this aircraft was called *Bol'shoi Bal'tisky* Type B.

The flight of May 13 lasted 10 minutes, the plane taking off and landing at the Komendantsky military airfield. Igor Sikorsky himself was the pilot,

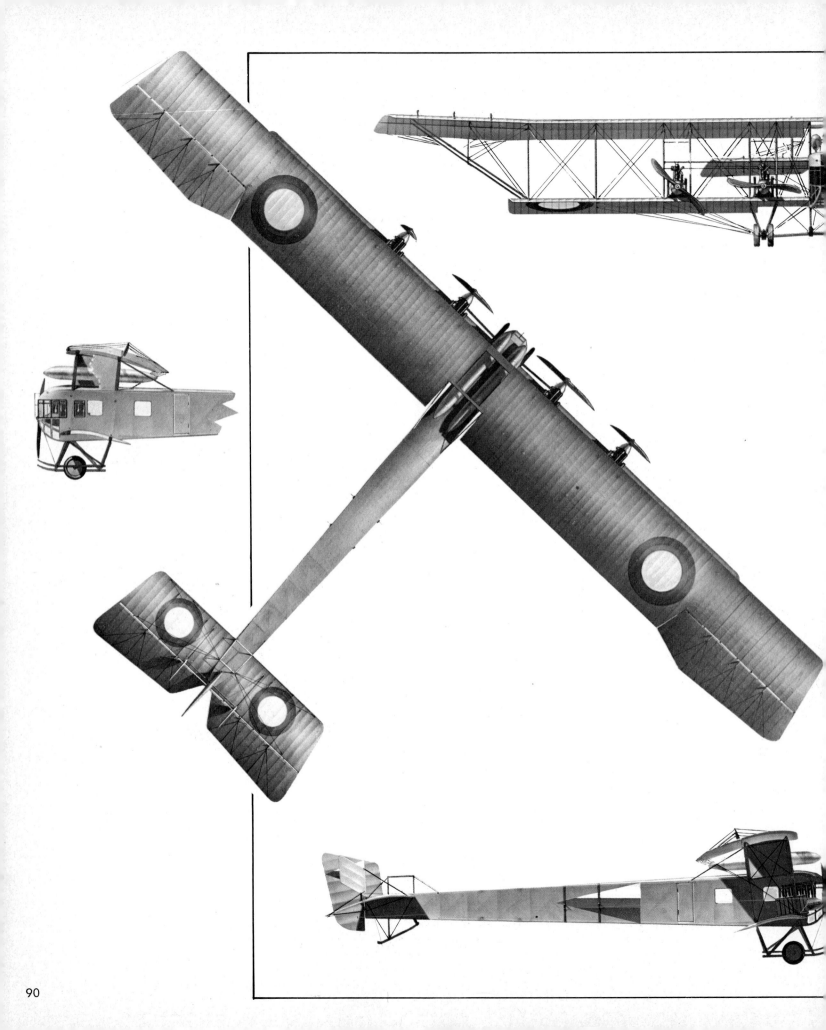

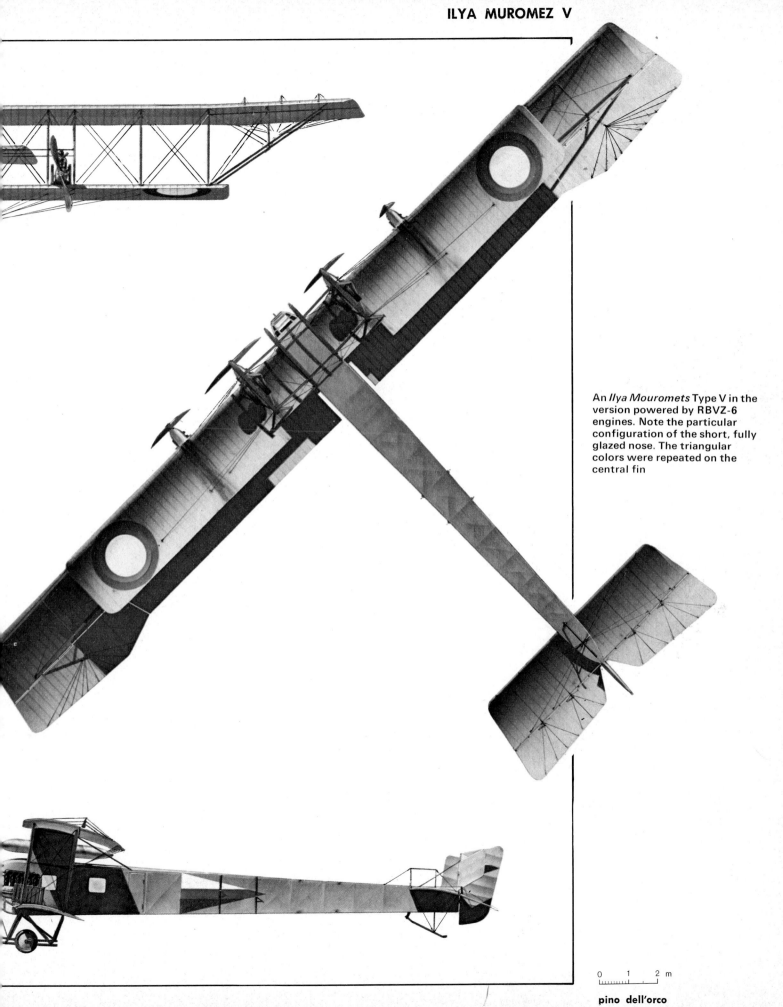

An *Ilya Mouromets* Type V in the version powered by RBVZ-6 engines. Note the particular configuration of the short, fully glazed nose. The triangular colors were repeated on the central fin

0   1   2 m

pino dell'orco

Top: *Nose of the* Bol'shoi Bal'tisky, *nicknamed* Le Grande, *in the version powered by four engines fitted in tandem pairs*
Center: *Interior of the cabin of the first four-engined I.M. fitted out for carrying passengers.* (Archivio Bignozzi)
Bottom: *The first I.M. coming in to land on skis. Note the high-mounted side engines.* (Archivio Falessi)

assisted by Capt. Gleb Alekhnovich and a mechanic, the latter sitting in the nose 'balcony'. The 10-minute flight revealed the weakness of various theoretical points and suggested practical solutions for the progressive development of giant aircraft.

After a few flights Sikorsky decided to separate the engines, finding that the rear propellers were contributing little thrust. On July 23, with his giant plane modified accordingly and rechristened *Russky Vityaz* (Russian Knight), he resumed flight tests, with improved results.

Meanwhile Sikorsky had been busy designing a true transport aircraft, larger and more comfortable than his initial efforts and incorporating all that he had learned from the *Bal'tisky* and *Vityaz*. He was also surely aware of the potential military value of such an aircraft, the largest then known and capable of carrying heavy loads over long distances. The *Russky Vityaz* had been irreparably damaged on the ground when an engine fell on it from a Voisin which broke up in mid-air overhead; but the *Vityaz's* engines were not damaged and could be re-used in the new plane, which was to be known as the *Ilya Mouromets* Type A, named after a hero in Russian mythology. The Type A was ready at the end of the year and was test-flown on December 11, 1913. This first flight nearly ended in disaster. Supplementary wing surfaces had been added to the main wings, increasing the total wing area to 182 m² (1959 sq ft), and this additional surface caused the plane to stall at about 50 m (165 ft) altitude. The Type A landed heavily but without great damage, and in January 1914 it took to the air without the supplementary wing area and performed satisfactorily.

The I.M. differed in several ways from its predecessors. The fuselage was entirely redesigned, the frontal balcony being eliminated, and replaced by a glazed nose section. The cabin was consequently enlarged and furnished more comfortably, with a table, sofa, armchair, *samovar,* light fixtures, heating, clothing compartment and toilet.

Technical description

Structurally the gigantic Sikorsky aircraft looked simply like an enlarged version of a typical biplane except that the dimensions and installations marked an entirely new departure. The fuselage cross section in the first model was surprisingly small, but in the I.M. series it was increased to equal the cabin height and broadened (including the center struts, which in the 1913 version were outside the cabin). On later series a crewman could use a trolley to travel from the cabin to the tail-end machine-gun position.

The basic airframe structure was of wood covered with fabric (except at the nose, where plywood was used instead). The cabin included the flight deck, which had dual controls only in the 1913 version (since later the second pilot served only as assistant and reserve pilot); and lounge space and freight compartments, which in the military version served to accommodate defensive installations and (from Type V onwards) interior bomb racks. Flight personnel could leave the cabin to get to the engines for minor repairs during flight or to reach the forward balcony which had a searchlight (in the 1913 version), or the outer nose platform and the topside platform in the early models of the I.M. Type Ye also had rudimentary armor protection—the floor of the pilot's cabin was covered by a 10-mm (0·39-inch) steel sheet and the back rests of the pilots' seats were similarly armored.

The two wings varied in span and chord. The upper wing tips were braced by slantwise struts and were slightly raised to give a very slight dihedral, minimal in the 1913 version, but increased later. In at least some versions of Type V the wings were slightly cambered. Only the upper wing had ailerons, which had slight warping at the tips and projected beyond the wing trailing edge. The center section of the upper wing was not covered in all military models after Type B and before Type Ye (i.e., Types V, G and D). Vertical diaphragms were positioned either above the inboard engines, on all engines, or between the fuselage and the upper wing.

The stabilizer was of exceptional span and chord, the latter in many cases exceeding the wing chord; it had considerable curvature to ensure maximum pressure differential under a wide range of loading conditions. The elevator was divided into two halves. The 1913 version originally had four rudders, but the efficiency of the design was such that they could immediately be reduced to two; the aircraft could be controlled even when two engines were shut off on the same side. On machines of the I.M. series there was usually only a single rudder with no fin, closely flanked by two smaller control surfaces.

The undercarriage included a complex of four skids, to which skis could be attached for winter use, or varying numbers of wheels: 16 in the 1913 version, 8 in the I.M.s, in four pairs apparently sheathed with a single tread for each pair. The tail skid sometimes consisted of two parallel elements.

The powerplant consisted of four water-cooled engines mounted in various combinations—either in pairs, with both tractor and pusher propellers

(Bol'shoi Bal'tisky Type B, I.M. Type D), or singly, mounted directly on the lower wing, with all propellers of the tractor type. Sometimes all or only the outboard engines were raised slightly above the lower wing, but aligned in any case, and sometimes the inboard (or outboard) engines were set slightly forward.

Development of the Sikorsky I.Ms

According to the system of designation adopted for Sikorsky aircraft, the 1913 version could be S.9 or S.12 and the later models would probably range from S.23 (I.M. Type B) to S.27 (I.M. Type Ye).

The name *Ilya Mouromets* was used to describe all Sikorsky four-engined military aircraft. The first aircraft of the I.M. series was acquired by the Russian Imperial Navy and shipped to the Libava (Liepaja/Latvia) naval base, where Sikorsky-designed floats with rubber-cord suspension were fitted. The two inboard Argus engines were replaced by two Salmson (Canton-Unné) radial engines delivering 140 hp each, and the outboard engines were mounted higher. In this four-engined seaplane configuration the aircraft made several successful flights, but no further orders were forthcoming.

The same arrangement for the engines, using 125- to 132-hp outboard engines and 140-hp inboard engines (all Argus), had been adopted for the second I.M., which, following the spectacular flight made by Sikorsky and Prussis to Kiev, had been dubbed the *Kievsky*.

The third version of the I.M. was designated Type V (the third letter of the Cyrillic alphabet, identical in form to the Roman B). Type V was considerably smaller than its predecessors, being designed on the basis of experience gained from previous models which could be of value in solving specific military problems. The Type V was also lighter and more compact, and part of the bomb load could be stowed inside. The Type V was the first I.M. designed specifically as a 4-engined bomber and made its first flight early in 1915. Thirty-two machines of this version were built.

In December 1915 a fourth version, Type G, went into production (G is the fourth letter of the Russian alphabet). The G was initially practically identical with the Type V but featured lengthened wing chord, increasing the wing area to 159·6 m² (1814·6 sq. ft). The power group of these first versions (Type G1) was mixed, varying from four 170-hp V-8 British Sunbeam Cossacks to two

220-hp V-12 French Renaults used together with two RBVZ engines, the last two in outboard positions. The armament had been strengthened on the basis of combat experience, being increased to five flexible machine guns (usually Lewis, sometimes Colt), but the need for even more defensive firepower was evident, especially in the aft sector, and Sikorsky, who followed closely the activity of his aircraft at the front, suggested the tail position, accessible to a gunner lying prone on the dolly mentioned above. The first tail-gun positions were fitted on the G2 and G3 variants, with corresponding variations in the configuration of tail elements, and at the same time the airframe was reinforced. A nose gun also appeared for the first time on the G2, and in the G3, of which 15 were built, two beam machine guns were added, making a total of six or seven guns. Of the series a total of 30 machines were built, including 20 G1s and G2s.

Not much is known about the Type D, except that it did not have its engines mounted in pairs. According to some sources the engines were Sunbeams, while others maintain that they were RBVZ-6s, which allowed a reduction in span from the regular 34·5 m to 30·87 m. Apparently only very few I.M. Type D machines were built.

When manufacture of the more powerful Renault engine under a licensing agreement got under way the design and construction of a bigger machine with improved defensive armament became possible. This was the I.M. Type Ye which carried a crew of seven. The wing span was increased to 38 m and the fuselage was redesigned to permit installation of two enormous fuel tanks protected by layers of special material. The nose was lengthened and of better aerodynamic shape, and the whole fuselage lengthened by several bays. Defensive armament normally consisted of seven machine guns, of which two were mounted in dorsal positions. The I.M.-Ye2 version, on which armor shielding was extended to the gunners' positions, carried eight machine guns and (experimentally) even a 50-mm quick-firing cannon. This variant of Type Ye was the last in the long series of I.M. bombers. A grand total of about 80 of these giant aircraft had been built when further production was halted by the revolution of October 1917.

How the Sikorsky I.M. Bomber was used in the War

The earliest military I.M., the *Kievsky,* was entrusted

Left: *The* Kievsky, *a désignation given to the second I.M. after its historic flight from Petersburg to Kiev. Note the turning platform on which a crew member is standing. The tail skid is composed of two parallel elements.* (Novosti)
Right: *I.M. Type V of the* Eskadra Vozdushnikh Korabl'ei *(Flying Ship Squadron).* (Archivio Bignozzi)

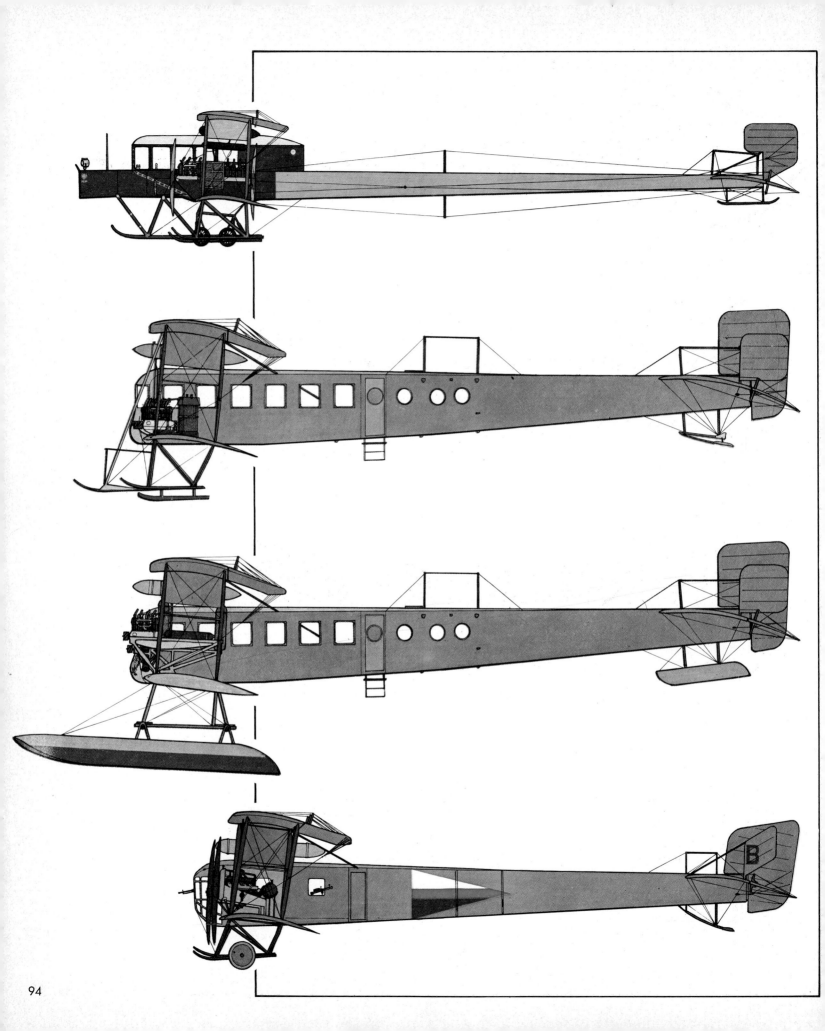

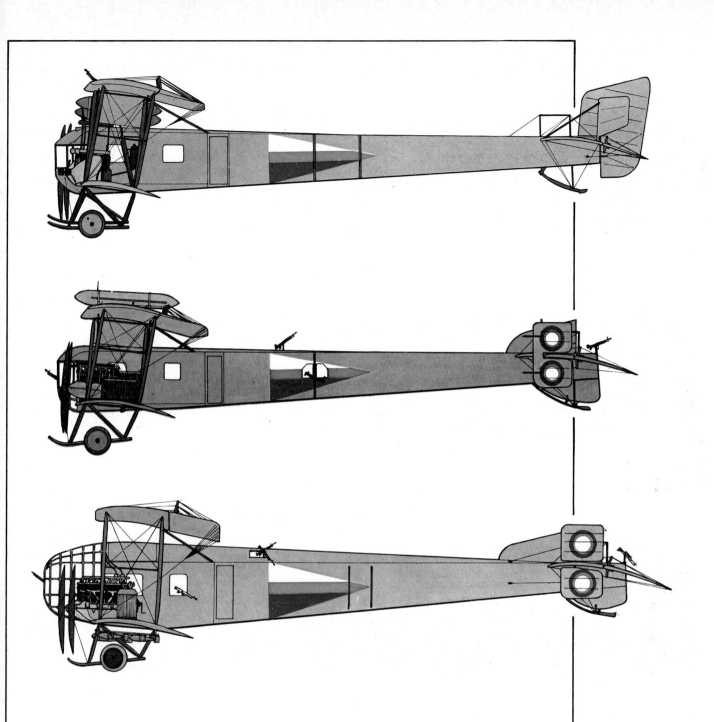

From top to bottom:
The *Bol'shoi Bal'tisky* in the
configuration powered by four
engines in tandem pairs
The earliest *Ilya Mouromets*
aircraft; note the skis
The earliest I.M. adapted as a
seaplane; the internal radial
Salmson engines have been
replaced by raised external
engines
I.M. Type V powered by
Sunbeam engines with frontal
radiators

From top to bottom:
I.M. Type V incorporating
various modifications—note the
pointed nose and the machine
gun mounted on the upper wing.
The engines are Argus
I.M. Type G2 with RBVZ-6
engines. The rudder is double
with a centrally mounted fin
I.M. Type E with Renault engines

Top right: *A group of officers of the EVK posing with a 300-kg (660-lb) bomb in front of an I.M.*
Top left: *Czar Nikolai II inspecting the* Russky Vityaz, *the second Sikorsky giant. The czar is on the 'balcony' and Sikorsky, wearing a pilot's helmet, is at the door of the cabin. This particular aircraft was one with separate engines instead of tandem pairs.* (Archivio Falessi)

Center: *Sikorsky (left) with his co-pilot, on the 'balcony' of the* Russky Vityaz. *The figure in the center is the Grand Duke Nikolai, Supreme Commander of the Tsarist armed forces.* (Archivio Bignozzi)

A rare photograph of the Russky Vityaz *in flight. This view brings out strikingly the long, thin fuselage characteristic of the earliest Russian giants.* (Archivio Bignozzi)

to Capt. G. G. Gorshkov, who gave the first demonstration of the potential of the big aircraft which the Russian military had procured for use as strategic reconnaissance planes. On June 4, 1914, he climbed to 2000 m with nine passengers and the next day he took up five passengers on a flight that lasted 6 hours 33 minutes. This was followed by the first bombing tests in July 1914. The bombs were hung externally and fighting was primitive but a promising start had been made. (Later on Captains Ivanov and Zhuravchenko were to design and build an efficient bombsight.) In October 1914 Sikorsky himself was to drop new types of bombs weighing from 20 to 40 kg (44 to 88 lb), releasing them manually through a tubular guide built into the floor of the fuselage.

On August 26, 1914, the Tsarist High Command ordered the first two I.M.s to the Northwest front for a period of operational trials. The result of this first wartime use was so disappointing that after nine weeks the order for 32 production aircraft was canceled, but the builders reacted sharply to the negative report of the military authorities. Sikorsky and his colleagues insisted that the complexity of the giant aircraft made it necessary for the pilots to have special training, and this training was decidedly lacking in the case of the men who first flew the I.M.s at the front.

The intervention of the Grand Duke Nikolai Nikolayevich, Commander-in-Chief of the Tsarist armed forces, settled the situation by accepting the proposal of the president of the RBVZ (M. V. Shidlovsky, a retired naval officer) to return to active service in command of a special unit equipped with the big aircraft. Pilots and technical support were to be RBVZ personnel and they were to undertake a period of technical and operational specialization.

On December 10, 1914, this unit, the EVK *(Eskadra Vozdushnikh Korabl'ei,* or 'Flying Ship Squadron'), was formed and equipped with the few I.M. Type B aircraft then available. The commanding officer was the newly re-activated Gen. Shidlovsky, and the base was at Yablonna near Warsaw where the EVK was part of the First Army, commanded by Gen. Odeshilidze. The initial actions carried out by the unit were reconnaissance sorties and bombing within a radius of 130 km (81 miles) from the base, and the targets were the railroad stations at Neidenburg, Soldau, Mlava, Plotsk and Willenburg. These raids were carried out beginning in February 1915, and it is known that on March 6 Capt.

Gorshkov's *Kievsky* dropped ten 16-kg (35-lb) bombs on Willenburg in a mission which lasted four hours, and on June 5 Capt. I. Bashko destroyed an ammunition train at Pryevorsk in Austria.

By this time the usefulness of the I.M.s was no longer questioned, and as soon as the unit achieved its planned equipment of 10 aircraft in the summer of 1915 it began to fly sorties with several aircraft working together against every important target. They accomplished a great deal, and their defensive power was such that the enemy – who had brought up additional fire power to combat the Russian giants – was hard-pressed to put up any effective opposition. The first German attempt at interception (on 6 July 1915) ended in the loss of two out of three German fighters which had attacked a single I.M.; the Russian bomber got away safely. As early as May 26 Capt. Alexi Pankratev had downed an enemy plane, flying the I.M. II (individual I.M.s were numbered with Roman numerals).

The offensive and defensive efficiency of the huge planes increased in successive models, and by December 1915 the EVK had carried out over 100 sorties; total weight of bombs dropped was about 20000 kg (22 tons), *with no losses due to enemy action.* In 1916 the giant Russian planes were even more active.

By the end of Russian participation in the war, the EVK's great planes had flown over 450 missions in three years and had dropped 65 metric tons of bombs with a loss of only three aircraft (two others had crashed owing to mechanical failure, some of it due to sabotage).

After the Russian-German armistice (December 15, 1917) several I.M.s were captured by the Germans. About 30 of them were destroyed by EVK personnel, while a few others joined the Bolsheviks and served as a nucleus for the new Soviet air arm. Still others were apparently flown by the White Army in the Civil War which followed the Russian October Revolution. The Soviets used them in the Northern Group of the 'Red Air Fleet of the Workers and Peasants Army' against the White forces in that area. In 1924 the last extant I.M. was assigned to the Serpukhov School of Aiming and Bombing. In the years 1921-22 one or more modified I.M.s were used by two experimental passenger and freight lines between Moscow and Sevastopol via Kharkov, and between Serapyl' and Yekaterinburg.

LOHNER L

An Austrian Lohner forced down in the Adriatic on March 29, 1916. The Lohner L was the most used Austrian two-seat reconnaissance seaplane against the Italians in the Adriatic theater. (Aeronautica Militare Italiana)

Before and during the war, the Austro-Hungarian empire had greater faith than the Germans in the wartime potential of seaplanes, and it was during those years that the Jacob Lohner firm of Vienna brought out a number of different models. Of these, the type known as the Lohner L was particularly successful. The L was a two-seat reconnaissance, patrol and bombing aircraft which was used extensively in the Adriatic area. In 1913 the Austrian Navy became the first to use seaplanes, during the Balkan war, assigning its first three seaplanes (French Donnet-Levèques) to the naval base at Kotor on the Balkan coast, later reinforcing them with American Curtiss and German Etrich aircraft.

In 1914 the Lohner factory patented its center-hulled biplane, the immediate forebear of the series of seaplanes which fought in the Adriatic skies until 1918. The first production aircraft were of Type E, with an 85-hp Hiero engine; 40 of these were built in 1914 and 1915. Type L represented

Specifications

Power plant	Austro-Daimler 140/180 hp
Upper wing span, *m*	16·20
Lower wing span, *m*	11·80
Total length, *m*	10·26
Height, *m*	3·85
Wing area, *m²*	53
Weight, empty, *kg*	1150
Weight, crew, *kg*	150
Weight, fuel and oil, *kg*	260
Weight, bombs, *kg*	200
Useful load, *kg*	600
Total weight, *kg*	1700
Maximum speed, *km/hr*	105
Flight endurance, *hrs*	4·0 (approx.)
Climb to 914 *m*	18·0 min
Climb to 1000 *m*	20·0 min
Ceiling, *m*	3500-4000

0   1   2 m

vincenzo cosentino

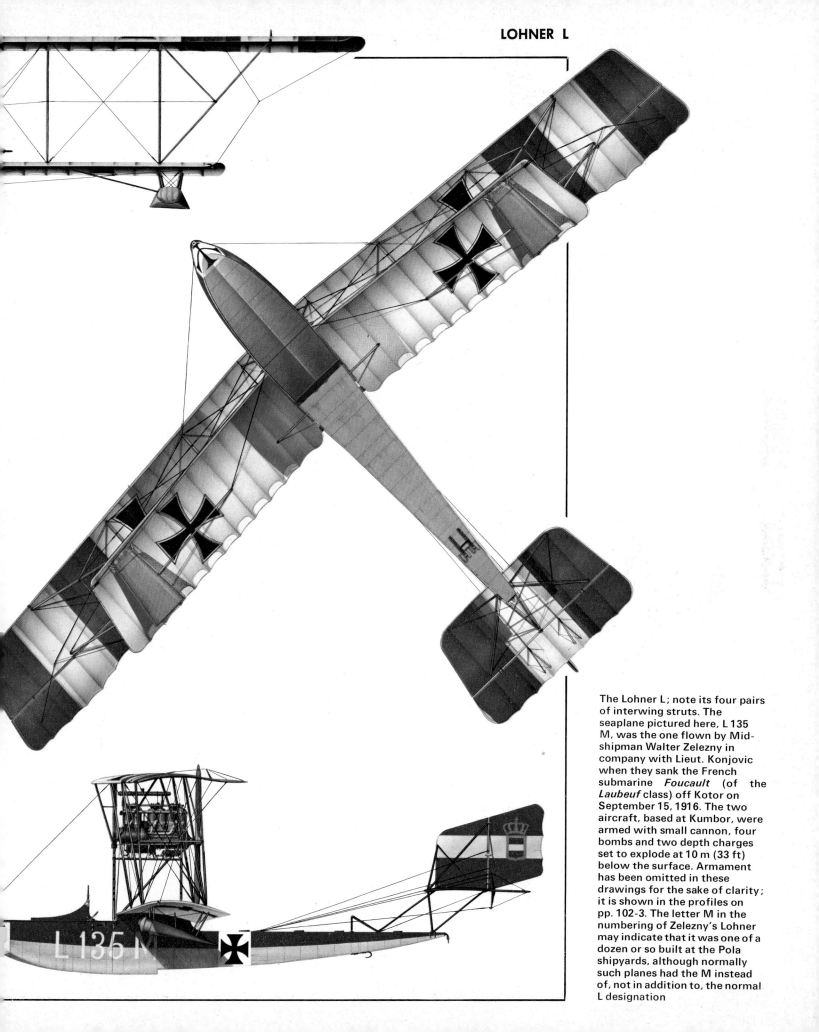

LOHNER L

The Lohner L; note its four pairs of interwing struts. The seaplane pictured here, L 135 M, was the one flown by Midshipman Walter Zelezny in company with Lieut. Konjovic when they sank the French submarine *Foucault* (of the *Laubeuf* class) off Kotor on September 15, 1916. The two aircraft, based at Kumbor, were armed with small cannon, four bombs and two depth charges set to explode at 10 m (33 ft) below the surface. Armament has been omitted in these drawings for the sake of clarity; it is shown in the profiles on pp. 102-3. The letter M in the numbering of Zelezny's Lohner may indicate that it was one of a dozen or so built at the Pola shipyards, although normally such planes had the M instead of, not in addition to, the normal L designation

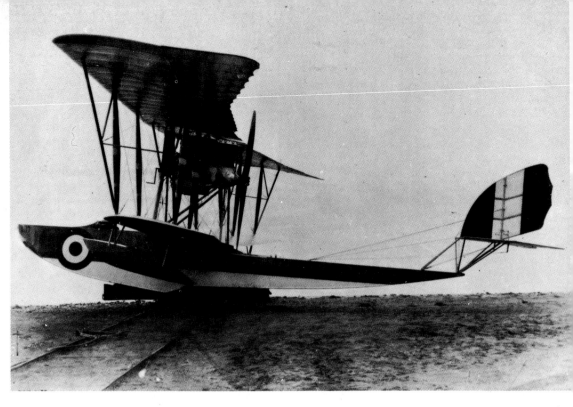

One of the Italian copies of the Lohner L—the Lohner-Macchi L.1, of which 140 were built after an Austrian seaplane had been captured. (Aeronautica Macchi)

a good step forward. Its dimensions were approximately those of the Lohner E, but it had a more powerful engine (usually a 140-hp Austro-Daimler), and eventually became the most popular of the Lohner planes.

Technical description

The Lohner L was of the type that was called 'sesquiplane', that is, a biplane with the lower wing a good percentage shorter than the upper. The wings were mounted directly onto the fuselage, with no interposed struts. The lower wing was rectangular, with slightly rounded tips; it had a dihedral of approximately 3° and a sweepback of approximately 10°. The number of wing struts varied from model to model (there were six pairs on the L). Only the upper wing had ailerons, which extended beyond the trailing edge. The wings were staggered by an 18° inclination of the forward struts. The arrangement of bracing wires on the Lohner machines was much more complicated than anything ever seen on German planes, but it did ensure a high degree of ruggedness.

Like other seaplanes of the day, such as the French-British FBA, the tail structure was supported by a system of struts and wires which, even when controlled with the greatest skill, could not ensure satisfactory maneuverability.

The fuselage, designed with particular care, was made of wood. In spite of its rather large forward cross section, the nose was of such a design that it combined superior seaworthiness with undiminished aerodynamic qualities.

The two-man crew were accommodated in front of the wings in side-by-side seats and protected by a small windscreen. The pilot had the port cockpit, the observer the starboard; the latter had a machine gun on a fixed mount, generally a Schwarzlose. In addition to this armament the Lohner L could carry from 5 to 50 kg of bombs or up to 200 kg of antisubmarine depth charges racked on the sides of the fuselage.

The power plant was either a 6-cylinder in-line 140-hp Austro-Daimler or a Hiero-Warchalowski engine of equal power. The engine, secured by three N-struts, drove a pusher propeller. However, the engine base was exposed and produced considerable drag. A honeycomb-type radiator was installed forward in a slightly elevated position. The fuel tanks, with an overall capacity of 200 liters (44 Imperial gallons), were installed in the fuselage behind the pilot's cockpit.

Instruments, rather rudimentary, were mounted on a small panel visible to both pilot and observer. Many Austrian seaplanes also carried a Telefunken transmitter powered by a 500-cycle generator driven by the engine. Very few had a radio receiver which was then still under development.

Seaplanes of that generation also had search lights and headlights with switches in the observer's cockpit. The observer also carried one or more Very pistols with a supply of flares protected by metal cartridges.

On several Lohner Ls captured by the Allies there was also a primitive bombsight, with a scale marking graduations of altitude based on theoretical constant speed. No drift correction device was available, however.

Development of the Lohner L

Together with the aircraft built by *Hansa-Branden-burgische Werke* the Lohner seaplanes were the principal machines used by the Austrian naval aviation in World War I. It would have been hard to find a naval pilot who had not flown one of these two types at least once. At first Austrian naval aviation had the very few seaplane pilots on its roster, and it was only towards the middle of 1914, as events and preparations for the war came to a critical point, that the commanding officer of the recently organized air corps accepted officers and a few noncoms for training. Shortly thereafter, when a school had been activated at Cosada near Pola, the intake was gradually increased. Courses

Steyr, were also assigned to training missions. A feature common to other two-seaters of the day was the lack of dual controls on trainers. About 30 Lohners staffed the Cosada training base, and other naval units had one or two. A reconnaissance seaplane (Type R), a three-seater with photorecon-naissance equipment in place of armament, was of questionable make: it may have been a Lohner product, or it may have come from another manufacturer.

The 1918 Armistice stripped Austria of its outlets to the sea, so none of the remaining seaplanes continued in active service. Lohners did, however, continue to play a role in the development of naval aviation elsewhere, especially in Italy, where towards the end of the war the *Aeronautica Macchi* had just begun to get organized for the production of seaplanes (Macchi was already building land-based fighters under license) when a Lohner, No. L 40, was forced down at Porto Corsini (Ravenna) during the night of May 27-28, 1915. The captured aircraft was sent to the Macchi factory at Varese, where it served as a prototype for production of the

in theory, given at the Valbandone airfield, included lectures on aircraft engines, aerodynamics, navigation and aerology (science of the whole free atmosphere).

The practical course included training in Lohners. In 1914-15 graduation requirements included the performance of a series of 'lazy eights' (aerobatic maneuvers consisting of two successive loops forming a vertical figure eight, with altitude, heading and attitude being approximately equal at the end of the maneuver as at the beginning) and repeated landings in a specified sea area. Later requirements included two hours of solo flight, climbing to 3000 meters (9843 ft), and various forced landings on the sea. When Austria entered the war, her naval aviation force included 21 officers and 8 noncoms, all pilots; during the conflict the Austrian naval aviation lost 91 pilots and 81 observers.

A total of 108 Lohner Ls were built and delivered according to the following schedule: 1914, 3 machines; 1915, 60 machines and 1916, 45 machines. By the time the Lohner E and L were retired from operations, several machines were modified for use as trainers. The Lohner K and S, which were essentially Lohner E unarmed seaplanes powered by 80-hp Oberursel rotary engines built by

Lohner-Macchi L.1, which eventually turned out to be the best seaplane of its time.

The Italian version was ready to fly in the record time of 33-34 days, and was test-flown by Cmdr. De Roberti at Schiranna on the Lago di Varese (Lake Varese) in northern Italy. The Macchi plant eventually built 140 Lohners, fitting them with the 150-hp Isotta-Fraschini V.4A engine and mounting a Fiat machine gun forward. One such aircraft was armed with a small cannon for antisubmarine work, and others carried a machine pistol in addition to the standard machine gun. As a flying machine the Lohner-Macchi L.1 was better than the FBA seaplane, although it did not perform quite so well on the water. It came to be recognized as the nucleus of the Italian Adriatic reconnaissance-bombing force and was the basis for a long, successful program in the development of Italian naval aviation.

Through a general lightening of the structure and a reduction of the struts from six to four pairs, and with a slightly more powerful engine, the 160-hp I-F V.4, Macchi produced the L.2, of which about 10 were built. The L.3 was the final, definitive Italian version of the Lohner and carried a useful load of 38% (rather than 26·5%) of the total weight, being thus notably superior to the Austrian original.

Left: *A Lohner-Macchi L.1 on Lake Varese*; right, *the same aircraft taxi-ing on water*. (Aeronautica Macchi, Aeronautica Militare Italiana)

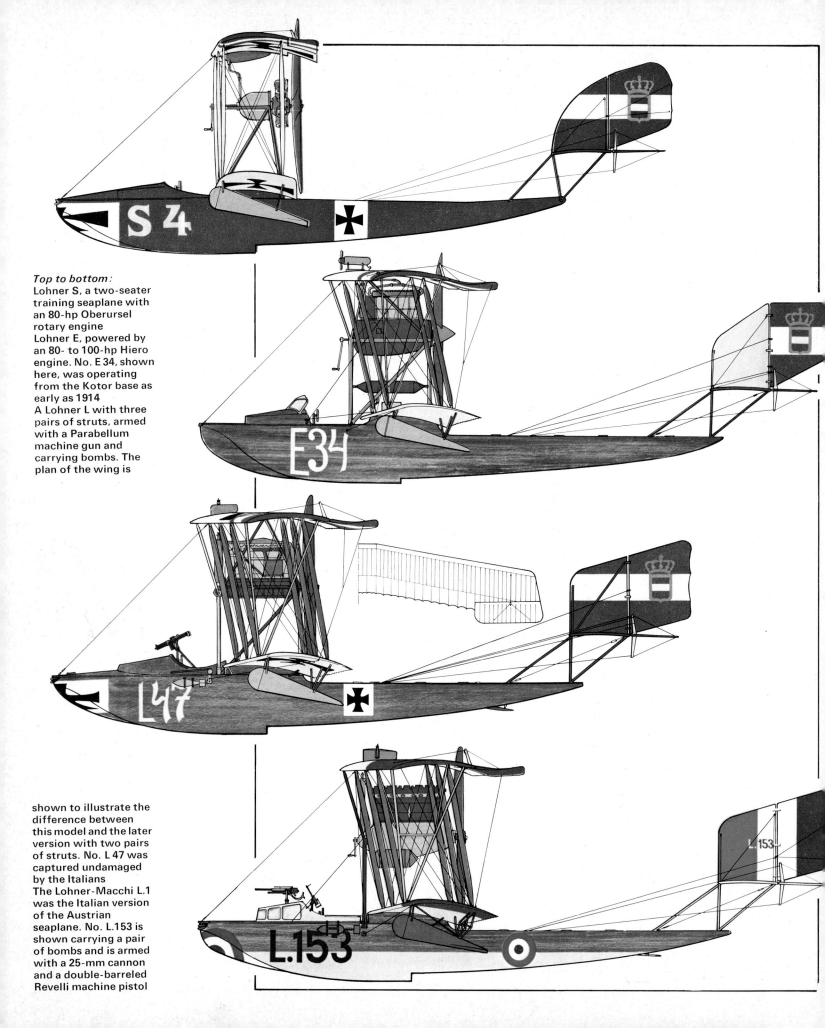

Top to bottom:
Lohner S, a two-seater
training seaplane with
an 80-hp Oberursel
rotary engine
Lohner E, powered by
an 80- to 100-hp Hiero
engine. No. E 34, shown
here, was operating
from the Kotor base as
early as 1914
A Lohner L with three
pairs of struts, armed
with a Parabellum
machine gun and
carrying bombs. The
plan of the wing is

shown to illustrate the
difference between
this model and the later
version with two pairs
of struts. No. L 47 was
captured undamaged
by the Italians
The Lohner-Macchi L.1
was the Italian version
of the Austrian
seaplane. No. L.153 is
shown carrying a pair
of bombs and is armed
with a 25-mm cannon
and a double-barreled
Revelli machine pistol

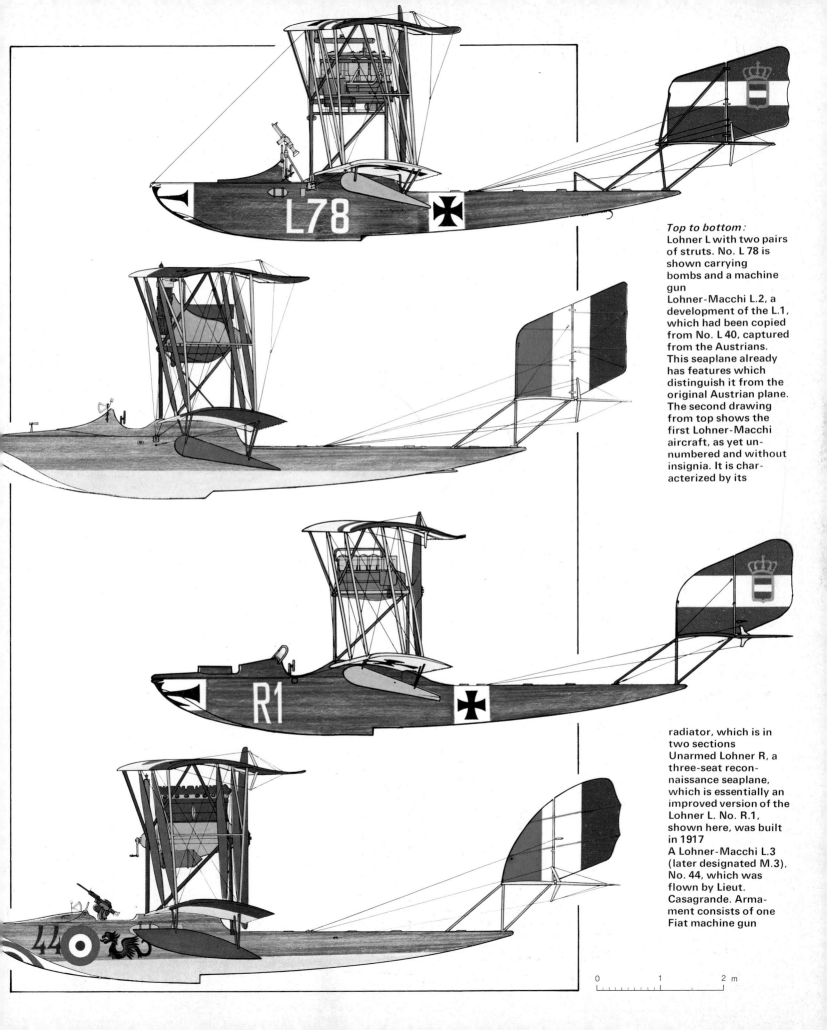

Top to bottom:
Lohner L with two pairs
of struts. No. L 78 is
shown carrying
bombs and a machine
gun
Lohner-Macchi L.2, a
development of the L.1,
which had been copied
from No. L 40, captured
from the Austrians.
This seaplane already
has features which
distinguish it from the
original Austrian plane.
The second drawing
from top shows the
first Lohner-Macchi
aircraft, as yet un-
numbered and without
insignia. It is char-
acterized by its

radiator, which is in
two sections
Unarmed Lohner R, a
three-seat recon-
naissance seaplane,
which is essentially an
improved version of the
Lohner L. No. R.1,
shown here, was built
in 1917
A Lohner-Macchi L.3
(later designated M.3),
No. 44, which was
flown by Lieut.
Casagrande. Arma-
ment consists of one
Fiat machine gun

0   1   2 m

How the Lohner L was used in the War

The Lohner seaplanes were used in many missions against Italian targets along the Adriatic coast, even before the beginning of the war, when several Lohner Es based at Kumbor reconnoitred the Kotor region. Such reconnaissance continued up to the early months of 1915. The first military actions showed how well developed the idea of collective sorties was among the Austrians even at that early date. The seaplane sorties were for the most part night bombing missions carried out by groups of six or seven planes at a time whenever the weather permitted. From May through October 1915 the Lohners bombed Venice, and in December and January 1916 they bombed Ancona, Rimini, Ravenna, Cervia, Mestre and Portogruaro; in the south Brindisi was hit on the night of May 31, 1916.

Austrian reports claimed that the Italian dirigible *Città di Ferrara* (City of Ferrara), which came down at sea near Pola on the night of June 15, 1915, had been hit by a Lohner seaplane (L.48) piloted by Lieut. Gustav Klesing (commander of the Pola seaplane base), after an aerial combat. The Italians reported that the *Ferrara* had been hit by artillery fire, although Lieut. Klesing, observing the stricken airship from above, may well have believed it to be his own victim. What isn't clear is why the Austrians should claim that there had been an aerial fight between the Lohner and the airship.

Gottfried Banfield, fighter ace of the Austrian naval aviation, shot down his first night victim flying a Lohner L. Near Trieste on the night of June 1, 1916, he gave chase to a Caproni Ca.3 bomber which had been lit up by an Austrian searchlight and brought it down. Banfield was also credited with numerous other missions while flying Lohners, including several victories against enemy fighter aircraft.

On June 12, 1916, the Austrian seaplanes inflicted heavy damage on the Italian destroyer *Zeffiro* and two torpedo-boat destroyers (TBDs), *Fuciliere*

and *Alpino,* in a battle off Parenzo. On September 15 of that same year two Lohners surprised and sank the French submarine *Foucault* in the Adriatic; the Austrians saved the French crew and took them prisoner. The *Foucault* was an old steam-driven boat of questionable military value, but the sinking of it by a seaplane is a milestone in the history of military aviation. The Austrians chalked up a number of other successes at the expense of the Italians: On September 9, 1917, they made a night attack on a dirigible repair hangar and blew it up, together with the airship M 8. A few weeks later, on September 26, a similar attack resulted in the destruction of the dirigible M 13.

From August 1914 through October 1918 the Austrian naval air corps lost a total of 74 seaplanes in dogfights, to antiaircraft fire or in accidents (crashes in test flights were numerous, although far less so with Lohner aircraft than with other types). In good part this was doubtless due to the vigorous search for new types of aircraft, combined with a lowering of quality control in the developmental phases. Quite frequently after new seaplane models had entered active service, they had to be recalled for modifications to make them safer.

Top, left: Above, *Lohner K and,* below, *Lohner L captured by the Italians. The Lohner K and S were used for training by the Austrian naval aviation*
Below, left: *Most Lohner L seaplanes, like this one, were powered by a 140-hp in-line Austro-Daimler engine*
Below, right: *The power plant used on Lohner-Macchi planes was usually the 150-hp Isotta-Fraschini V.4A, as shown here.* (Aeronautica Militare Italiana, Archivio Apostoli)

MORANE-SAULNIER N

A Morane-Saulnier Type N of the Royal Flying Corps, with Lieut. T. H. Bayetto in the cockpit. (Photograph by Robert E. Sheldon)

The first time the *Société Anonyme d'Aéroplanes Morane-Saulnier* showed its aircraft at the *Salon Aéronautique* in Paris, in 1911, it made a tremendous impression on the assembled technicians and *aficionados* because it exhibited not less than *four* excellent monoplanes. Its prestige was further enhanced when the famous airman Roland Garros joined Morane-Saulnier as test pilot. Thanks to Garros' suggestions the firm was ready by 1913 to offer its first production models—the G and H monoplanes, which differed practically only in cockpit layout: Type G was a two-seater, Type H a single-seater.

On the eve of World War I the Morane-Saulnier Type L—a direct descendant of the Type G but designed as a 'parasol' monoplane (with the main plane mounted on a canopy above the fuselage)—was one of the fastest reconnaissance monoplanes in the French air corps. Its speed and maneuverability were such that when the war came the best pilots could intercept all German planes. Besides being noted as one of the first natural interceptors in aviation history, the Type L gained its fame as

Specifications

	Type N	Type I	Type V
Power plant	Le Rhône 9C	Le Rhône 9J	Le Rhône 9J
Horsepower	80	110	110
Wing span, *m*	8·15	8·24	8·75
Length, *m*	5·83	5·81	5·81
Height, *m*	2·25	2·50	2·50
Wing area, *m²*	11	11	—
Weight, empty, *kg*	288	334	—
Total weight, *kg*	444	510	—
Maximum speed at S/L, *km/h*	144	176	165
Climb to 1000 *m*	4·0 min	2 min 50 sec	3 min 20 sec
Climb to 2000 *m*	10·0 min	6 min 20 sec	8·0 min
Climb to 3000 *m*	—	12·0 min	12·0 min
Ceiling, *m*	3000	3500	4000
Flight endurance	1 hr 30 min	1 hr 45 min	—

the first true fighter of all time embodying that special harmony of aircraft, armament and system of aiming.

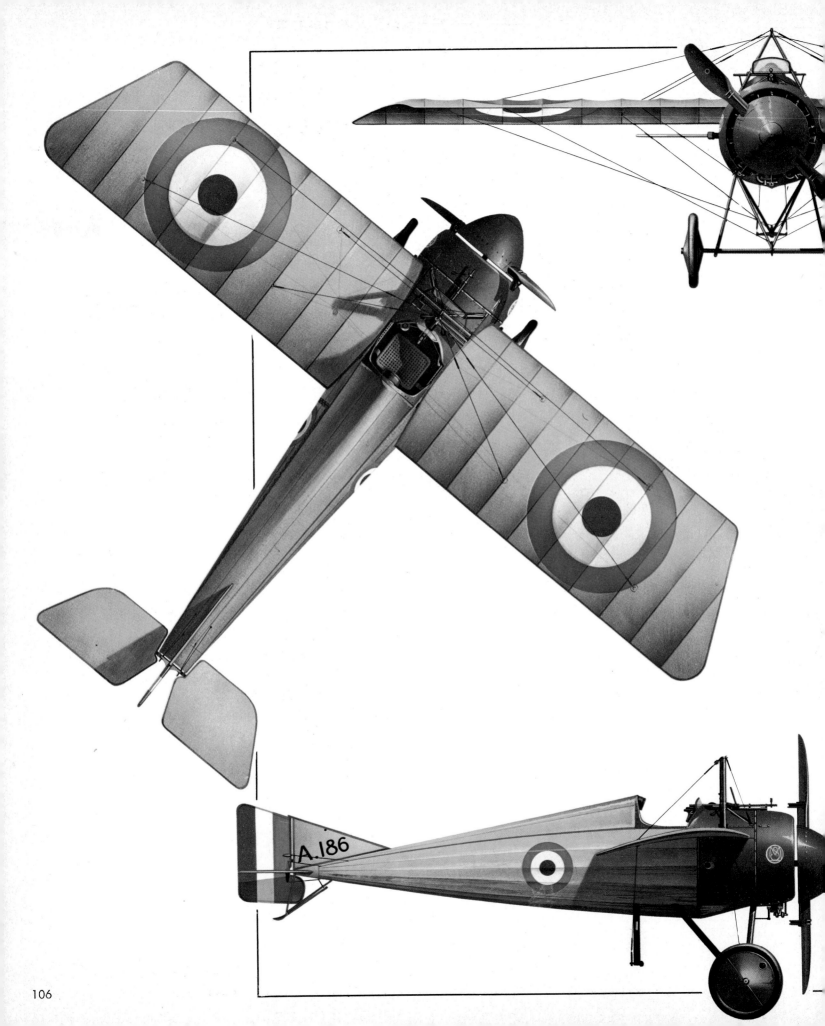

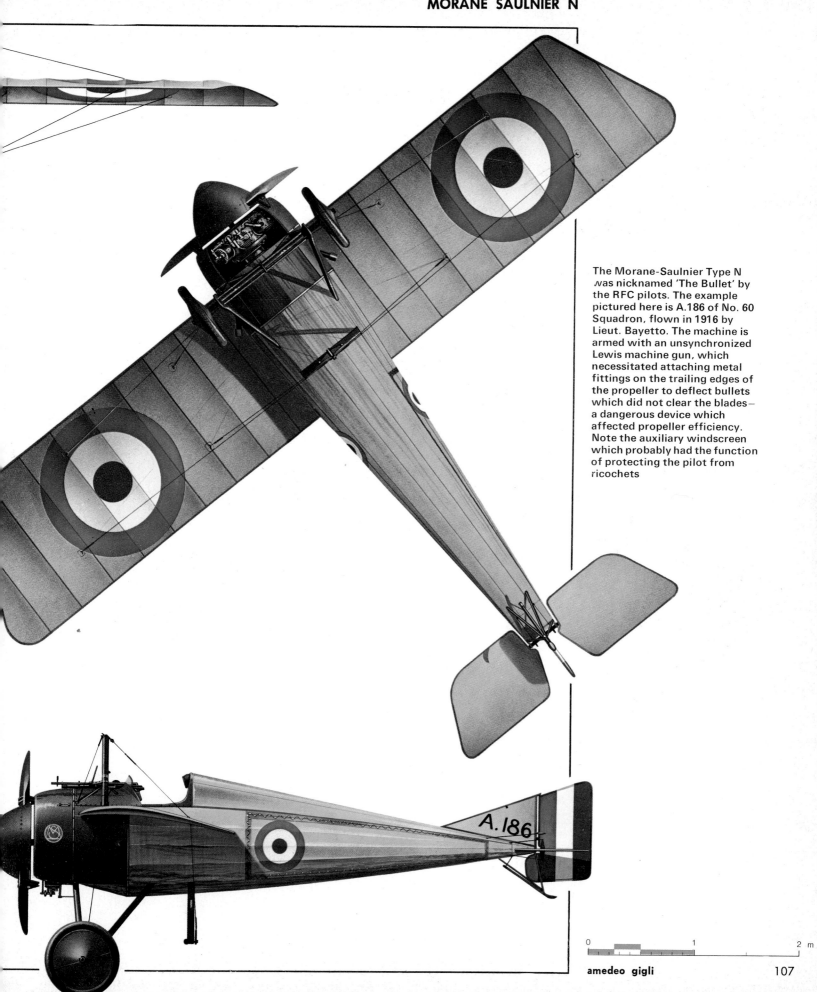

The Morane-Saulnier Type N
was nicknamed 'The Bullet' by
the RFC pilots. The example
pictured here is A.186 of No. 60
Squadron, flown in 1916 by
Lieut. Bayetto. The machine is
armed with an unsynchronized
Lewis machine gun, which
necessitated attaching metal
fittings on the trailing edges of
the propeller to deflect bullets
which did not clear the blades—
a dangerous device which
affected propeller efficiency.
Note the auxiliary windscreen
which probably had the function
of protecting the pilot from
ricochets

A.186

0   1   2 m

Above: *A Morane-Saulnier parasol monoplane of No. 3 Sqn., RFC.*
Below: *A Morane-Saulnier Type L parasol monoplane in service with the RFC. The first of these planes was built in 1913*

The next model, the Morane-Saulnier Type N, made its debut at the Aspern (Vienna) air meet in June 1914, piloted by Roland Garros, and it made a strong impression, partly because of its clean lines, reminiscent of those of the Deperdussin monoplanes designed by Louis Béchéreau. The Type N, however, was simpler in design and used conventional materials. Its performance was not brilliant at the Aspern meet, possibly because it had been completed and sent there in too much of a hurry without adequate tests at home. Garros took first place only in climbing competition (in spite of an unsuitable propeller), establishing a record of 1000 m in 2 min 29 sec; the machine was powered by an 80-hp Gnôme.

On the last day of the Aspern meet, Archduke Ferdinand and his wife were assassinated at Sarajevo. Europe was on the brink of war.

The Morane-Saulnier Type N (which in the *Aviation Militaire* books was known as the MS. 5C 1) appeared at the front shortly after Roland Garros was captured by the enemy in April 1915. This particular Type N was piloted by Garros' friend Eugène Gilbert of *Escadrille* MS 23 and carried the proud name *Le Vengeur* (The Avenger) on the fuselage. At first the Type N had no official designation, but it was later marked as MS 388, and its performance was good enough to convince the French authorities to order a series for operational use.

Technical description

The original Saulnier Type N was a typical monoplane of medium span, quite similar to its forebears, the Types G and H. It was built of wood, with a well streamlined fuselage, but its most characteristic feature was the large propeller spinner completely covering the engine.

The wing, set at shoulder-level, was rectangular and built around two stout spars with nine wing ribs on each side of the center section, with inner bracing of steel wires. The wing structure was fabric-covered except for plywood skinning at the wing roots for better access to the cockpit. There were no ailerons, lateral control being handled by wing warping. These warping controls necessitated the use of a rather complex network of wires terminating above and below the wing.

The fuselage consisted of an inner truss structure of wood, and had a circular cross section achieved by constriction of the wooden framework by stringers. Most of the fuselage was fabric-covered, except for a small aluminum panel ahead of the pilot's cockpit. The engine cowling and spinner were also of aluminum. The airframe of the Morane-Saulnier Type N has been frequently called monocoque, although it wasn't: it was wholly a truss structure, and the term monocoque was doubtless misapplied because the outer appearance of Type N was similar to the fuselages of contemporary Deperdussin monoplanes, which were among the first to have a rigid plywood shell.

As in other Morane-Saulnier models, the undercarriage had M-struts with a rubber-cord shock absorber system, the usual arrangement in those early years. The stabilizer, fin and rudder were of limited area and consisted of a fabric-covered wooden framework. The rudder extended above and below the stabilizer, and the lower section was protected by a sturdy landing skid.

The engine was an 80-hp Gnôme rotary in early planes, later often replaced by the 110-hp Le Rhône 9J rotary on Types I and V, covered by a metal cowling which left the lower cylinders open. As mentioned above, the most characteristic external feature of the Type N was the enormous spinner, which had originally been actually hemispherical with a pronounced hub. The spinner, affectionately nicknamed *la casserole* ('the kettle') by ground crews and pilots alike, covered the engine entirely and gave a good profile to the nose. Although this was good aerodynamically, it prevented adequate cooling of the engine. On later models the 'kettle' was considerably reduced in size, with corresponding improvement in engine cooling (and access for maintenance).

The fixed gun, mounted slightly to starboard of the pilot, was usually a 7·7-mm Vickers or Lewis machine gun. As early as 1914 Raymond Saulnier had worked on a synchronization system, basing his experiments on a Hotchkiss machine gun which

he had acquired from the army, but he abandoned the project because of the difficulty in retaining reliable ammunition after a few duds had seriously damaged his propeller. This was unfortunate, because Saulnier was on the right track when he was obliged to give up his research and fall back on a system of steel wedges set into the propeller trailing edge to repel bullets—a crude and potentially dangerous system, because it both lowered the propeller efficiency and diverted bullets in unpredictable directions.

Operationally the aircraft was quite efficient, but only in the hands of expert pilots, as were practically all these early monoplanes which had very sensitive controls and, as a result, were extremely maneuverable. One of their negative points was the rather high landing speed.

Only 49 Morane-Saulnier Type·N₃ were built, and it is not known how many were actually used by the French air corps. In the summer of 1915, 10 Morane monoplanes were ready for operational service, with the newly designed spinner replacing the large 'kettle' as fitted on Gilbert's plane. The fuselage aft of the cockpit had also been redesigned, and the stabilizer had been reshaped into two tapered trapezoids (see drawing, p. 106).

Development of the Morane-Saulnier N

The Morane-Saulnier Type N was preceded by Type G which appeared in 1915 and was put into production almost immediately.

The Type P marked a return to parasol highwing configuration. At first it was a two-seater, later a one-seater, in which the most interesting

characteristic was the armament—two synchronized Vickers machine guns mounted on the engine cowling, which made it probably the first Allied fighter armed with two guns.

In April 1916 the design of the Type U was finished. This version had stronger airframe structure and rigid wing bracing; it is not known whether it was ever built or not, but the absence of armament in surviving drawings would seem to indicate that it was an experimental model. It did lead, however, to the Type AC, which appeared in the autumn of 1916, with a similar rigid wing bracing. The Type AC was armed with a single synchronized Vickers machine gun, partly faired over. At least one experimental Type AC aircraft carried two Vickers guns. A total of 31 machines of this type were built, but few operational details are known of its service life: no French squadron was wholly equipped with the Type AC, although some units had a few of them in the spring of 1917. Two were sent for trials to the Royal Flying Corps in January 1917.

How the Morane-Saulnier Type N was used in the War

Details on the active service of the Morane-Saulnier Type N in the French squadrons are scarce, since only a few aircraft were actually delivered, and even these were soon replaced by the contemporary Nieuport fighters, which had been ordered in quantity.

Two highly respected French aces often flew these planes—Jean Navarre of the *Escadrille* MS 12 and the famous pioneer of aerobatics, Adolphe Pégoud, who achieved six victories with Morane-Saulniers.

The British used this French machine because their only indigenous fighter, the Bristol Scout, could not be supplied in sufficient quantities to satisfy the requests of the Royal Flying Corps. The French Type N was the only one available to oppose the Fokker threat at the crucial moment.

The French airman Adolphe Pégoud, one of the early aerobatic pilots, about to take off on a reconnaissance flight at the controls of a Morane-Saulnier parasol monoplane. (Photograph by Safara)

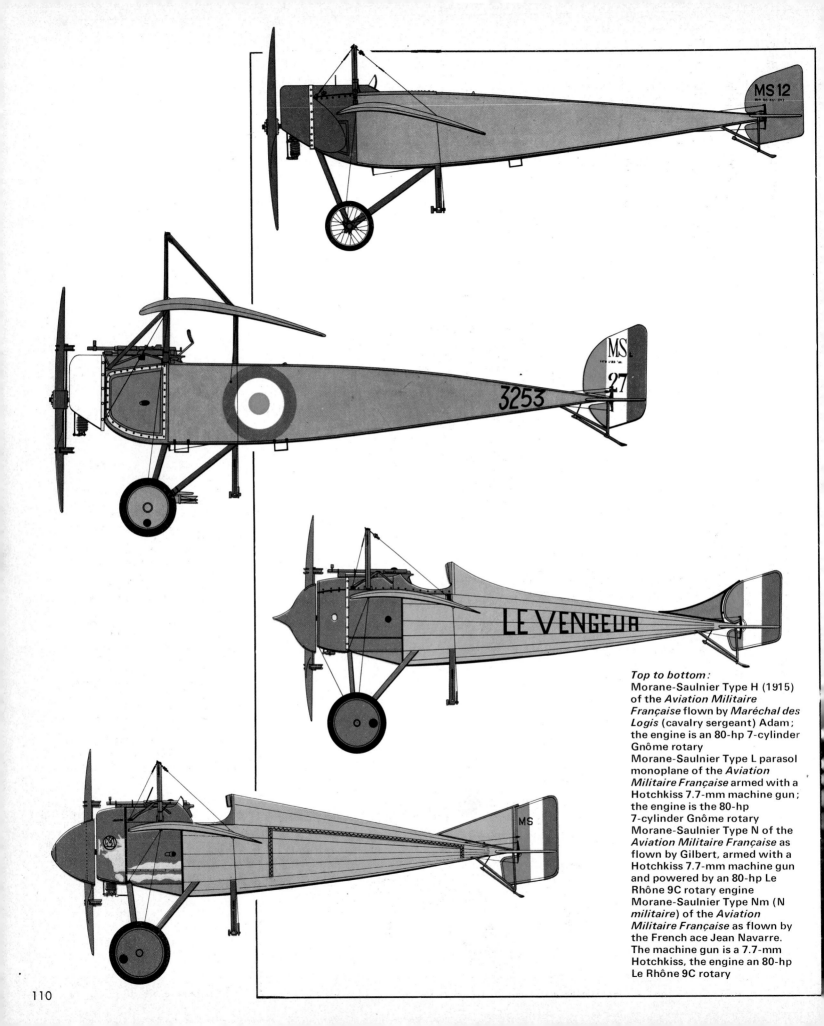

Top to bottom:
Morane-Saulnier Type H (1915) of the *Aviation Militaire Française* flown by *Maréchal des Logis* (cavalry sergeant) Adam; the engine is an 80-hp 7-cylinder Gnôme rotary
Morane-Saulnier Type L parasol monoplane of the *Aviation Militaire Française* armed with a Hotchkiss 7.7-mm machine gun; the engine is the 80-hp 7-cylinder Gnôme rotary
Morane-Saulnier Type N of the *Aviation Militaire Française* as flown by Gilbert, armed with a Hotchkiss 7.7-mm machine gun and powered by an 80-hp Le Rhône 9C rotary engine
Morane-Saulnier Type Nm (N *militaire*) of the *Aviation Militaire Française* as flown by the French ace Jean Navarre. The machine gun is a 7.7-mm Hotchkiss, the engine an 80-hp Le Rhône 9C rotary

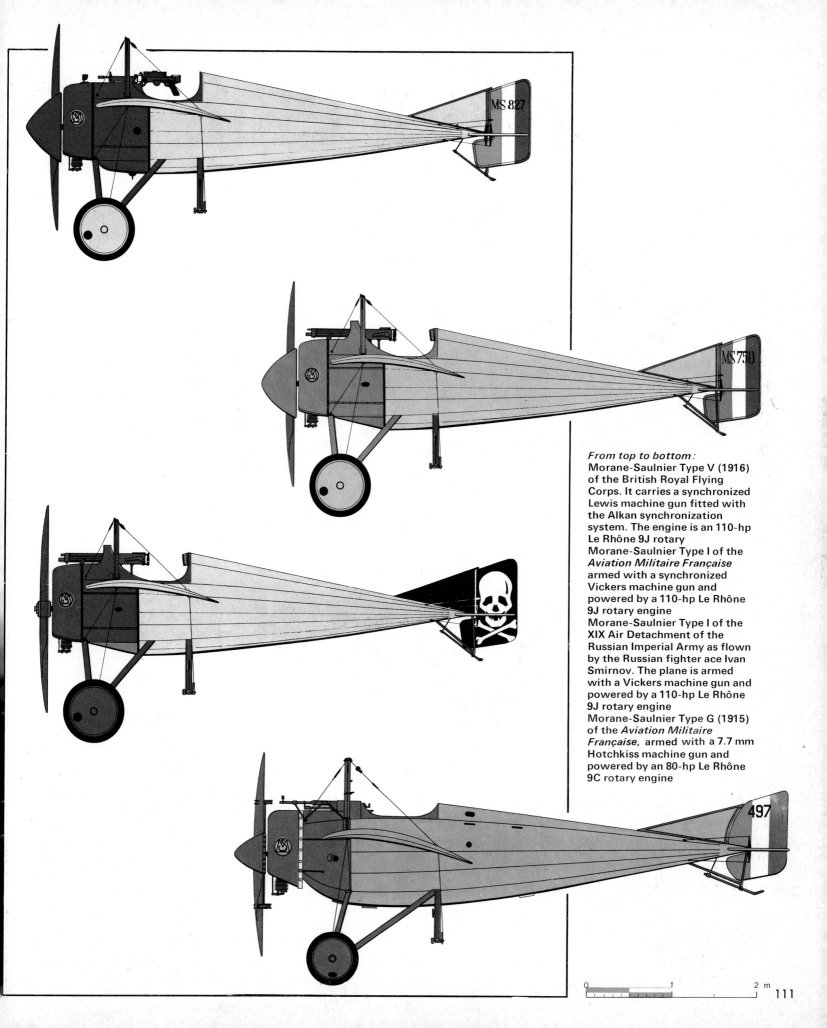

From top to bottom:
Morane-Saulnier Type V (1916) of the British Royal Flying Corps. It carries a synchronized Lewis machine gun fitted with the Alkan synchronization system. The engine is an 110-hp Le Rhône 9J rotary
Morane-Saulnier Type I of the *Aviation Militaire Française* armed with a synchronized Vickers machine gun and powered by a 110-hp Le Rhône 9J rotary engine
Morane-Saulnier Type I of the XIX Air Detachment of the Russian Imperial Army as flown by the Russian fighter ace Ivan Smirnov. The plane is armed with a Vickers machine gun and powered by a 110-hp Le Rhône 9J rotary engine
Morane-Saulnier Type G (1915) of the *Aviation Militaire Française,* armed with a 7.7 mm Hotchkiss machine gun and powered by an 80-hp Le Rhône 9C rotary engine

Top: *A Morane-Saulnier Type BB (or MS7), a two-seat biplane which was powered by either an 80- or 110-hp Le Rhône rotary engine. Note the ring-mounted rear machine gun*

The first three Moranes were assigned on an experimental basis to three British units who were asked to test their performance. Their judgment was favorable, perhaps prematurely so, but convinced Maj.-Gen. Trenchard to place an order: 24 Type N machines were commissioned by the Paris office of the British Aviation Supplies Department in January 1916, and the first Type N was delivered on March 18, 1916. The new aircraft was assigned to Nos. 1, 3, 4 and 60 Squadrons of the RFC, and was soon dubbed 'The Bullet' because of its unmistakable spinner fuselage shape.

As soon as other British pilots started flying the Type N their reports were disturbing. They found that at altitude the wing loading was excessive, above 3000 meters there was a strong tendency to stall, and that flying was difficult in bad weather. One report ended, 'The Bullet is far from being a good aircraft and is pretty hard for an average pilot to fly'. It was not much of an improvement over its predecessor, the Type L, which was noted for its lack of stability and tendency to go into a tailspin.

The manufacturers accepted the rough criticism, but within a few weeks announced that they had successfully tested an 11-square-meter wing with a modified profile. The new wing was eventually mounted on several of the RFC machines, and from pilots' reports it is clear that the overall performance was improved, even to the point of giving the pilots an advantage over the contemporary Fokkers. Incidentally, apart from its unique spinner, the 'Bullet' so resembled the German fighter that the British repainted some of the metal parts— the engine cowling and spinner—in red so that their own aircraft might be rapidly identified in the air.

The Bullets were fairly active during the Battle of the Somme (1916), but suffered serious losses, including their commander, Maj. F. E. Waldron. The situation which was created immediately thereafter is clearly revealed in an official memorandum dated July 24, 1916, in which replacements are requested for at least one of the Flights which made up No. 60 Squadron, RFC. When aerial warfare was resumed on August 23 two units had been wholly re-equipped

with Nieuports, and from then on the Morane-Saulnier Type N was gradually retired from active operations until wholly replaced by the new Type Vs.

The earliest monoplane powered by a 110-hp rotary engine—the Type I—was completed in March 1916. It was simply a Type N fitted with a more powerful engine and incorporated some improvements suggested by various pilots who had flown it: strengthening of the undercarriage, substitution of a smaller spinner and a differently-shaped engine cowling. But there were still faults—now it was the limited flight endurance of the new model, which was only 1½ hrs instead of the 3 hours demanded by the British RFC.

In this way, there originated the Type V, slightly larger (with an increased wing span and chord) and fitted with two fuel tanks (main and supplementary) in the fuselage which gave the new aircraft the required flight endurance. The engine was still the 110-hp Le Rhône rotary and the armament was usually a synchronized Vickers machine gun, although on one Type V two Vickers were mounted experimentally. Most Type Vs carried the Cadroy-Cordonnier gun synchronizing system which avoided loss of propulsion efficiency, but a few machines had the Altrano synchronizer. Of the 12 of this type delivered to the British there are unfortunately no operational reports available, and it is also not known whether the French ever used the Type V in combat.

The Russians also used the Morane-Saulnier monoplane: a few Type Ns were delivered to the Imperial command in 1916, and it was reported that the 'Dux' plant in Moscow had made at least one copy. Be as it may it is known that several Morane-Saulnier monoplanes were flown by the Russians on the Rumanian and Southwestern fronts and that at least 11 were still in active service in July 1917. The Russian fighter ace, Ivan Smirnov of the 19th Squadron, won at least 12 victories while flying such an aircraft.

To summarize, the Morane-Saulnier monoplanes (Types L, H, and the N which they inspired) were the forebears of the first family of modern fighters— the German Fokker *Eindeckers*. These famous German fighters were based both structurally and aerodynamically on a Morane-Saulnier Type H which Anthony Fokker had managed to pick up, while the capture of Garros' Type L with its rudimentary system for firing through the propeller speeded up the eventual solution of the problem, the invention of an efficient synchronizing device which was the foundation of Fokker's success.

Bottom: *The Morane-Saulnier Type N was the first aircraft (in 1914) to be armed with a machine gun which could be fired through the propeller*

BRANDENBURG C.I

On the evening of April 7, 1916, shortly before sunset, Maj. Francesco Baracca, a well-known Italian airman, grounded his first enemy plane. He was at the controls of a Nieuport *Bébé*, the enemy pilot was flying a Brandenburg C-I (No. 61.57), which most reports, official and otherwise, described at the time as an Aviatik, probably because of its remarkable similarity to that machine, an Austrian reconnaissance aircraft then in use.

Shortly before the war the Triestine millionaire Camillo Castiglioni had bought the *Hansa und Brandenburgische Flugzeugwerke,* and the pioneer aircraft designer, Ernst Heinkel, had been appointed director of engineering and design. This gave the Austrians the opportunity to make use of Heinkel's remarkable creative talents.

Certainly the C-I, which Heinkel had designed in 1915, was one of the most successful projects of the wartime period, in both its lines and performance. The latter was better than anything the competition could offer in the way of fighters and for a good three years the C-I was the backbone of the *Aufklärungskompanien,* the Austrian reconnaissance detachments which normally were supplied with from 8 to 10 aircraft each, of which 5 or 6 might be reconnaissance planes and the other 3 or 4 fighter escorts.

Specifications

Horsepower	160	200	220	230
Wing span, *m*	12·25	12·25	12·25	12·25
Total length, *m*	8·45	8·45	8·45	8·45
Height, *m*	3·33	3·33	3·33	3·33
Weight, empty, *kg*	770	800	820	830
Total weight, *kg*	1310	1310	1320	1350
Maximum speed, *km/hr*	140	155	158	160
Climb to 1000 *m, min-sec*	—	0:55	0:50	0:50
Climb to 5000 *m, min-sec*	6:55	4:30	4:00	4:00
Ceiling, *m*	5800	5800	6000	6000
Flight endurance	3 hrs	—	—	—

Above: *The Brandenburg C-1 forced down by Maj. Francesco Baracca near Medeuzza on April 7, 1916. It was C-I 61.57, an UFAG-built machine with a 160-hp Daimler engine.* (Aeronautica Militare Italiana)
Bottom, left: *Detail of the same aircraft.* (Archivio Bignozzi)

113

429.29

Brandenburg C-1 429.29, a machine of Phönix Series 429 (the fourth and final variant of the 29 series), built in 1918. The camouflage, standard on Series 429, was unusual among C-Is; it was used by the Austrians on the Italian front toward the end of the war

The C-I was designed in Germany, but the 'Big Brandenburg,' as it was called to distinguish it from the 'Little Brandenburg,' a two-seater trainer built by the same factory, was turned out on a production basis not only by the *Hansa-Brandenburgische Flugzeugwerke* but also by two Austrian firms, the *Phönix Flugzeugwerke* of Vienna and the *Hungarische Flugzeugfabrik A. G.* (Ufag).

Technical description

The Brandenburg C-I was a sleek two-seater biplane with extremely clean lines, perhaps the handsomest plane built in the early years of the war.

The upper wing was rectangular, with no rounding except on the tips, without sweepback and with a dihedral of about 5°. The ailerons were of generous proportions. A characteristic feature was the four inboard-inclined wing struts and the marked forward stagger of the top mainplane. Span of the two wings was nearly equal, with the lower wing slightly shorter. The wing itself was of a double-spar construction, with 15 wooden ribs in each half wing. The wing structure was covered with plywood and fabric. The upper wing was joined to the fuselage by metal tubing, and both struts and axle of the undercarriage were of similar tubing.

The cross section of the fuselage was trapezoidal forward and at the center and rectangular toward the tail. The profile was aerodynamically sound. The fuselage structure was almost entirely of wood, except for the nose, which was covered partly in plywood and partly in fabric. The stabilizer, attached to the top decking of the fuselage, was nearly triangular and rather short. The fin, relatively small and triangular on the earliest machines, was later enlarged in area for greater directional stability; the rudder was of generous proportions.

The pilot and observer occupied a single roomy cockpit, an arrangement which the designer thought would encourage collaboration between the two. The observer manned a Schwarzlose machine gun, the standard defense weapon of Austrian reconnaissance aircraft, fitted on a semicircular mount. The Brandenburg C-I was also used on light bombing missions: it could carry one fragmentation bomb of 80 kg and two 10 kg incendiaries, for a maximum load of 100 kg. The observer had an optical sight for bomb aiming and a rudimentary but efficient system of bomb release. Bombs could be racked either beneath the fuselage or below the lower wing.

At the beginning of 1917 the machine gun mount was raised to the level of the upper wing to permit forward fire, over the propeller; the pilot's seat was protected by a mica screen. However, this modification proved unsatisfactory and was not continued.

On later models a fixed Schwarzlose machine gun was fitted to the left of the pilot, under the radiator. On Series 29 and later a fixed machine gun was mounted on the upper wing; it was fired by the pilot via a length of flexible cable. The gun was belt-loaded, with 500 rounds to the belt; the rear machine gun could take two belts. Brandenburgs with armament also had a special sighting device consisting of a telescopic sight mounted on one of the wing struts coupled with an indicator notch etched on the dashboard. Planes on reconnaissance missions also carried camera equipment.

The C-I was one of the earliest aircraft to have dual controls. The observer also had one-way wireless communication with the ground, the transmitter being powered by a generator mounted under the nose of the plane, behind the propeller.

On machines used for night bombing missions, special mufflers were installed which not only silenced the engines but also concealed exhaust flashes from ground observers. However, this device was not successful, since it heated up excessively.

Above, left: *Nose of the Brandenburg C-I 369.124, built at the UFAG plant, with a 200-hp or 230-hp Hiero engine. The wings have been removed before this photograph was taken at an Italian airfield.* (Archivio Bignozzi)
Center, left: *UFAG 64.07, with a 160-hp Daimler engine. The armament, which is visible in the photograph, consisted of two Schwarzlose machine guns, of which the wing-mounted weapon was belt-fed.* (Aeronautica Militare Italiana)
Bottom, right: *Another view of the C-I captured in 1916 and repainted in Italian colors.* (Archivio Bignozzi)

The Brandenburg C-I was powered by any one of several engines, ranging from the 160-hp Daimler to the 230-hp Hiero. On some machines the cylinder heads were covered, but as on most planes of the day, the engines were usually partly unprotected. On the earlier models the radiator was sunk into the right wing; later the standard design had the radiator mounted above the engine ahead of the upper wing.

The main fuselage tank was fitted in the fuselage ahead of the cockpit. In the later models it had a capacity of 250 liters; there was also a reserve tank holding 25 liters. Flight endurance was more than 5 hours at cruising speed.

series:

PHÖNIX PRODUCTION
Series no. 23: Daimler, 160 hp.
Series no. 26: Austro-Daimler, 160 hp.
Series no. 27: Austro-Daimler, 185 hp.
Series no. 29: Austro-Daimler, 210 hp.
Series no. 29.5: Hiero (Fiat), 200 hp.
Series no. 429: Hiero (Fiat), 230 hp.
*Continuation of series 29, 129, 229, 329.
UFAG PRODUCTION
Series nos. 61, 62, 64, 67, 68: Austro-Daimler, 160 hp.
Series no. 63: Mercedes D.III, 160 hp.
Series no. 69: Hiero (Marta), 200 hp.
Series no. 169: Benz Bz.IVa, 220 hp.
Series no. 269: Austro-Daimler, 200 hp.
Series no. 369: Hiero, 230 hp.

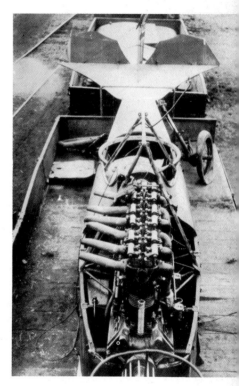

Even when carrying a full load the C-I was capable of brilliant performance, with great stability and an ease of piloting seldom found in other aircraft types of the same category. It was a reliable plane and a safe one, with excellent climbing speed. It could take off and land in a fairly short space, especially as more powerful engines became standard equipment.

Upper left: *Three Brandenburgs of different production series at the Pergine airfield on the Italian front.* (Aeronautica Militare Italiana)
Upper right: *A damaged Brandenburg which has been dismantled for transport on a railroad flatcar. In the foreground, the engine, a 220-hp Benz. The plane itself was of Series 169, a variant of the UFAG Series 69 with a newly designed stabilizer.* (Archivio Bignozzi)

Development of the Brandenburg C-I

Brandenburg C-Is were built under license by Austrian and Hungarian factories in 18 different

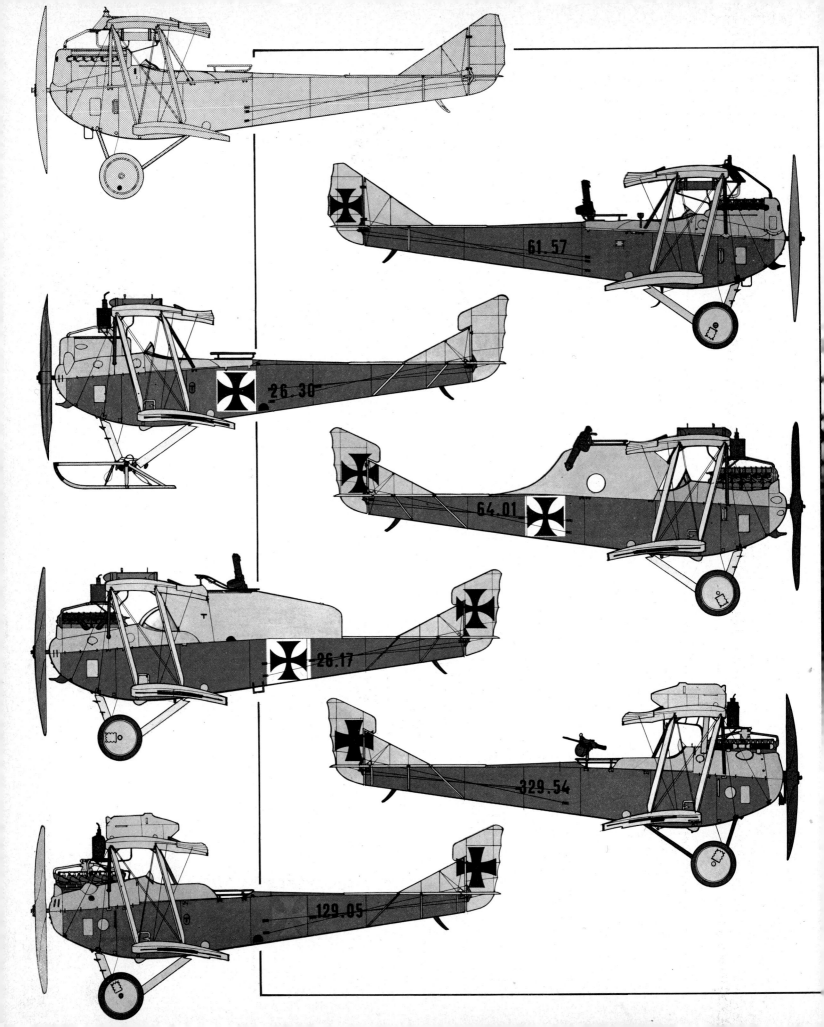

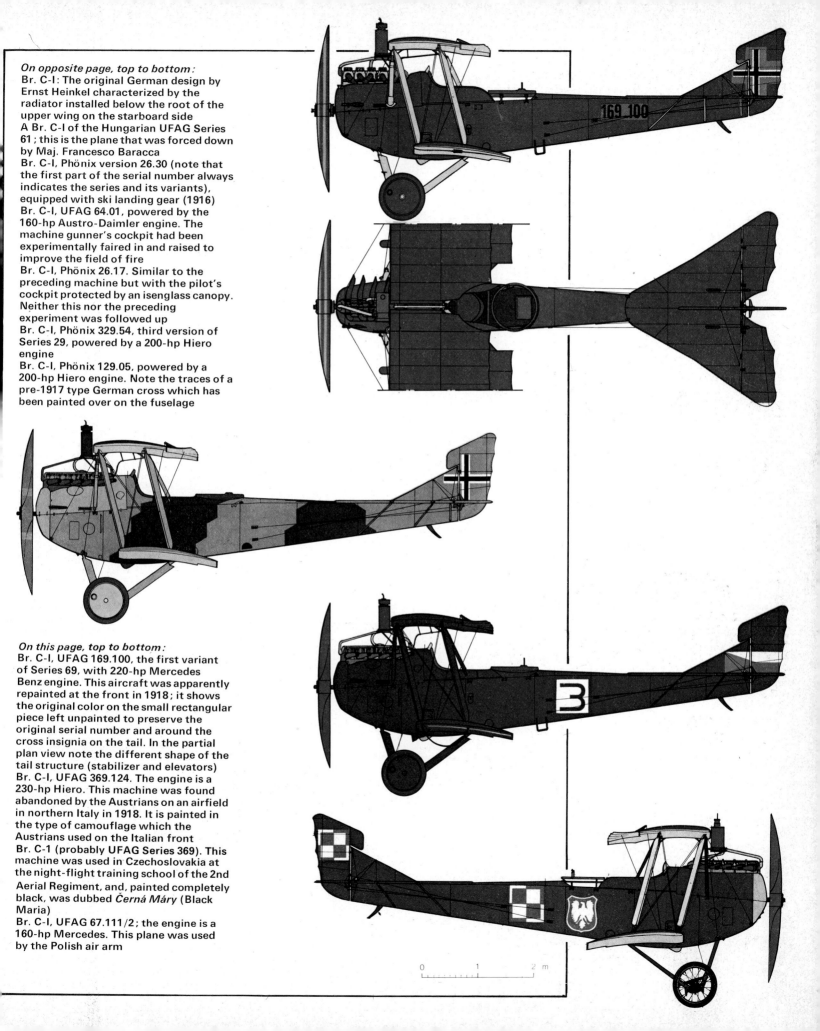

On opposite page, top to bottom:
Br. C-I: The original German design by Ernst Heinkel characterized by the radiator installed below the root of the upper wing on the starboard side
A Br. C-I of the Hungarian UFAG Series 61; this is the plane that was forced down by Maj. Francesco Baracca
Br. C-I, Phönix version 26.30 (note that the first part of the serial number always indicates the series and its variants), equipped with ski landing gear (1916)
Br. C-I, UFAG 64.01, powered by the 160-hp Austro-Daimler engine. The machine gunner's cockpit had been experimentally faired in and raised to improve the field of fire
Br. C-I, Phönix 26.17. Similar to the preceding machine but with the pilot's cockpit protected by an isenglass canopy. Neither this nor the preceding experiment was followed up
Br. C-I, Phönix 329.54, third version of Series 29, powered by a 200-hp Hiero engine
Br. C-I, Phönix 129.05, powered by a 200-hp Hiero engine. Note the traces of a pre-1917 type German cross which has been painted over on the fuselage

On this page, top to bottom:
Br. C-I, UFAG 169.100, the first variant of Series 69, with 220-hp Mercedes Benz engine. This aircraft was apparently repainted at the front in 1918; it shows the original color on the small rectangular piece left unpainted to preserve the original serial number and around the cross insignia on the tail. In the partial plan view note the different shape of the tail structure (stabilizer and elevators)
Br. C-I, UFAG 369.124. The engine is a 230-hp Hiero. This machine was found abandoned by the Austrians on an airfield in northern Italy in 1918. It is painted in the type of camouflage which the Austrians used on the Italian front
Br. C-1 (probably UFAG Series 369). This machine was used in Czechoslovakia at the night-flight training school of the 2nd Aerial Regiment, and, painted completely black, was dubbed Černá Máry (Black Maria)
Br. C-I, UFAG 67.111/2; the engine is a 160-hp Mercedes. This plane was used by the Polish air arm

0   1   2 m

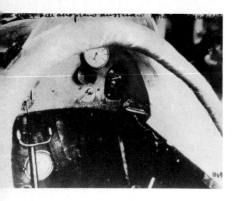

How the Brandenburg C-I was used in the War

At the beginning of the war the Brandenburg C-I was considered by all participants except the French to be a long-range reconnaissance plane. Later, when the mobility of the fronts virtually put an end to land reconnaissance, short-range recce and artillery target observation were also assigned to the reconnaissance pilots. The Austrians selected the Brandenburg as the vehicle for these missions and within a few months, with the cooperation of the German aircraft industry, they were able to marshal a sizeable fleet of aircraft of a performance capability such as to challenge many of the Allied fighter planes. Before the formation of bombing squadrons, the bombing function too was assigned to reconnaissance aircraft, and the first large-scale operational mission in which Brandenburg C-Is were mentioned in official dispatches was one on May 14, 1916, when a squadron of them attacked Italian positions at Ponte Piave.

Although many C-Is were used throughout the war, very few operational details have come down to us, to a great extent because of the reticence which prevailed in official circles in those days.

Several episodes are known however: On July 11, 1916, an Austrian sergeant-major, Joseph Siegel, set out in a C-I and flew southwest over the Austrian-Italian border, continuing on over Brescia and Parma, then over the Apennines to La Spezia, southeast of Genoa, where he dropped five bombs before returning to his base — a solo flight of some 400 km (248 miles) over enemy territory. His outward trip was quiet enough, but after the bombing he was pursued by Italian fighters and his homeward trip was far from peaceful.

The destruction of the Italian dirigible M-4 was also credited to a C-I of the *Fliegerkompanie* based at Aissovizza. On the night of May 3 the dirigible had bombed Ljubljana, and was then intercepted by the Austrian recce aircraft on its return. This machine was flown by the Austrian ace Benno von Fernbrugg, who had started flying C-Is early in 1916 and eventually achieved five victories with this type.

The C-Is remained on active duty until the autumn of 1917, when they were gradually replaced by the more modern Phönix C-I and the UFAG C-I, two planes which were clearly faster and better armed. Both were derived from a Brandenburg C-II prototype designed by Heinkel and built in 1916.

Top: *Detail of pilot's cockpit in a Brandenburg C-I, final series.* (Archivio Bignozzi)
Bottom: *A Brandenburg C-I captured by the Italians at Lentis in the Friuli region in May 1917. The serial number was Phönix 29.70, and the engine was a 200-hp Hiero. Note the typical enclosure of the fixed machine gun on the upper wing and the auxiliary fuel tank*

CAPRONI Ca.3

Top: *Caproni Ca.3, Serial No. 2387, which took part with 35 other bombers in the raid on Pola, one of the heaviest bombing operations in which Capronis ever participated. The squadron dropped 200 bombs, a record for the day.* (Aeronautica Militare Italiana)
Bottom: *One of the few 450-hp Capronis which were modified by fairing over the center nacelle*

Specifications

	Ca.3	Ca.3 mod.	Ca.56a
Power plants (Isotta-Fraschini)	V.4B	V.4B	V.4B
	3×150 hp	3×150 hp	3×150 hp
Wing span, *m*	22·74	22·74	22·74
Length, *m*	11·05	11·05	11·05
Height, *m*	3·84	3·84	3·84
Wing area, *m²*	95·64	95·64	95·64
Weight, empty, *kg*	2300	2600	2400
Total weight, *kg*	3890	4000	3900
Maximum speed, *km/hr*	140	140	130
Ceiling, *m*	4800	4500	—
Climb to 1000 *m, min-sec*	8:00	8:00	6:00
Climb to 3000 *m, min-sec*	—	—	24:00
Climb to 4000 *m, min-sec*	40:00	65:00	—

The year 1913 marks the birth date of the bombing aircraft expressly designed and built as such, and its inventor was Gianni Caproni, a famous Italian designer and manufacturer of airplanes. It was in fact through Caproni that it was first possible for the theory of Jules Douhet—who considered the airplane the decisive factor in modern warfare—to gain credence.

The design for a three-engined bomber which Caproni finished in 1913 called for a machine of exceptional size for that day, and one with the total power requirement shared by a number of engines. In that day there was nothing like it except the Russian *Ilya Mouromets* created by Sikorsky, but the Caproni differed from all other designs in its structure and the daring conception of the power plant.

The power group in the Caproni design consisted of three Gnôme rotary engines. In the first draft of the design these were to be mounted one behind the other in the central nacelle, one driving a pusher propeller directly, the other two driving tractor propellers at the noses of the twin fuselages by means of a transmission. A special differential

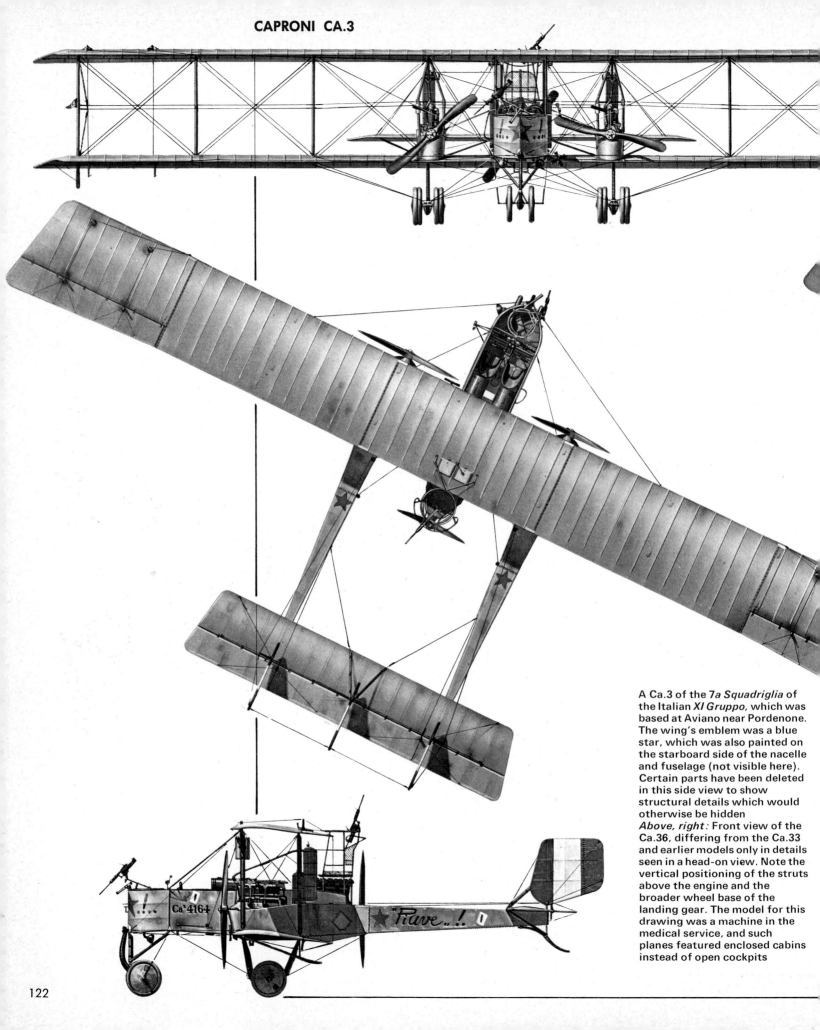

CAPRONI CA.3

A Ca.3 of the *7a Squadriglia* of the Italian *XI Gruppo,* which was based at Aviano near Pordenone. The wing's emblem was a blue star, which was also painted on the starboard side of the nacelle and fuselage (not visible here). Certain parts have been deleted in this side view to show structural details which would otherwise be hidden

Above, right: Front view of the Ca.36, differing from the Ca.33 and earlier models only in details seen in a head-on view. Note the vertical positioning of the struts above the engine and the broader wheel base of the landing gear. The model for this drawing was a machine in the medical service, and such planes featured enclosed cabins instead of open cockpits

Insignia of squadrons equipped
wholly with Caproni aircraft
during the war

pino dell'orco

had a slight positive rake and consisted of five sections—center section, port and starboard root sections, and two outboard sections. The cockpit/nacelle unit and the two fuselages were all attached to the center section. Both upper and lower outboard wing sections had ailerons joined by steel cables. The wings were of double-spar construction, the spars being of ash connected by compression ribs and drag wires; wing ribs were both single and double (with the former of spruce and ash, the latter of poplar and ash). The ailerons were of similar structure and material. Struts were made of ash, spruce and Oregon spruce, bracing wires were of steel cable. The entire covering was doped fabric.

Top: *The Italian* XI Gruppo *(Bomber Wing), based at Aviano near Pordenone, consisted of six squadrons wholly equipped with Caproni Ca.3s.* (Museo Caproni, Taliedo)
Center, left: *In the spring of 1917 Caproni bombers powered by 300-hp engines were based at Comina. This photograph shows the 'Ace of Spades' of the 8a Squadriglia with its crew: observer, Capt. Barbarisi, pilots, Lieut. Gori, Lieut. Pagliano, and mechanic-gunner, Pvt. Zamengo.* (Archivio G. Apostolo)
Bottom left: *Installation and launch tests for 800-kg (1764-lb) torpedo were carried out at Venice in August 1917.* (Museo Caproni, Taliedo)
Center spread: *A group of Ca.3s of the 11th Bomber Wing on the field at Aviano in the summer of 1917.* (Museo Caproni, Taliedo)

transmission made it possible for both tractor propellers to be driven by a single engine when necessary.

Such a layout of the power units had evident advantages, but to avoid complications which would have delayed commissioning of the aircraft—or caused Caproni's proposal to be rejected altogether—his revised design featured three independent engine-propeller combinations. Using the same 80-hp Gnômes as specified in the first design, the Caproni bomber was test-flown in October 1914 by Emilio Pensuti.

Government approval of a proposal for 12 trimotors of this type was slow, and the order was forthcoming only in June 1915, specifying Fiat A.10 engines of 100-hp each as power plants. These planes were to be designated Ca.1 (which became Ca.32 in the revised postwar system of designations. Delivery of the first 12 Capronis was completed in October 1915, followed by 150 more with the Fiat engines. On nine other aircraft (known as Ca.2) the central engine was a 150-hp Isotta-Fraschini V.4B.

Useful load, flight endurance and general flying performance were very good, and the Italian pilots were able to carry out what were, for that day, heavy bombing missions against distant, strategically important targets.

The Caproni's successes at the front soon led Italian military authorities to request modifications. Three 150-hp Isotta-Fraschini V.4Bs increased the total power from 300 to 450 hp, and this meant an increase in maximum breaking load of 300 kg. These new demands were not easy to meet quickly, and it was almost a year later that the first Caproni Ca.3 (or Ca.33 in the postwar system of designation) took off, lifted aloft by its astounding 450 hp.

Technical description

The 450-hp Caproni was a twin-fuselage biplane of impressive dimensions. The wings, of equal span,

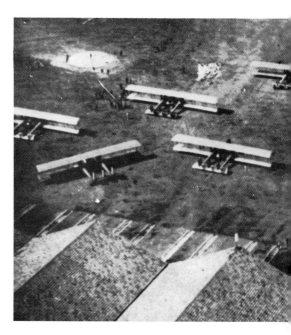

Each of the two fuselages, which were identical, consisted of wooden framework built around four ash longerons, and braced with wire. The fuselage was also fabric covered.

The tail assembly included a stabilizer of tubular metal structure braced with sheet metal struts, elevator and three rudders. The rudder frames were of metal tubing braced with wood. The two outer rudders were completely movable about their axes, and only the center rudder was hinged to a fin.

The central cockpit-nacelle element was also built around four longerons joined fore and aft by steel tubing, centrally trussed and strengthened with steel bracing wires. The forward section of the cockpit ahead of the wing leading edge was covered with fabric, the rest with plywood.

The main landing gear consisted of two independent axles, each with adjustable twin wheels. The nose landing gear was also two-wheeled (see drawing, p. 123). Each fuselage was equipped with a wooden skid, and the lower wing with wing tip skids.

Two fuel tanks, of lead-sealed sheet metal, held 315 liters (70 gallons) each, and were fitted behind the pilot's and co-pilot's seats. The oil tanks, one for each engine, had a capacity of 25 liters (9·9 gallons) each.

The crew consisted of two pilots, a rear gunner and an observer. The latter's cockpit was in the nose, ahead of the engines, and was armed with a ring-mounted machine gun. Pilot and co-pilot sat side by side just behind the observer and had dual controls. Accommodation for the tail gunner was beneath the trailing edge of the center wing section above the pusher engine; his machine gun was also ring-mounted. A single instrument panel served both pilots; instruments were few and included compass, tachometer and manometer.

Development of the Caproni Ca.3

All 250 of the 450-hp Caproni Ca.3s which the Italian government had ordered were delivered by the end of 1917. In November of that year the *Commissariato Generale,* the Italian military procurement agency, ordered an additional score of Ca.3s. The original plan had been to order 50 more Caproni bombers but there were not enough engines available. Deliveries of this additional batch of planes were completed in February 1918.

Meanwhile the 450-hp version had appeared in France, where it was built under license first by the REP, a firm founded by the pioneer aeronautical engineer Esnault-Pelterie, and later by the SAIB. French aircraft manufacturers produced 86 Ca.3s, differing from the Italian original only in the occasional use of a French engine (such as the 130-hp Canton-Unné) in the center position.

One of the very first attempts during the war to use aircraft for fast transport of the wounded was made in a Ca.3. In Caproni bombers adapted for

these missions there was accommodation for two seriously wounded casualties on stretchers installed over the two fuselage sections and completely enclosed by cowlings; two other casualties could be accommodated in the cabinized central section with the crew.

One Ca.3 was experimentally armed with a flexible 25-mm canon in the nose, but it was not a success and was not followed up.

A version which was called the Ca.3 Mod. (for *modificato,* modified) differed by incorporating certain changes in the wing root attachments so that the port and starboard wing sections could easily be installed and removed, while the center section remained fixed. The Ca.3 Mod. was built for a short while at the Savigliano plant during the war, then production was resumed in 1923 and continued until 1926; 153 Ca.3 Mod. (later called the Ca.36) machines were completed, and of these 144 were delivered to the *Regia Aeronautica,* as the postwar Italian air arm was called.

Although by the mid-20s these aircraft were obsolete, they still gave a good account of themselves in the colonies, where they were appreciated for their simplicity, safety and reliability.

The Ca.36 was also adapted to the needs of the medical corps, and was able to accommodate eight casualties in the cabin (four on suspended stretchers, four in seats). A medical officer or nurse was included as the second member of the crew.

The 450-hp Caproni was also modified as a civilian aircraft, with space for six passengers, and several machines of this type also found employment in the official mail service between Padua and Vienna. These were known as Ca.56a.

The Ca.5 series (later designated Ca.44, 45, 46, 47) were larger aircraft, powered by engines developing a total of 600 hp.

How the Caproni Ca.3 was used in the War

The first bombing missions in which the new Caproni airplanes took part took place in August 1915. Among the earliest operations were those directed against Aisovizza, Castegnevizza, Adiussina, Bainsizza, Ljubljana, the Alpine valleys and the battle over Pergine during which Caproni pilots and gunners brought down three enemy aircraft. Capt. Salomone, who was part of a Ca.1 crew raiding Ljubljana, was hit, but nevertheless brought his Caproni back to the base, and thus became the first aviator to win the *Medaglia d'Oro* (Gold Medal), the Italian equivalent of the Victoria Cross or the American Congressional Medal of Honor. Italian bombers also played an important part in the spring offensive of 1917, taking part in both day and night operations of great efficiency.

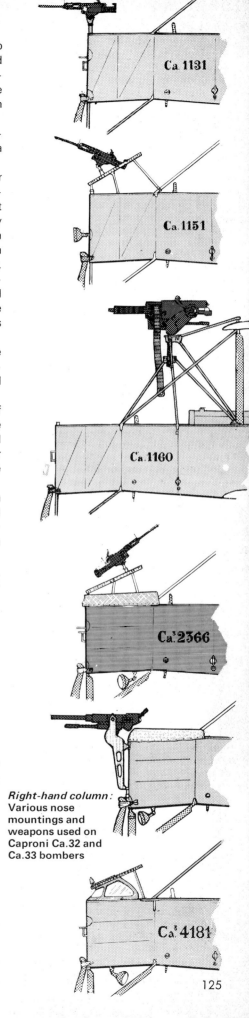

Right-hand column: **Various nose mountings and weapons used on Caproni Ca.32 and Ca.33 bombers**

125

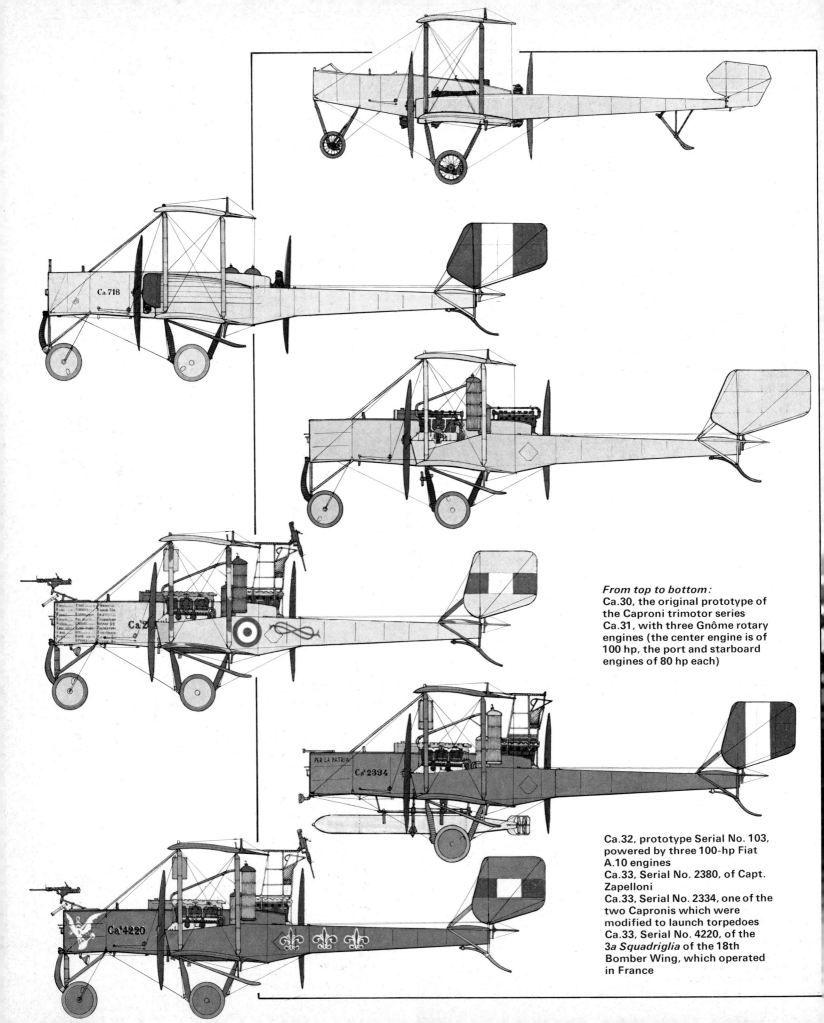

From top to bottom:
Ca.30, the original prototype of
the Caproni trimotor series
Ca.31, with three Gnôme rotary
engines (the center engine is of
100 hp, the port and starboard
engines of 80 hp each)

Ca.32, prototype Serial No. 103,
powered by three 100-hp Fiat
A.10 engines
Ca.33, Serial No. 2380, of Capt.
Zapelloni
Ca.33, Serial No. 2334, one of the
two Capronis which were
modified to launch torpedoes
Ca.33, Serial No. 4220, of the
3a Squadriglia of the 18th
Bomber Wing, which operated
in France

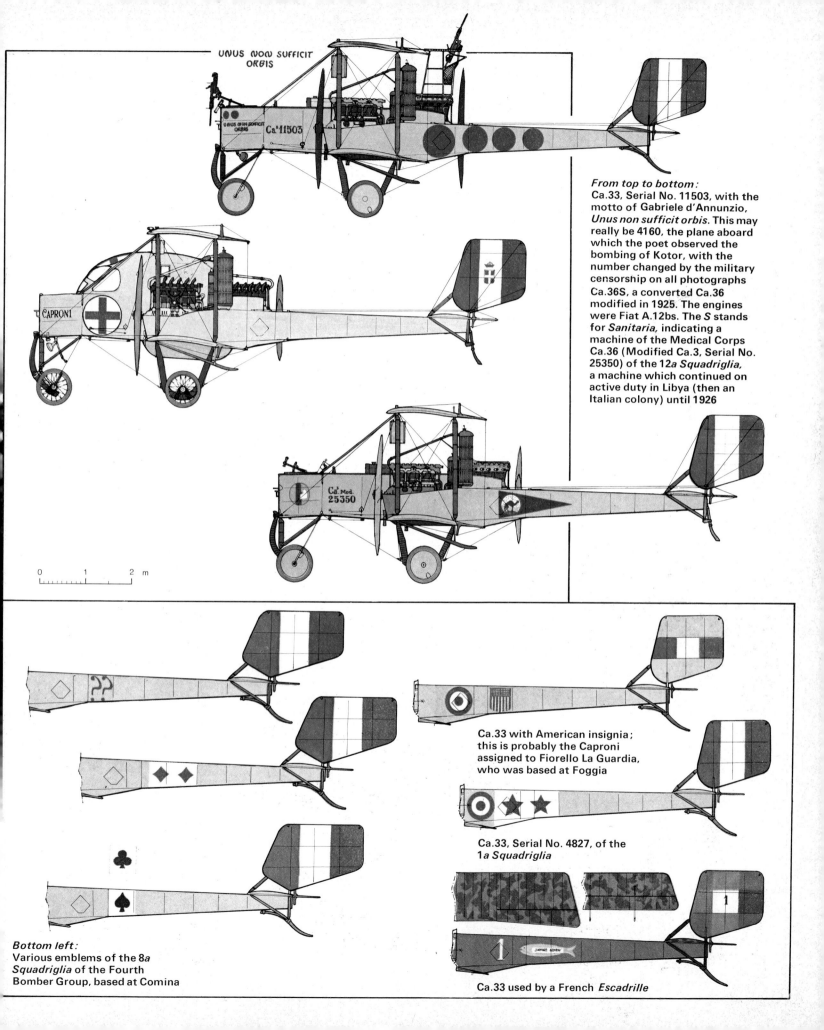

UNUS NON SUFFICIT ORBIS

Ca.ª 11503

CAPRONI

Ca.ª Mod. 25350

From top to bottom:
Ca.33, Serial No. 11503, with the motto of Gabriele d'Annunzio, *Unus non sufficit orbis*. This may really be 4160, the plane aboard which the poet observed the bombing of Kotor, with the number changed by the military censorship on all photographs
Ca.36S, a converted Ca.36 modified in 1925. The engines were Fiat A.12bs. The *S* stands for *Sanitaria*, indicating a machine of the Medical Corps
Ca.36 (Modified Ca.3, Serial No. 25350) of the 12*a Squadriglia*, a machine which continued on active duty in Libya (then an Italian colony) until 1926

0 1 2 m

Ca.33 with American insignia; this is probably the Caproni assigned to Fiorello La Guardia, who was based at Foggia

Ca.33, Serial No. 4827, of the 1*a Squadriglia*

Bottom left:
Various emblems of the 8*a Squadriglia* of the Fourth Bomber Group, based at Comina

Ca.33 used by a French *Escadrille*

Almost from the very beginning of combat flights the virtues of the Caproni were obvious. For example: of all the 300-hp machines which took part in the bombing of Aisovizza, there was scarcely a plane that had not been hit by anti-aircraft fire but they all returned safely. During the bombing of Ljubljana, one Caproni was two hours late in getting off the ground, but it flew on alone to the target, dropped its bombs, took its fair share of flak and returned to the base. Often the anti-aircraft fire did a great deal of damage, but the Caproni was rugged enough to get back to the base the great majority of times, often after having brought down several enemy planes.

The 300-hp Capronis continued to be intensely active during the Austrian counteroffensive of early 1917, a period when every effort was being made to ready its 450-hp successor.

In March 1917, in fact, the first deliveries of these more powerful aircraft were made to the *IV Gruppo* (4th Bomber Wing) which was based at San Pelagio. The first operations involving large numbers of these bombers, however, did not take place until June, when the *XI Gruppo* (11th Bomber Wing) based at Padua gave good support to ground troops in a battle at Ortigara and also bombed Pola and Tarvisio. Other groups flying Ca.3s were at Ghedi (14th Bomber Wing), Comina and Campoformido (4th), Aviano (11th) and Verona (9th). Two squadrons were based at Tahiraga in support of Italian troops in Albania.

Of particular value in that summer of 1917 were the incursions made by Caproni bombers over Assling, a vital railroad junction and an industrial center of prime importance, and over the valley of Chiapovano. In 12 days, from August 2 to 14, Italian

airmen hit the enemy where it hurt most in five raids on Chiapovano, three on Pola, and two on Assling.

The new aircraft also inspired the warlike ambitions of the poet d'Annunzio when he gave his support to a plan to bomb the naval base at Kotor off the Balkan coast. A special detachment of Caproni bombers was set up, known as *Distaccamento A. R.* (Detachment A.R.), the cover name being suggested by the commander's name, Armani. Gianni Caproni, designer of the bombers, was skeptical of the whole operation, but d'Annunzio was right, and the operation was carried out with brilliant success.

When Italian ground troops were forced to withdraw on the Tagliamento and Piave rivers, the Caproni units were tireless in their support, inflicting serious damage on enemy lines of communications and troop concentrations.

In July 1917 it was decided to use Ca.3s to launch torpedoes against Austrian naval vessels in their well-established bases at Pola, Kotor and Sebenico. This involved some difficult problems for the torpedoes meant an additional 400 kg (880 lb) over the normal war load. Experiments carried out at Venice were successful, but the preparation of the squadron took so long that only one operation was feasible before the war ended.

One Italian bombing unit was also active in France. The *XVIII Gruppo* (Bomber Group) commanded by Capt. De Riso was sent there at the specific request of the French High Command. This group consisted of three squadrons, based first at Longvic, then at Ochey. Flying 450-hp Ca.3s, the Italians hit targets on the Marne and supply centers north of Rheims, Thionville, Sablon, St.-Quetin and Metz.

A squadron of Caproni aircraft was also operated by the Italian navy for reconnaissance work along the Istrian coast. Eventually this unit also took part in bombing missions.

The name of Caproni is also associated with the highly publicized exploit over Vienna toward the end of August 1917, when two 450-hp Caproni Ca.3s of the *4a Squadriglia* were prepared for this propaganda flight dreamed up by d'Annunzio. Auxiliary fuel tanks were installed, thus increasing the range of the aircraft to about 900 km (560 miles). Room for these auxiliary tanks was made by removing bomb racks and armament. But the project didn't get off the ground that year, and when it finally took place a year later it was with the SVA scouts from 'Serenissima' Squadron not with the Ca.3s.

Capronis were also used at the 8th Training Center for American pilots at Foggia, where their qualities of toughness and maneuverability were highly rated. One training instructor is on record as having performed a loop and a roll at an altitude of about 2000 m (6562 ft).

Many American pilots who had earned their wings in Caproni trainers took part in bombing sorties together with Italian airmen. Two Ca.3s were sent to the US in 1918, followed by two technical missions, to make publicity flights for the Third War Loan.

Top: *Experimental version of the Ca.3, designated Ca.35. The engines are the regular 150-hp Isotta-Fraschinis. Note the faired-over center nacelle and 25-mm nose cannon.* (Museo Caproni, Taliedo)
Center, left: *A Caproni Ca.5 of the Italian air corps. The Ca.5 had three engines developing a total of 600 hp, and for this reason it was often known as the Ca.600*
Bottom: *The first night raid carried out by a Caproni squadron took place on January 6, 1917, when the railroad station of Nabresina was bombed. The Capronis also bombed the area around Monte Querceto, this detachment being under the command of Capt. Falchi.* (Museo Caproni, Taliedo)

FOKKER E I_E IV

The Fokker E I. The great influence of both the Morane-Saulnier and Hanuschke monoplanes is obvious. Note, however, the rudder, which is unmistakably of Fokker design. (Museo Caproni, Taliedo)

Specifications

	E I	E II	E III	E IV
Power plant	Oberursel U-O, 80 hp	Oberursel, 100 hp	Oberursel U-I, 100 hp	Oberursel U-III, 160 hp
Wing span, *m*	8·95	8	9·52	9·52
Total length, *m*	6·75	7·30	7·30	7·50
Height, *m*	3·18	2·79	2·79	3·07
Wing area, *m²*	∞16	∞14	∞16	∞16
Weight, empty, *kg*	357	398	398	465
Total weight, *kg*	562	609	608	723
Maximum speed, *km/h*	130	141	145	150
Climb to 1000 *m, min-sec*	7:00	5:00	—	—
Climb to 2000 *m, min-sec*	—	—	12:00	8:00
Ceiling, *m*	—	—	3500	—
Flight endurance, *hrs-min*	1:30	1:30	2:45	1:30

The first fighter plane which brought fame to Anthony Fokker was, curiously, based on a French aircraft. The armament which made the Fokker monoplane for several months the most feared of all enemy aircraft among Allied pilots was also French in origin—and the Fokker was feared by the Allies, to the point where a British Member of Parliament referred to the B.E.2cs as 'Fokker fodder'.

Anthony Fokker had had a fair number of flops before he finally managed to buy a damaged Morane-Saulnier Type L for 500 marks. Once he had repaired the French machine and tried it out, he immediately realized how wrong his previous approach had been, and with a characteristic Fokkerian lack of principle he set about 'designing' an exact duplicate of the Morane-Saulnier. A few

days after his trial flight, Fokker dismantled the machine and used the pieces as patterns for the principal elements of his own construction which was designated the M 5. Fokker's assistant, a young aeronautical engineer named Martin Kreutzer, introduced a number of improvements, and in this way the Fokker M 5 became substantially superior to its French prototype.

The M 5, a two-seater, was built in two versions, the M 5k (for *kurz*, or 'short'), with a span of nearly 9 m (29·5 ft), and the M 5l, with a span of approx. 11 m (36 ft). The former was the version from which the E I was derived, eventually leading to its progressive developments E II, III and IV.

A second episode, entirely unforeseeable, brought the new German machine and French aviation to-

Fok EⅢ419/15

amedeo gigli

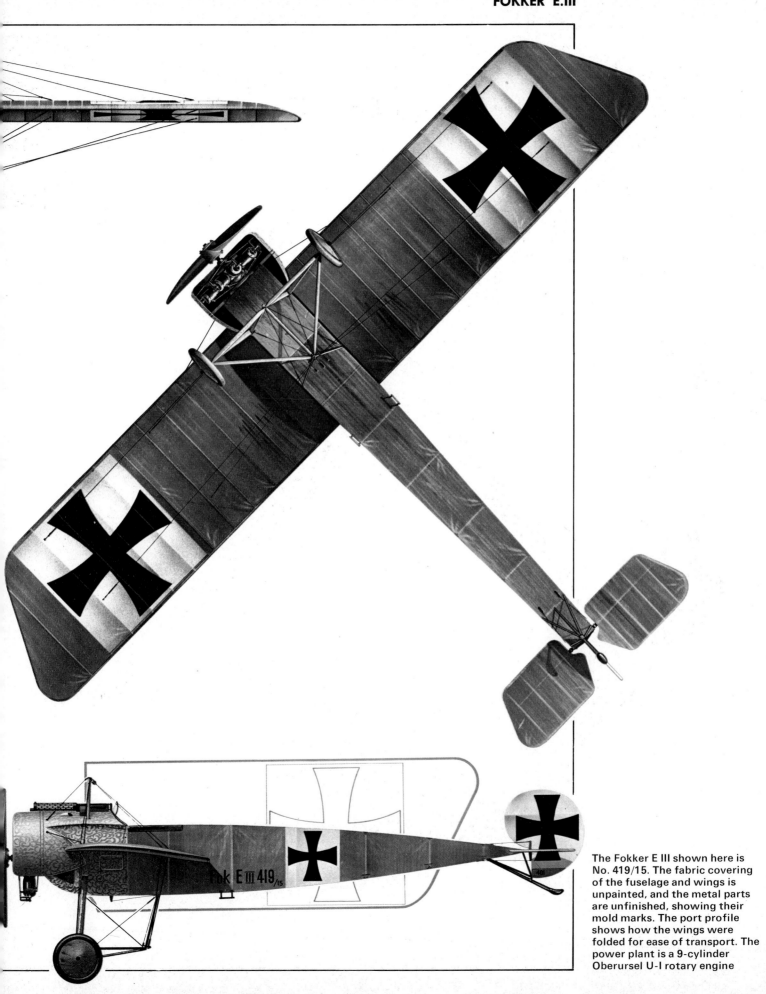

The Fokker E III shown here is No. 419/15. The fabric covering of the fuselage and wings is unpainted, and the metal parts are unfinished, showing their mold marks. The port profile shows how the wings were folded for ease of transport. The power plant is a 9-cylinder Oberursel U-I rotary engine

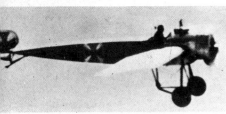

Top: *Anthony Fokker in the cockpit of his M 5k/MG, preparing to give a demonstration of the synchronization device for the Parabellum machine gun*
Center: *One of the few extant photographs of a Fokker E I in flight.* (Nowarra)
Bottom: *The German Capt. Bahr and his Fokker E I. Note the intricate system of landing and flying wires*

gether again—the forced landing of the first French ace Roland Garros behind the enemy lines in April 1915. Garros did not succeed in burning his plane, another Morane-Saulnier Type L parasol armed with a single fired Hotchkiss machine gun fitted with a very rudimentary device which made it possible to fire through the rotating propeller blades; the aircraft fell in German hands in almost undamaged condition. A curious feature in this episode is that although both the Germans and Russians had done research on synchronization mechanisms, Garros used the crudest of devices, which was simply to embed steel wedges in the trailing edges of his propeller to fend off any shots that didn't get through the rotating blades. Even so Garros had been able to shoot down five German aircraft in 20 days, and the Germans were delighted to have captured the famous 'secret weapon' which had enabled the French to force down so many of their aircraft. The first German attempts to copy Garros's weird 'synchronizer' ended in catastrophe, because the German Parabellum MG 14 was so powerful that the bullets instead of ricocheting off the armored blades demolished the whole propeller. Later experiments with a device developed by Heinrich Luebbe, a watchmaker whom Fokker had recruited, and Fritz Haber were wholly successful, and in a few months the new Fokker monoplane armed with an efficiently-synchronized machine gun had gained such importance as to constitute the prime element in German air superiority at the front.

Technical description

The total production of the various Fokker fighting scout monoplanes derived from the M 5k amounted

to about 450 machines, and the E III version (constituting the bulk of this total) can be considered typical of the other three types as well.

The Fokker E III had a fuselage which was a simple structure of welded steel tubing, very closely copied after the Morane-Saulnier monoplanes. This permitted an easy arrangement of armament mounts and, indeed, made it possible to adapt the M 5k (which came from the Schwerin works as the 216th plane completed) as the first prototype of the new fighter.

The greater part of the fuselage was fabric-covered, but the nose was protected by two aluminum panels. To decrease drag the width of the fuselage was reduced by about 5 cm (2 in) from that of the Morane-Saulnier; this modification also improved visibility from the cockpit, which had a manual sliding panel in the floor for downward visibility.

However the undercarriage was radically different from that of the French aircraft; the wheel base was increased from 1·5 to 2·0 m (4·9 to 6·6 ft), although this arrangement did not prove to be very satisfactory.

The wing planform was rectangular, with the typical positive rake at the wing tips. Structurally there were two stout main spars, with two connecting elements, steel drag wires, and 13 ribs in each half wing. All in all, the Fokker wing was superior to the Morane-Saulnier, not only because of its greater strength but also on account of its superior aerodynamic characteristics, due to closer spacing of the ribs which permitted more accurate construction of the wing profile. The wing was completely covered with fabric, except for two ply-wood strips along the roots.

The tail control surfaces, of limited area, were built of a steel tubing framework covered with fabric. The entire rudder was movable and protected by a rugged tail skid (a small fin was installed on a few machines to increase stability). Flight controls included rudder pedals and a control stick for the warping mechanism which was eventually to be replaced by ailerons. (Control by warping meant that the wing could not be very rigid.) The whole wing was connected to the upper cabane and under-carriage by a veritable maze of landing and flying wires.

The engine was a 9-cylinder, 100-hp Oberursel U I rotary, driving a 2·53-m (8 ft 4-inch) dia. two-bladed wooden propeller. The engine mount was of steel, with a cylindrical cowling covering all but the three bottom cylinders.

The fuselage section between the engine and the pilot's cockpit accommodated a divided tank for oil and reserve fuel, while the main fuel tank was aft of the cockpit. The reserve fuel was gravity-fed to the engine, the fuel from the main tank being pressure-fed by a pump driven by the engine or, in an emergency, by a hand pump.

Visibility from the pilot's cockpit was excellent. The cockpit was sufficiently roomy to accommodate a second crew member behind the pilot. Instrumentation was rudimentary, and instead of being installed on an instrument panel the various dials were mounted on the sides of the cockpit. In addition to the flight controls there were, on the control stick, the trigger connected to the machine gun, and a switch for cutting out a certain number of cylinders, thus permitting some regulation of engine power.

Armament was one (or, rarely, two) LMG 08/15 7·92-mm synchronized machine gun, mounted on the top decking of the forward fuselage, slightly to the right of the centerline. The rate of fire of the LMG 08/15 was originally 400 rounds per minute, but this was soon raised to 600. Before the introduction of an optical sight on the E III, the aiming device on the E I had been a crude arrangement consisting of a headrest for the pilot permitting him to define the line of fire with his body.

All things considered the E III was not an aircraft of brilliant performance. The Oberursel rotary engine was not very reliable, and it usually developed a good 10 per cent less than its rated power. Engine power also decreased directly with altitude, and for this reason the Fokker monoplane was unable to operate above 3000 m (9800 ft); at the same time drag was very high because of the many landing and flying wires which hampered performance to a marked degree. One Fokker monoplane captured by the British achieved 140 km/hr (97 mph) at sea level and 126 km/hr (78 mph) at 3500 m (6890 ft). The maximum rate of climb, little more than 3·5 m/sec (11·5 ft/sec) at ground level, was only 0·4 m/sec (1·3 ft/sec) at 3500 m, which meant that it took approximately 30 minutes to climb to 3000 m. Maneuverability at that altitude was virtually nil.

Empty and loaded weights were 398 and 608 kg respectively (878 and 1341 lb), but production aircraft often had much higher empty weight, with the result that the useful load had to be limited to avoid excessive decrease in flight performance.

Development of the Fokker E I - E IV Fighters

The first of the Fokker fighter monoplanes, the E I, was simply an M 5k armed with a synchronized machine gun; the gun was originally a Parabellum, which was soon replaced by the more efficient LMG 08/15. The aircraft was personally presented by Anthony Fokker to the German air detachments operating on the French front in the period from May to July 1915. This aircraft was powered by an 80-hp Oberursel rotary engine and carried enough fuel for 2 hrs flying.

A curious spinoff of the E I was an experimental version in which the whole airframe was entirely covered with celluloid to reduce its visibility practically to zero. Other variants were distinguished by modifications designed to improve the armament.

The E II, derived from the E I (and sometimes designated as E 14), was an effort to improve flight characteristics. The prototype was powered by the usual Oberursel 80-hp rotary engine but even with the 100-hp Oberursel the E II was not, all things considered, a very satisfactory aircraft. In the hope of increasing its maximum speed, Fokker had reduced the wing area to approximately 14 m² (150 sq. ft), with a span of approximately 8 m (26·25 ft), but the poor aerodynamics of the E II offset the increased speed almost entirely and both rate of climb and maneuverability were far inferior to those of the E I.

The next model, the E III, proved to be the most successful of all Fokker monoplanes. For some reason, the manufacturers continued to use the same designation M 14 to describe the E III as they had for the E II. The principal new features of the E III were an increase in span and wing area. The engine was the same 100-hp Oberursel that had driven the E II. Since German engine production could not keep up with the demand, the E III was often powered by engines of other makes, and sometimes the substitution was made not only because of shortages but in an effort to increase horsepower. Thus an 80-hp Le Rhône rotary salvaged from a captured Nieuport might serve, or a Goebel Goe I (100 hp) or a Siemens-Halske 90-hp engine might be tried experimentally. Neither of these German engines, however, was generally available until the Fokker monoplanes were already obsolescent.

Top to bottom:
A Fokker monoplane with wings folded for transport
A Fokker E II, identifiable because of the improved engine cowling. (Nowarra)
Head-on view of Max Immelmann's Fokker armed with three machine guns. (Nowarra)
Fokker E IV, recognizable by its double radial engine. (Museo Caproni, Taliedo)

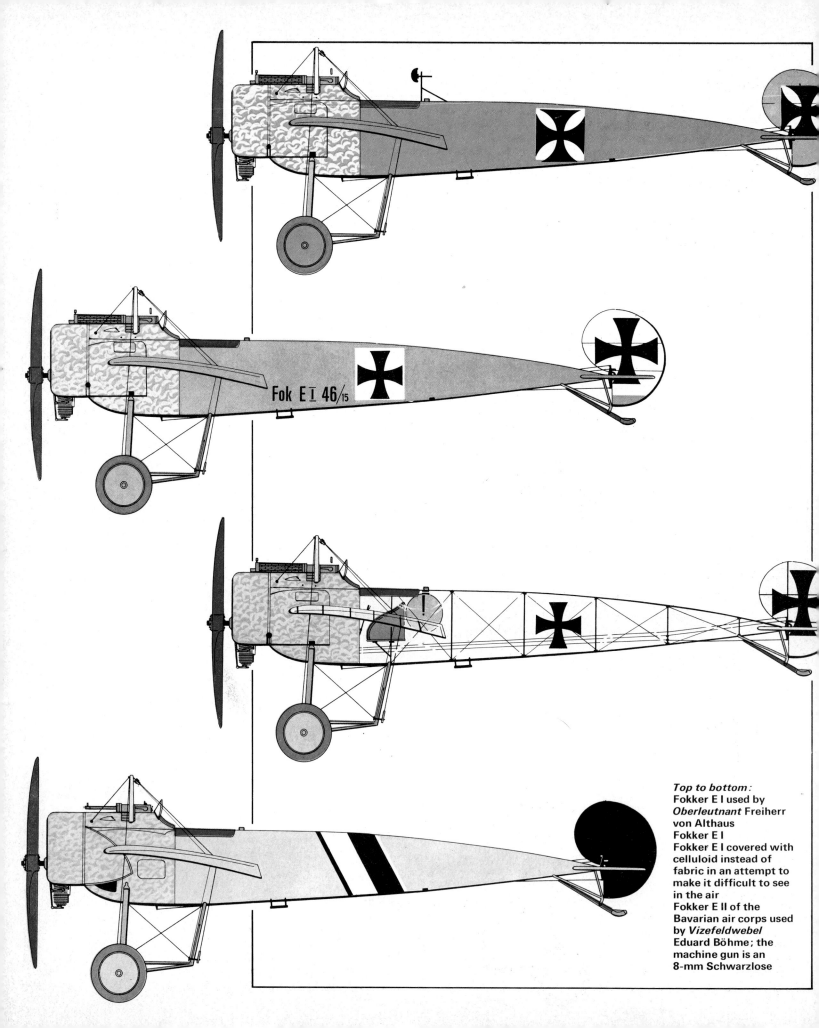

Top to bottom:
Fokker E I used by
Oberleutnant Freiherr
von Althaus
Fokker E I
Fokker E I covered with
celluloid instead of
fabric in an attempt to
make it difficult to see
in the air
Fokker E II of the
Bavarian air corps used
by *Vizefeldwebel*
Eduard Böhme; the
machine gun is an
8-mm Schwarzlose

Fok E I 46/15

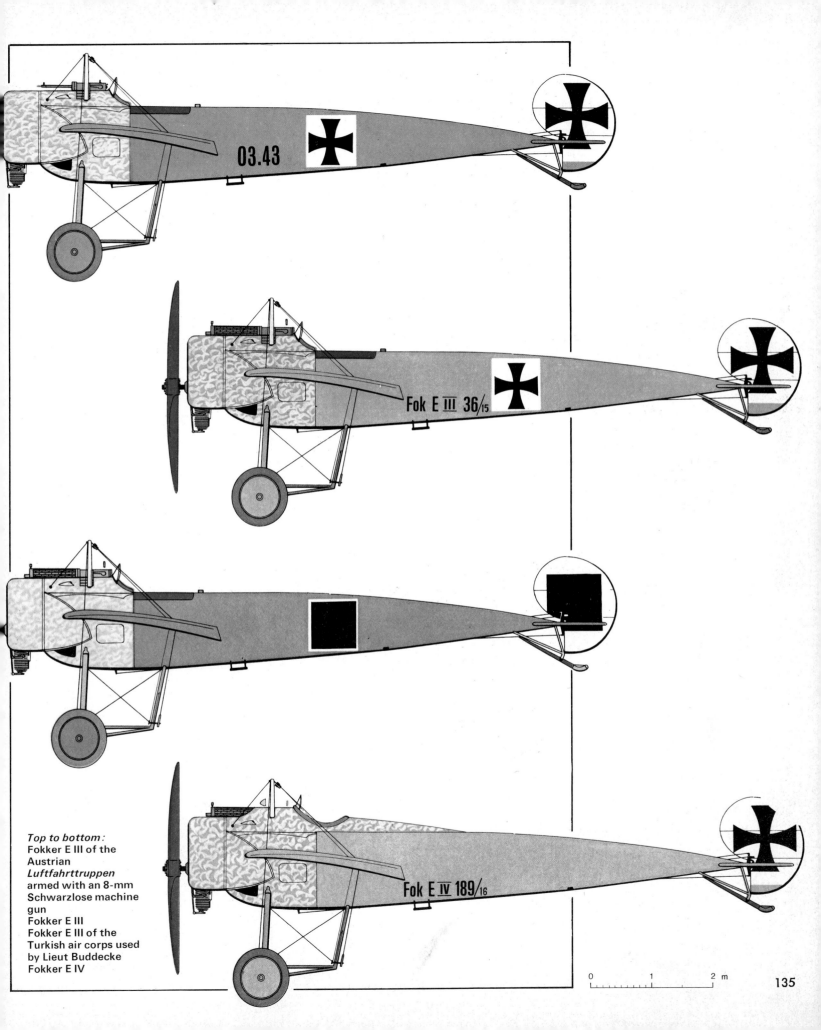

03.43

Fok E III 36/15

Fok E IV 189/16

Top to bottom:
Fokker E III of the
Austrian
Luftfahrttruppen
armed with an 8-mm
Schwarzlose machine
gun
Fokker E III
Fokker E III of the
Turkish air corps used
by Lieut Buddecke
Fokker E IV

0   1   2 m

The final version of the series was the E IV, which carried the powerful armament of two machine guns which outclassed anything the Allies had flying at the time. German fighter pilots, equipped with a backup weapon in case of jamming, had a distinct advantage. The E IV was heavier than earlier models and had a more powerful engine, the 160-hp Oberursel U III double rotary. Both engine and cockpit were skilfully faired to reduce drag, but in spite of the optimism inspired by good performance returned by the prototype the new fighter was a disappointment. In fact, the high speeds in both level flight and in climbing were never achieved by Fokker E IV production aircraft, and maneuverability was noticeably inferior.

The German fighter ace Max Immelmann ordered an E IV powered by a captured 160-hp Le Rhône engine. He then fitted *three* machine guns synchronized to fire through the propeller blades, mounting them with the barrels pointing upward at about 15°. It was a lethal combination, but the weight of the armament was a distinct disadvantage, and Immelmann's formula was soon abandoned.

Structurally all these monoplanes were very similar, and even armament and arrangement of fuel tanks, etc., did not differ greatly from one to the other (from the E II on, there was a rear fuel tank in all models). One successful innovation was the ease of dismantling and reassembling the aircraft, together with the characteristic folding wings for transport (the wings folded back against the fuselage).

How the Fokker Monoplanes were used in the War

Until the spring of 1915 the Allies had enjoyed a decided superiority in the air, so that the appearance of the new Fokkers came as an unpleasant surprise.

As soon as Fokker had delivered his monoplanes, such German aces as Boelcke, Immelmann and Udet began to chase the Allied machines. They had firm orders not to get involved in dogfights except over their own lines, the idea being to keep the secret of the successful German synchronization from falling into Allied hands. This consideration, of course, hamstrung the natural aggressiveness of the German airman, but even so the qualities of the new plane and the skill of the German pilots impressed the British and French, who had to suffer some heavy losses in the air.

An example: In August 1915, during an attack on Saarbrücken, a French bomber wing lost not less than nine aircraft to Fokker pilots, and the Fokker monoplanes played an important part in the air umbrella which the Germans created over Verdun during their bloody offensive of February 1916.

The Fokker monoplanes were rightly feared by the Allies: but they could also be very dangerous to their own pilots, who on more than one occasion heard the sickening sound of their propellers splintering from the firepower of an LMG when the synchronizer slipped out of phase. It may be that the German ace Max Immelmann died in an accident of this kind, although exactly how he was killed has never been established.

Among the many German flying units which were equipped with Fokker monoplanes there were at least nine *Feldfliegerabteilungen* (Field Air Detachments) and four *Kampfeinsitzerkommandos* (Single-seat Combat Groups), plus German naval units and Home Defense units. Fokker monoplanes were also used in Palestine and Turkey, and toward the end of 1916 several E IIs were still in active service on the Russian-German front. A certain number of E Is, IIs and IIIs were turned over to the Austrian air corps. and rearmed with 8-mm Schwarzlose machine guns.

Fokker monoplanes unquestionably were of fundamental importance in the development of the fighter plane; in fact, after 1915 designers of such aircraft rarely used any other basic concept than the single-engine single-seat monoplane with fixed armament. However the success of the Fokker monoplane lasted for only a brief period, since by 1916 the new Allied fighters (the French Nieuport 11s, the British D.H.2s and F.E.2s) had abruptly changed the balance of power in the air. But even in this development the Fokker played an important part, since it was this aircraft that set off the feverish competition for constant technical improvement which became (and remains) the prime concern of military aviation.

A Fokker E III captured by the French. Allied airmen are inspecting the aircraft; note that the wing insignia have been hidden by branches to avoid provoking attack from friendly planes overhead. (G. B. Jarrett Collection)

BRÉGUET 14

Left: *The Bréguet 14 was one of the earliest successful examples of metal-skinned aircraft. It was one of the French planes built in greatest numbers, the total production being about 8000 machines*
Below: *One of the earliest Bréguet 14 A2s, a reconnaissance plane equipped with flaps along the trailing edge of the lower wing*

Specifications

	14 A2	14 B2
Power plant	Renault, 300 hp	Renault, 300 hp
Upper wing span, *m*	14·64	14·36
Lower wing span, *m*	12·40	13·66
Total length, *m*	8·87	8·87
Height, *m*	3·0	3·0
Wing area, *m²*	47·5	59·2
Weight, empty, *kg*	1000	1025
Useful load, *kg*	310	514
Speed at 4000 *m, km/hr*	184	165
Climb to 4000 *m, min-sec*	15:20	26:00
Flight endurance, *hrs-min*	3:45	3:30
Ceiling, *m*	6100	5200

Among the most durable planes of the war, in the sense that they continued to be built and used over a longer period of time before being replaced by newer machines, was the Bréguet XIV, also known as the Bréguet 14 from 1918 on. One reason for the longevity of this remarkable airplane lay in its technical innovations, such as the use of duralumin alloy in its structure. Louis Bréguet had been among the first aircraft pioneers in France to use metal air frames even in his earliest model, the biplane which he built and powered with a 50-hp Antoinette engine, and flew himself way back in 1909. In the years just before the war, he built a series of all-metal airframe biplanes with rear-mounted engines and pusher propellers.

Then Michelin brothers decided to donate 100 aircraft to the French nation. These planes were to be built in the Michelin factory at Clermont-Ferrand, and the design chosen was the Bréguet BU-3, an aircraft of the Voisin type with a central fuselage nacelle and 200-hp Canton-Unné engine. The product was immediately christened the BUM and otherwise known as the Bréguet-Michelin. Its development was fast, at first with a model designated SN-3 (which was awarded first prize for an aircraft designed specifically for the bombing of German factories in the Essen region), followed later by the Bréguet IV, V and VI, which became pro-

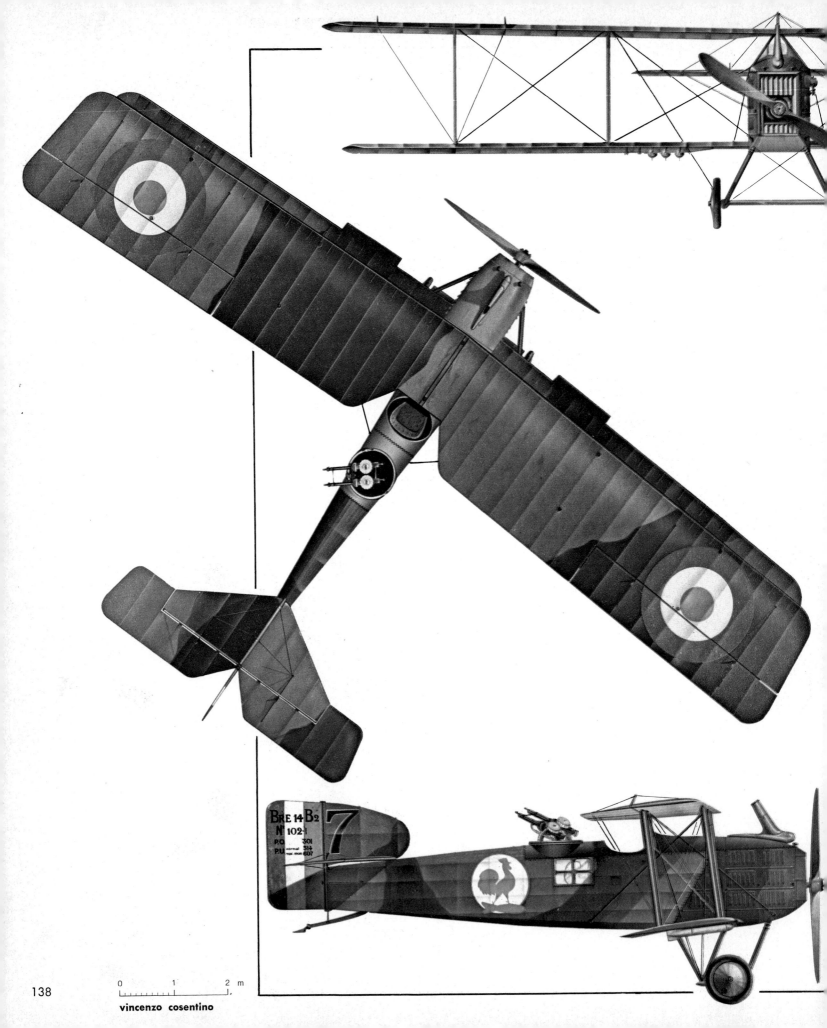

BRE 14 B2
N° 1024
P.O. 301
P.U. normal 514
P.U. max. mon 607

7

0 1 2 m

vincenzo cosentino

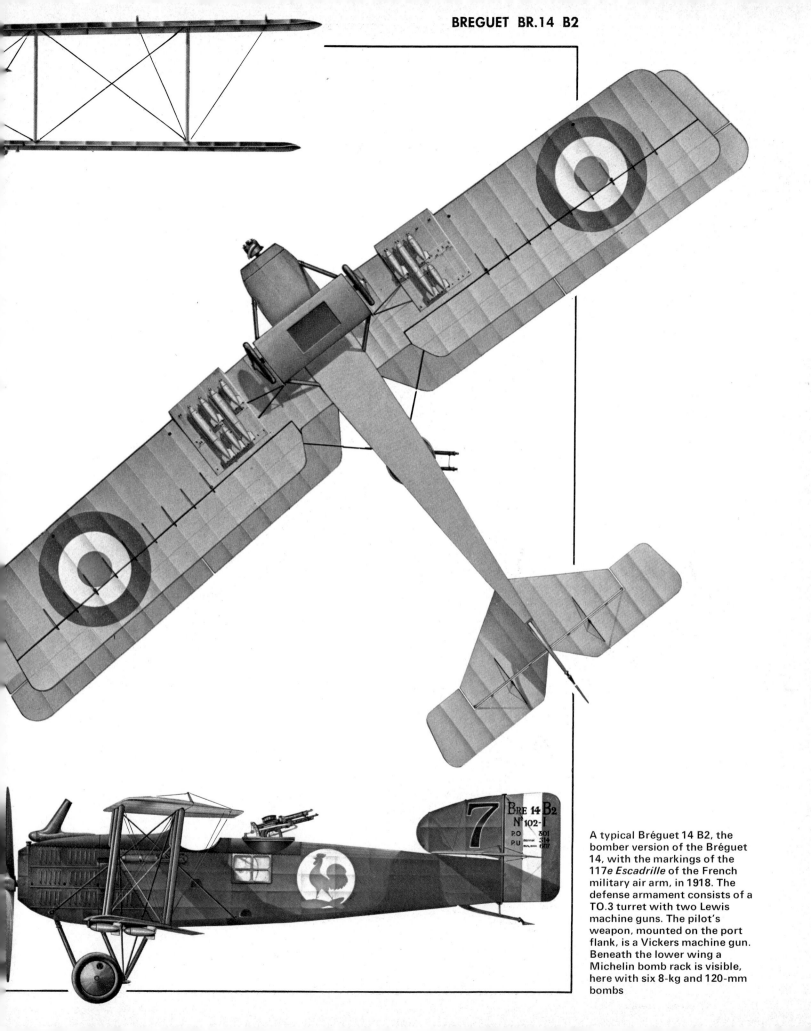

A typical Bréguet 14 B2, the bomber version of the Bréguet 14, with the markings of the 117e *Escadrille* of the French military air arm, in 1918. The defense armament consists of a TO.3 turret with two Lewis machine guns. The pilot's weapon, mounted on the port flank, is a Vickers machine gun. Beneath the lower wing a Michelin bomb rack is visible, here with six 8-kg and 120-mm bombs

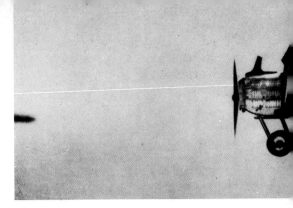

duction models, but whose performance was considerably reduced because of the heavy armament load imposed upon them.

When the manufacture of these aircraft was finished in 1916 the Michelin factory was faced with a critical period. It was at that point that Louis Bréguet proposed a new design, the Bréguet XIV, which marked a revolutionary advance over his previous designs in that it had a forward-mounted engine driving a tractor propeller and in the extraordinary use of light alloy, rare in aircraft construction but already traditional on German airships.

The project was approved by the *Section Technique de l'Aéronautique* (STAé), the official body controlling the construction of military aircraft, which suggested the 200-hp Hispano-Suiza engine. Bréguet, however, preferred the 275-hp 12-cylinder Renault, an engine which had already proved itself when used on the Bréguet V.

On November 21, 1916, only six months after proposal of the new plane, the Bréguet 14 prototype was first flown at Villacoublay. Louis Bréguet himself was the pilot, his passenger being the aeronautical engineer Vuillerme, who had contributed significantly to the design calculations.

Top, center spread: Bréguet 14 B2, the bomber which first saw action with the French military aviation in April 1917. Its sturdy airframe proved equal to the heavy assignments given to it
Bottom: Many different engines were tried out on the Bréguet 14. Here a 380-hp 12-cylinder Liberty engine has been installed. (Service d'Information et de Rélations Publiques des Armées)

Technical description

Like earlier Bréguets, the Br. 14 was not outstanding for its lines, but it was nevertheless a highly flexible aircraft in so far as its use was concerned, and its esthetic shortcomings were to a great extent offset by its extraordinary toughness, which ensured its active service for many years after the war.

The fuselage was of a classic rectangular cross section, built around four duralumin longerons with tubular bracing elements of the same diameter as the longerons. Thus the whole airframe was a powerful truss structure with steel braces and bracing wires. The longerons were also of light alloy structure, rectangular in cross section, with wooden (oak or ash) veneer at the points of attachment of the rigidizing elements. The outer elements were reinforced with steel plating. The wing ribs were built up of layers of plywood faced with ash, while the wing roots had two layers of 3-mm plywood flanged with poplar.

All other components of the aircraft—tail structure, movable control surfaces, landing gear—which were subjected to vibration or stress continued to be made of welded steel tubing. The quality of such a structure was confirmed by static tests carried out on the Bréguet wing, and it was soon reconfirmed by the ease with which the Bréguet responded to rigorous test flights under adverse weather conditions.

Other characteristic elements of this French biplane were the enormous rectangular frontal radiator, the engine cooling with many ventilation slots in the side panels, the slight negative rake of the wing tips, absence of dihedral in the lower wing, and the exceptionally rugged undercarriage.

Ailerons were fitted only on the upper wing. Other noteworthy features included the very limited inverse stagger of the wings (the leading edge of the upper wing was slightly aft of the lower) and the considerable streamlining of the stabilizer.

Some of the very earliest examples of the Bréguet 14 A2 (the reconnaissance version of the 14) had rudimentary automatic flaps along the training edge of the lower wing, similar to those which were to be fitted on the later bomber version (Br. 14 B2). These flaps moved through a very limited range and were not controlled by the pilot but by a series of elastic cables whose tension could be separately regulated and which forced the flaps down when the forward speed fell below 100 km/hr (62 mph). For higher speeds the action of the apparent wind was sufficient to return the flaps to their original position.

Development of the Bréguet 14

Bréguet production did not cease after the Armistice; it continued until 1926, by which time over 800 Bréguet 14s had been manufactured—a record never beaten by any other Bréguet model.

Many units of the French air arm were equipped with the Br. 14 even after the war, and it was used in the colonies under the designation 14TOE

Bréguet 14 B² Moteur Liberty 380 H

the *Lignes Aériennes Latécoère* (Latécoère Air Lines) were flying 106 Bréguets carrying passengers and mail to South America, and one of these planes was even equipped for in-flight refueling. The French aircraft were also used for commercial service in Belgium, Brazil, Siam and Sweden.

The Bréguet 14 A2 was the immediate forebear of the Br.16 Bn2, which had a greater wing area, with six interplane struts to port and starboard, instead of the four struts used on the Br.14. Bomb racks beneath the lower wing could take up to 460 kg (1015 lb) of bombs. Eventually the Br.16 Bn2 replaced the Voisin for night bombing missions.

A two-seater fighter plane, the Br.17C2, was also a descendant of the Bréguet 14. Readied just before the Armistice, it was used to equip several peacetime squadrons.

It is difficult to determine exactly when the last Bréguet 14 flew, but it was certainly many years after the first design was conceived by Louis Bréguet. One of these outstanding aircraft can be seen at the *Musée de l'Air* at Chalais Meudon.

Left: *Toward the end of 1917 three French reconnaissance squadrons were equipped with Bréguet 14 A2s.* (Archivio Apostolo)
Below, top: *Known as the Bréguet 14T, this civil version was developed after the Armistice; it could accommodate two passengers in an enclosed cabin. Two auxiliary fuel tanks were attached to the lower surface of the upper wing either side of the fuselage.* (Archivio Apostolo)
Below, bottom: *Bréguet 14H, the seaplane version of this well-known French aircraft, with a central and two lateral floats.* (Archivio Apostolo)

(*Théâtre des Opérations Extérieures,* Theater of Colonial Operations).

Immediately after the Armistice several Bréguets were active in the air arms of Brazil, China, Czechoslovakia, Denmark, Finland, Greece, Japan, Poland, Portugal, Siam and Spain. In 1923 70 machines powered by the 400-hp Lorraine-Dietrich engine were procured by China and Manchuria. A few Bréguets were built under license in Spain and Japan (by the Nakajima Co. in the latter case) and used as trainers.

Besides its long and significant military career the Bréguet 14 played an important part in the early history of postwar commercial aviation. A series of long-distance flights also added to the laurels of the Bréguet, such as a double crossing of the Mediterranean by Lieut. Roget and Capt. Coli, a 1600-km (1000-mile) flight which was completed on January 26, 1919; and a 1900-km (1180-mile) flight from Paris to Kenitra, Morocco, which the same pilots made in 11 hours and 15 minutes.

Bréguet also added to its prestige by making the first airmail flights. After a few experimental sorties, Louis Bréguet organized the *Compagnie des Messageries Aériennes* (Air Postal Co.), with flights connecting Paris to Lille, Brussels, London and Marseilles on a regular schedule.

The passenger version of the aircraft was known as the Bréguet 14T. It could accommodate two passengers in an enclosed cabin, extra fuel being carried in two tanks attached to the under surface of the upper wing. These were the machines which were used by Pierre Latécoère, organizer of a corporation for the operation of the air lines. In 1925

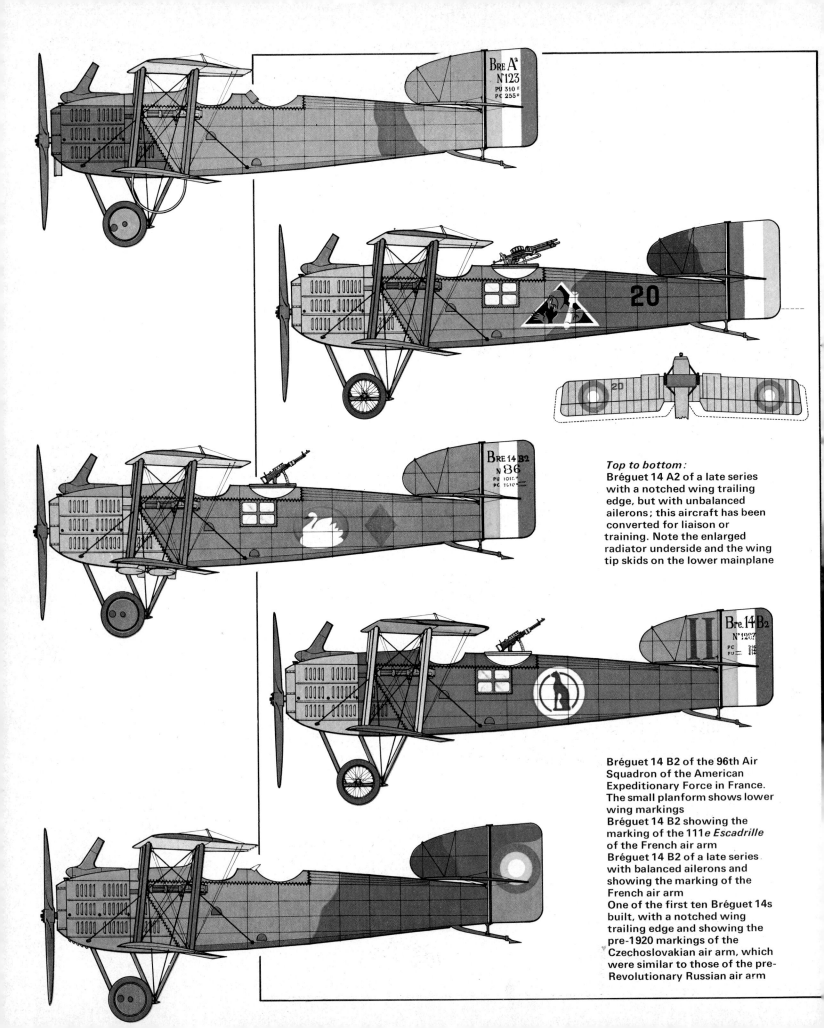

Top to bottom:
Bréguet 14 A2 of a late series with a notched wing trailing edge, but with unbalanced ailerons; this aircraft has been converted for liaison or training. Note the enlarged radiator underside and the wing tip skids on the lower mainplane

Bréguet 14 B2 of the 96th Air Squadron of the American Expeditionary Force in France. The small planform shows lower wing markings
Bréguet 14 B2 showing the marking of the 111e *Escadrille* of the French air arm
Bréguet 14 B2 of a late series with balanced ailerons and showing the marking of the French air arm
One of the first ten Bréguet 14s built, with a notched wing trailing edge and showing the pre-1920 markings of the Czechoslovakian air arm, which were similar to those of the pre-Revolutionary Russian air arm

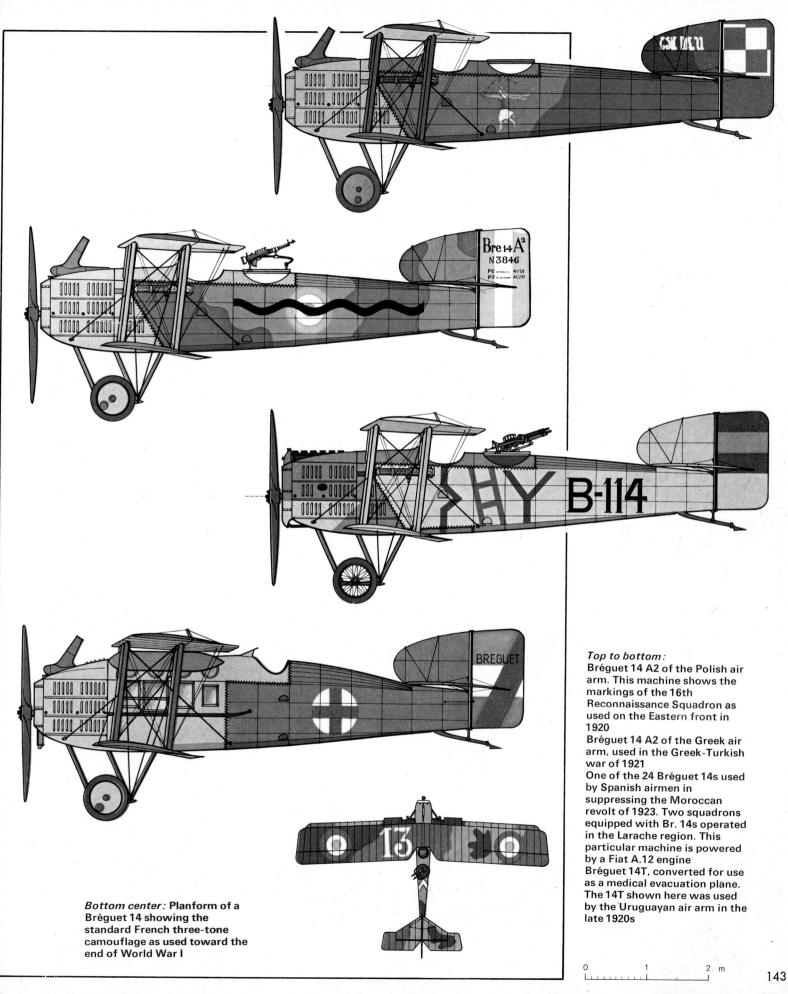

Top to bottom:
Bréguet 14 A2 of the Polish air arm. This machine shows the markings of the 16th Reconnaissance Squadron as used on the Eastern front in 1920
Bréguet 14 A2 of the Greek air arm, used in the Greek-Turkish war of 1921
One of the 24 Bréguet 14s used by Spanish airmen in suppressing the Moroccan revolt of 1923. Two squadrons equipped with Br. 14s operated in the Larache region. This particular machine is powered by a Fiat A.12 engine
Bréguet 14T, converted for use as a medical evacuation plane. The 14T shown here was used by the Uruguayan air arm in the late 1920s

Bottom center: Planform of a Bréguet 14 showing the standard French three-tone camouflage as used toward the end of World War I

0   1   2 m

143

and either one or two ring-mounted 7·7-mm Lewis machine guns in the rear cockpit.

Soon Bréguets began to replace the Sopwith 1½ Strutter, and at the end of 1917 they were used to equip three reconnaissance squadrons (BR 11, 35 and 227), four heavy artillery spotting detachments (Br. 202, 209, 218 and 220), and six bomber squadrons (Br. 66, 108, 111, 121, 126 and 127).

Toward the middle of 1918 there were not less than 71 squadrons equipped with Bréguets on the Western front, with additional five in Serbia, three in Greece, six in Morocco and eight in Macedonia.

The rugged Bréguet airframe stood up remarkably well to its heavy operational use on all of these fronts, and in spite of the wide range of missions for which it was selected the basic design was changed very little as time went on. The most important modification, perhaps, was the adoption of plywood ailerons to improve lateral control.

The standard power plant was always the 300-hp Renault, but many other engines were tried experimentally. Among the most interesting of such installations were the 400-hp Renault 12K, the 260-hp Fiat A.12, the 300-hp Fiat 12bis, the 400-hp Liberty 12 and the 285 and 370-hp Lorraine-Dietrich. But none of these engines made the difference that was achieved by installation of the 320-hp Renault Fe 12 with the Auguste Rateau turbosupercharger, which permitted maximum power up to 5500 m (18000 ft). This particular Bréguet 14 was never used during the war, but its development continued after the Armistice with more than satisfactory results, establishing a record of 183 km/hr at 7000 m (114 mph at 23000 ft).

A single-seat bomber was also tried out experimentally. An auxiliary fuel tank was installed in the pilot's cockpit, with the pilot moving aft to the observer's position. It was hoped that this version might be able to reach as far as Berlin, but this ambitious goal was never achieved and developmental work was stopped.

Another version of the basic Br.14 proved useful in 1918, when four Bréguets were converted into ambulance planes on the Aisne front. Others, designated Br.14S, were widely used in Morocco and Syria in 1926-27. Each of these aircraft was equipped to transport two casualties on stretchers.

In 1918 the 2e and 3e Escadrilles of the Belgian air arm were re-equipped with Bréguet 14 A2s powered by Fiat A.12 or A.12bis engines. The United States bought 376 Bréguet 14s in Europe in 1918, about half of them with Fiat engines. Some of these were used for training, while others were assigned to night reconnaissance.

The Bréguet 14 was never used by the French naval air arm, although two seaplane models were built. The first of these (Br.14H) had a central float and two smaller side floats, while the second, completed in February 1924, had two ordinary side floats.

The total tonnage of bombs dropped by Bréguet 14s during the war reached 1880 metric tons.

Top: *A version of the Bréguet 14 developed toward the end of the war is this two-seat fighter, designated Br.17 C2. It was used by some units of the French air arm after the Armistice*
Center: *Close-up of the pilot's cockpit of a Bréguet belonging to 9th Air Squadron of the US Army Air Service*

Bottom: *Cross-section view of the Bréguet 14. Bréguets were powered by a wide variety of engines, including Renault, Fiat, Liberty, Hispano-Suiza and Lorraine models. Its maximum speed was 208 km/hr (129·24 mph) and its maximum ceiling reached 6350 m (20833 ft). It had a useful load of 615 kg (1353 lb) and a maximum flight duration of 5 hrs.*

How the Bréguet 14 was used in the War

Even on its earliest test flights the Bréguet 14 showed itself to be a wholly successful plane. But Bréguet still had a hard fight on his hands to get the French military authorities to accept it. The first official order was received on March 6, 1917, requesting 150 aircraft, and this was followed on April 4 by a second order for 150 Br.14 A2s.

Once the bureaucrats had recognized the qualities of the new aircraft, production ballooned: In the spring and summer of 1917, 330 machines were ordered from the Darracq factory, 50 from Henry and Maurice Farman, and 200 from Paul Schmitt. Two further orders, for 250 and 125 aircraft, were received by Bréguet in July and September 1917, and others for 75 and 170 machines were received by Schmitt and Farman respectively. A final order for 600 planes was issued in December 1917, calling for the production of 300 each by Bellanger and SIDAM.

The Bréguet was produced in two versions, the 14 A2 and the 14 B2, for reconnaissance and bombing respectively. The prototype of the latter was delivered to the French military authorities in April 1917. It differed from the reconnaissance version in that the side panels of the fuselage were transparent, it had a longer wing span (13·60 instead of 12·4 m), resulting in an increase of about 2 m² in the wing area: it also had a Michelin bomb rack on the underside of the lower wing, with a capacity of 32 bombs weighing 8 kg (17·6 lb) each. Both versions were commissioned in active service in the summer of 1917, with approximately the same defensive armament—a fixed 7·7-mm Vickers for the pilot,

ALBATROS

Top: *Albatros D.II of* Jasta *9 on the Western front*
Center: *With the D.III the Albatros structure began to have V-struts between the wings*
Bottom: *Another view of the Albatros D.III showing the fine design of its nose. Note the enormous exhaust*

Specifications

	D.I	D.II	D.III	D.V	D.Va	W.4
Engine power, *hp*	160	160	185	200	200	160
Wing span, *m*	8·50	8·50	9·05	9·05	9·05	9·50
Length, *m*	7·40	7·40	7·33	7·33	7·33	8·50
Height, *m*	2·95	2·64	2·98	2·70	2·70	3·65
Wing area, *m²*	22·90	24·50	20·50	21·20	21·20	31·60
Weight, empty, *kg*	647	637	661	620	687	790
Total weight, *kg*	888	898	886	852	937	1070
Maximum speed, *km/hr*	175	175	175	165	187	155
Climb to 1000 *m, min-sec*	6:00	5:30	3:20	4:00	4:00	6:30
Climb to 2000 *m, min-sec*	9:00	—	7:15	8:50	—	—
Climb to 4000 *m, min-sec*	—	26:00	18:08	22:50	22:08	to 3000 m in 23:00
Climb to 5000 *m, min-sec*	37:00	—	—	—	—	—
Ceiling, *m*	5000	5200	5500	5700	5700	3000
Flight endurance, *hrs-min*	1:50	1:30	2:00	2:00	—	3:00

On August 5, 1916, Robert Thelen, aeronautical engineer at the *Albatros Werke GmbH* of Johannisthal, presented the prototype of a single-seat scout biplane which he had designed with the collaboration of two assistants, Gnaedig and Schubert.

The new biplane was designed with a view to replacing the various fighter monoplanes of the German air arm, which by then were getting rough treatment at the hands of the Allied pilots with their new D.H.2 and Nieuport 11 aircraft.

The prototype, Serial No. D 423/16, met with immediate success. It was powered by a 160-hp Mercedes D.3 engine and had a maximum speed of over 170 km/hr (105·6 mph) and a high rate of climb which let the pilot reach 1000 m (3280 ft) in a little over 6 minutes. The new aircraft had a ceiling of 5200 m (17060 ft), extraordinary for the time, and, moreover, gave its best performance at that altitude. Another advantage of the new plane was its fire power, which was about twice that of other fighters. It carried two 7·92-mm synchronized Spandau machine guns, at a time when most other aircraft had only one fixed weapon shooting through the propeller blades.

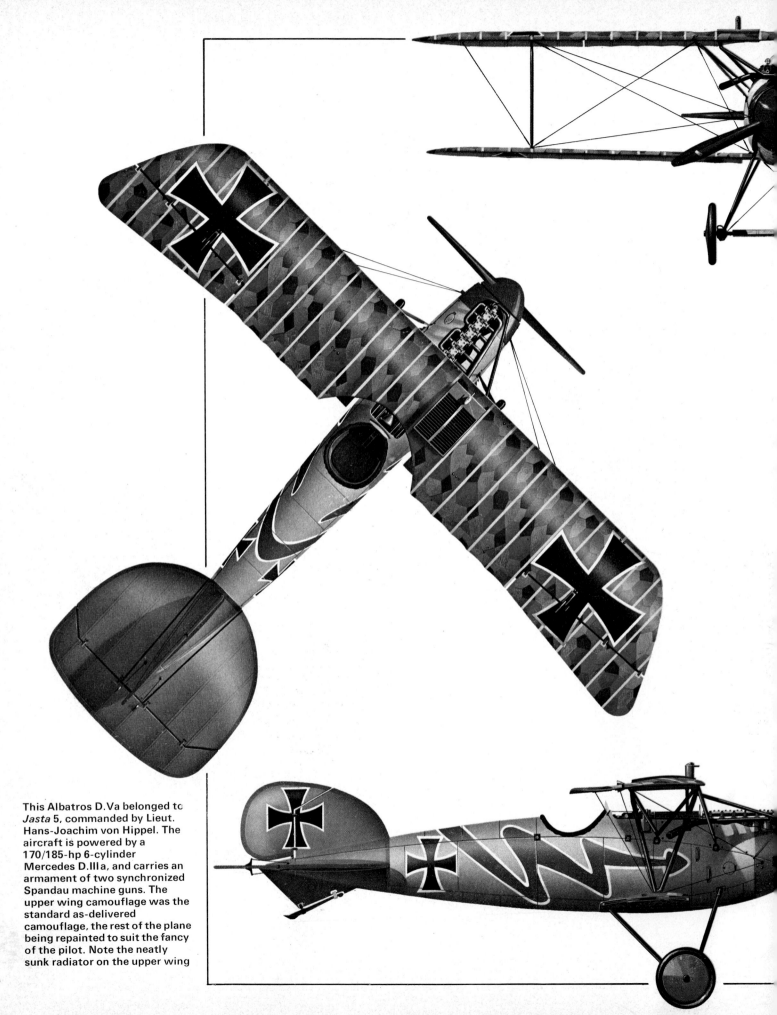

This Albatros D.Va belonged to *Jasta* 5, commanded by Lieut. Hans-Joachim von Hippel. The aircraft is powered by a 170/185-hp 6-cylinder Mercedes D.IIIa, and carries an armament of two synchronized Spandau machine guns. The upper wing camouflage was the standard as-delivered camouflage, the rest of the plane being repainted to suit the fancy of the pilot. Note the neatly sunk radiator on the upper wing

ALBATROS D.Va « BLITZ »

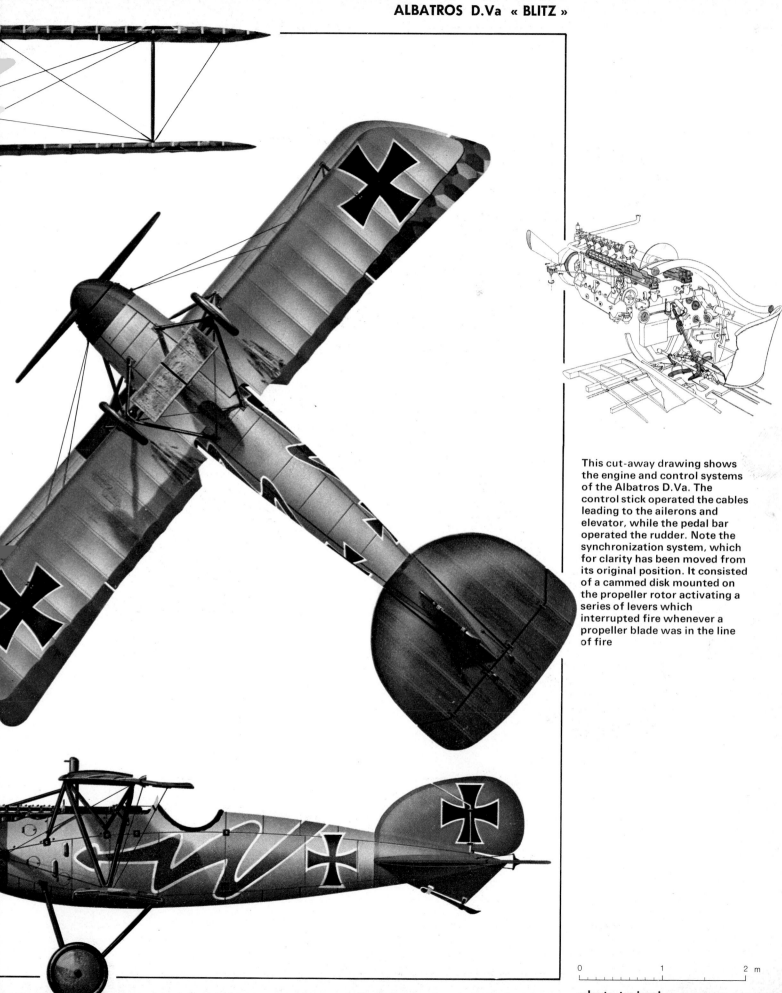

This cut-away drawing shows the engine and control systems of the Albatros D.Va. The control stick operated the cables leading to the ailerons and elevator, while the pedal bar operated the rudder. Note the synchronization system, which for clarity has been moved from its original position. It consisted of a cammed disk mounted on the propeller rotor activating a series of levers which interrupted fire whenever a propeller blade was in the line of fire

0   1   2 m

roberto terrinoni

Apparently the Albatros D.I was less maneuverable than the monoplanes built by Fokker, Pfalz and Euler, particularly because of its greater wing loading, but even so it met with the instant approval of the military and was put into production with very few changes.

The new Albatros began to reach the operational units in September 1916, just when German airmen were being reorganized into *Jagdstaffeln* (fighter squadrons) which were popularly abbreviated as *Jastas*. Each *Jasta* consisted of six fighters which had the task of ensuring air supremacy over their allotted sector so that other operational aircraft could work in safety.

Technical description

The general airframe structure of the Albatros biplanes was quite traditional, at least so far as wing and tail structures were concerned. The wings were of wooden construction built around two box spars, with single bays formed by parallel struts on the D.I and D.II and by V-struts on the D.III and D.V. The tail structure consisted of a welded tubular steel framework covered with fabric, quite orthodox in structure but unusual in shape and with an extraordinary feature in that the fin was positioned forward of the stabilizer hinge, which made it possible to utilize a one-piece elevator. Both stabilizer and rudder were faired. The undercarriage was of a conventional tubular steel V-type which fitted into sockets attached to the fuselage. A sizeable tail skid protected the tail assembly.

The fuselage, however, was far from being orthodox. It was of a semimonocoque structure, with six spruce longerons joined by very light ($\frac{3}{8}$ in.) plywood formers. The outer covering consisted of three-ply wooden sheets, screwed onto the frame and contributing considerably to its rigidity. This structure was, of course, much more complex from a production point of view than the traditional trussed and slab sided structure, but the advantages were great, particularly in lightness and smoothness of surface and in the possibility for refinements of streamlining. Later engine cowling

was improved to continue the clean lines of the fuselage and bulbous spinner was added. In the D.V the fuselage section was more rounded than in previous models.

Development of the Albatros D.I-V

The D.I had an inherent drawback which was common to many biplanes—extremely limited upward and forward visibility, a serious defect which in fact caused the death of the ace Oswald Boelcke, who died in a tragic collision between his own Albatros and another flown by his comrade Erwin Böhme. This was remedied by modifications leading to the design of the D.II, in which the upper wing was lowered to within 40 cm (15·75 in.) of the fuselage.

Several aircraft, which were given the designation D.IIa, had a streamlined Teeves und Braun radiator instead of the cumbersome, boxlike Windhoff radiators which, mounted on the sides of the fuselage, had partly spoiled the clean lines of the earlier models.

When these various changes were introduced production of the D.I was terminated after about 60 planes had been built. It was followed on the production lines by the D.II (also built by the LVG), and deliveries of the new fighter soon began to reach operational units. (After the war the D was given the designation L.15, the D.II being known as the L.17.)

At the same time designers at the Albatros Werke were trying to improve the maneuverability of the basic aircraft by redesigning the wings from scratch. Thelen, following the design of the Nieuport, reduced the lower wing chord considerably and replaced the parallel interplane struts with V-struts to increase the rigidity of the structure. The upper wing was also modified, the span being increased by about 0·5 m (1·6 ft). The resultant reduced wing loading gave lower maximum speed, but not to the point where it was serious problem; rather, it notably improved maneuverability and the rate of climb. The radiator was firmly attached under the wing, usually at the centerline but sometimes to starboard to avoid scalding the pilot in case of a puncture in combat.

The next model, the D.IV, used the equal-chord wings of the D.II but with a more powerful engine and a fuselage of round cross-section. The performance of this model did not meet military standards, however, and the new engine, a 220-hp Daimler D.4, also caused its problems.

The following D.V retained the oval fuselage designed for the D.IV and the efficient wing structure of the D.III. This new version was powered by the Mercedes D.3 engine, but with higher compression ratio and oversize cylinders and pistons, increasing the power to 200 hp. The fin was enlarged and the rudder was rounded (these changes were also incorporated on some of the last D.IIIs).

Top: *In the D.V the designers introduced a fuselage with an oval cross section.* (Archivio Apostolo)
Bottom: *The D.Va was a variant of the V incorporating a slightly lowered upper wing and a return to the control system used on the D.III.* (Archivio Apostolo)

As usual, other minor changes were introduced on later machines, such as the occasional addition of a headrest for the pilot and a different arrangement of aileron control cables. The latter characterized the plane which was designated D.Va, and the aileron cable arrangement was similar to that first used on the D.III (with the cables running through the lower wing).

The D.Va was the version produced in the largest machines—some 1600 aircraft, all told—although its performance was not remarkably better than that of the D.III.

A seaplane version was built for the German Navy and given the designation W.4 (for *Wasserflugzeug*); it entered active service at the end of 1916. The fuselage was based on that of the D.I with longer wing span (and consequently greater wing area); floats of various shapes were tried experimentally to determine the optimum form. The initial W.4 seaplanes still had the old Windhoff radiator, eventually replaced by the Teeves und Braun. Later W.4s had ailerons on both upper and lower wings. Overall performance was only slightly inferior to that of the D.I.

In the heyday of the triplane, the Albatros Werke also came out with a tailplane based on the D.V airframe, but the result did not justify putting it into production. This model was given the designation L.36. (The Albatros Werke produced a different design of triplane, the L.39, with a 195-hp Benz engine based on the D.X, the last of the D series, which was also built in a number of other experimental variants.)

In February 1918 a D.Va with a 185-hp BMW.IIIa reached an altitude of 10500 m (34500 ft), although this figure was based on readings of an uncorrected barograph.

How the Albatros D fighters were used in the War

The *Jagdstaffeln* or *Jastas* came into being as a development of the *Kampfeinsitzerkommandos* of the German air detachments fighting on the French front. *Jasta 1* was activated on August 23, 1916, at Berthincourt, followed four days later by *Jasta 2* at Laguincourt. The latter was commanded by Capt. Oswald Boelcke, the German ace who first pro-

posed organization of the *Jagdstaffeln*. Among his men was the then 24-year-old Manfred von Richthofen, his prize disciple who was later to outstrip his mentor as a skilful and fearless fighter pilot.

At the beginning of September three Albatros D.Is were delivered to *Jasta 2*, together with two Fokker D.IIIs and a Halberstadt D.II. Of these three models, certainly the best was the Albatros, and this was soon demonstrated in test flights and mock combat; indeed, the other two types were quickly relegated to secondary missions and fighter-pilot training classes.

On September 17, 1916, for the first time, *Jasta 2* took off nearly complete. There were five aircraft, including one flown by von Richthofen. Soon Boelcke sighted eight B.E.2 bombers escorted by six F.E.2b two-seater fighters. He maneuvered to cut off their retreat, then pounced on them from altitude out of the sun. The sudden attack caught the British by surprise and their formation broke up. In the furious combat which followed, each of the German pilots shot down a British plane, for a total of five.

On October 28, 1916, *Jasta 2* took off with all six of its planes for a regular patrol along the front in search of action. It was a cloudy, rainy day. Near Flers the six Albatros met two De Havillands which were flying at lower altitude, and naturally they attacked. Perhaps the Germans were over-confident because of their clear advantage. Two German planes attacked one of the British, and in the excitement the undercarriage of one plane hit the upper wing of the other. The latter, flown by Boelcke, left the fray and started circling toward the ground. Suddenly the upper wing broke off and the Albatros disappeared into the clouds and crashed. When the *Jasta* returned to Laguincourt the German pilots learned that their chief was dead.

By the end of the year at least 35 *Jastas* had been activated and the roster of aces included Hans-Joachim Buddecke of *Jasta 4*, Manfred von Richthofen of *Jasta 11*, Karl Allmenröder, also of *Jasta 11*, and Werner Voss of *Jasta 10*—only a few among the many German fighter aces who became famous in the dogfights against outstanding British and French pilots.

In January 1917 there were 214 D.IIs at the front, and the D.IIIs had begun to arrive. In four months, the number of D.IIs had been reduced by

Top left: *The Albatros D.IIIs of von Richthofen's famous 'Flying Circus', each with the paint job preferred by the pilot.* (Archivio Apostolo)
Top right: *Albatros D.Vs on a German airfield. Note the different colors of these planes, painted like the D.IIIs according to the taste of each pilot.* (Archivio Apostolo)
Bottom right: *Austrian Albatros D.IIIs at an air base near the Italian front.* (Agenzia Marka)

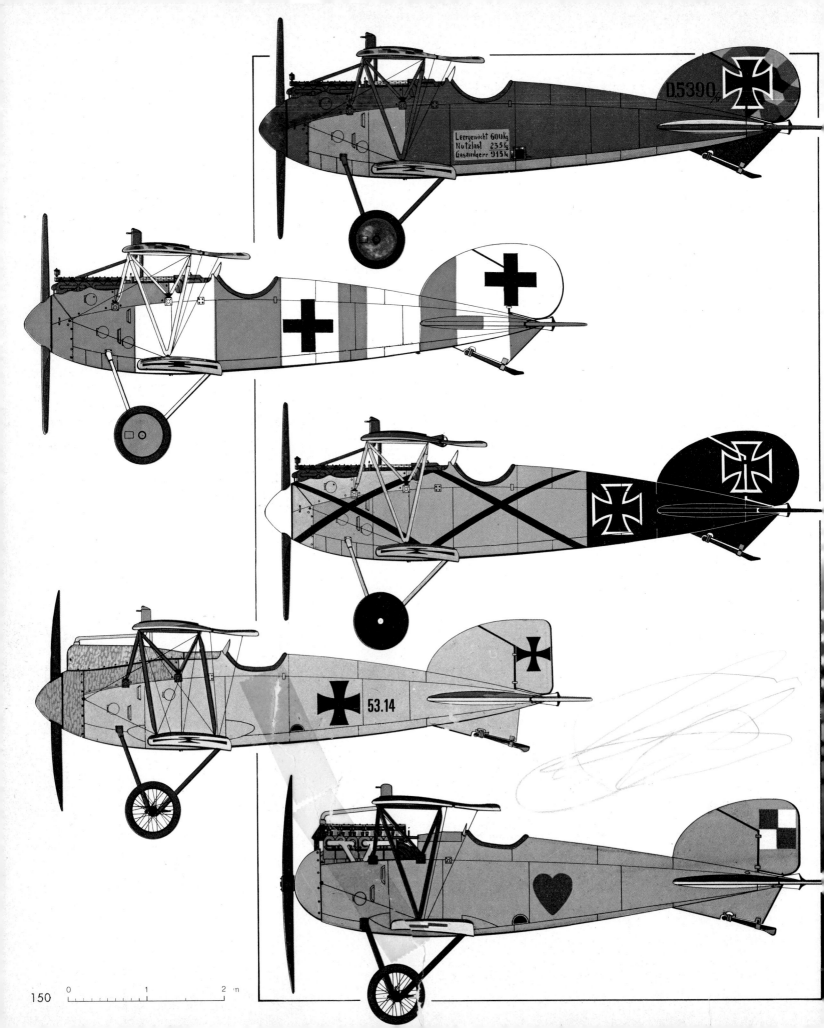

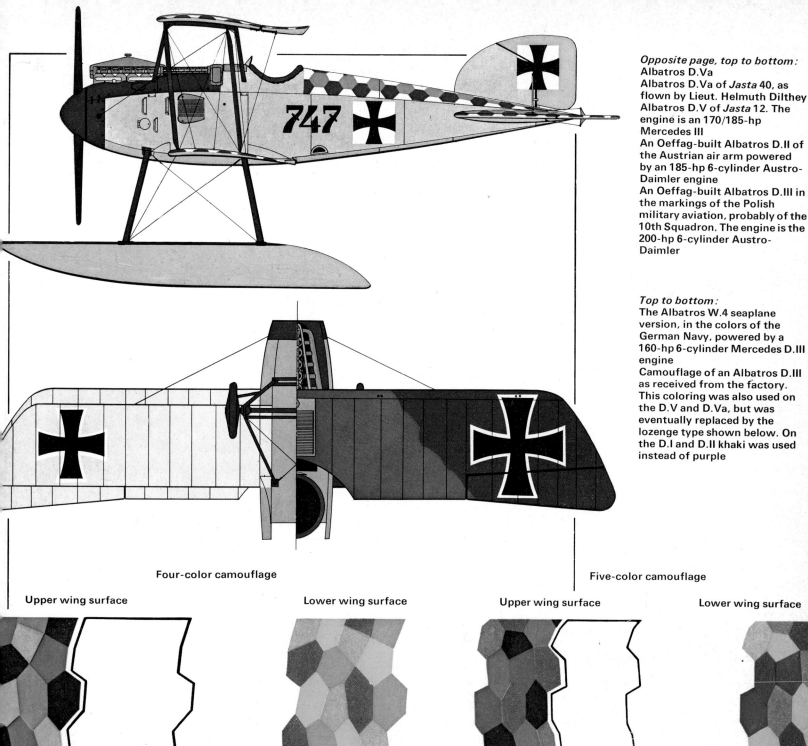

Opposite page, top to bottom:
Albatros D.Va
Albatros D.Va of *Jasta* 40, as flown by Lieut. Helmuth Dilthey
Albatros D.V of *Jasta* 12. The engine is an 170/185-hp Mercedes III
An Oeffag-built Albatros D.II of the Austrian air arm powered by an 185-hp 6-cylinder Austro-Daimler engine
An Oeffag-built Albatros D.III in the markings of the Polish military aviation, probably of the 10th Squadron. The engine is the 200-hp 6-cylinder Austro-Daimler

Top to bottom:
The Albatros W.4 seaplane version, in the colors of the German Navy, powered by a 160-hp 6-cylinder Mercedes D.III engine
Camouflage of an Albatros D.III as received from the factory. This coloring was also used on the D.V and D.Va, but was eventually replaced by the lozenge type shown below. On the D.I and D.II khaki was used instead of purple

747

Four-color camouflage

Five-color camouflage

Upper wing surface

Lower wing surface

Upper wing surface

Lower wing surface

The white outlines show the interlocking of successive unit strips. These lozenge designs were supplied by a number of manufacturers in a variety of four- and five-color arrays. The areas here colored orange might be ochre or beige if printed by a different supplier; the violet might be more or less red or blue, and so on

151

half. Meanwhile the Austrian plant of the Oeffag at Wiener-Neustadt had begun producing the Albatros (20 aircraft of series 53 with 185-hp Austro-Daimler engines), and in this way the Albatros also began to operate on the Italian front.

The *Jastas* had begun to receive the D.III in January 1917. It was a time of great German air power, which was to culminate three months later in what the British called 'Bloody April'. In ground fighting the Battle of Arras was drawing to a close, and in the air German fighter aces were winning many victories over the courageous French and British pilots. It was at this time that the Germans started painting their aircraft in bright livery, with each pilot choosing his own colors and insignia.

All British pilots knew of the 'Pink Lady', which was an all-pink Albatros flown by a pilot with delicate, rather effeminate features. Before long the myth of a German girl pilot who was avenging her husband, killed in the war, became widespread.

Manfred von Richthofen flew an Albatros which was painted red, which led to his nickname of 'the Red Baron'. His squadron-mates feared that the Red Baron might become too popular a target among the enemy, so they asked permission to paint their aircraft the same color. This was granted, and soon Allmenröder was flying a red Albatros with white wing tips and spinner, while others varied the red with black rudder and stabilizer, and so on.

Another famous Albatros pilot was Eduard von Schleich, nicknamed 'the Black Knight'. A brilliant and skilful pilot, he took part in many a dogfight, surviving the war with a total of 35 victories. This record was tied by the foremost Austrian ace, Godwin Brumowsky, who also often flew the Albatros. Other Austrian aces included Frank Linke-Crawford (27 victories) and Josef Kiss.

The D.III was also built, like the D.II, by UFAG, its production running in Series 532, 153 and 253, all powered by the 185-, 200- or 225-hp Austro-Daimler engines. On the Italian front the D.III was used extensively if account is taken of both Austrian and German units which fought against Italy from October 1917 to the spring of 1918 (*Jastas 1, 31* and *39*).

German D.IIIs also fought in Macedonia and Palestine, flying a special 'tropical' variant sporting two radiators instead of one.

As early as December 1918 the first Polish air units had acquired some 10 Albatros D.IIIs. The Polish government then ordered 38 additional D.IIIs from UFAG, plus many others from Germany (all delivered secretly) where the Albatros Werke was still turning them out under the new designation L.20. The Poles received about 15 of these machines early in 1920 and used them in actions first against the Ukraine, then the Bolsheviks. Thus the elegant Albatros continued to soldier on well beyond the Armistice.

And, finally, in 1920 Czechoslovakia procured several Albatros L.17s to equip its first fighter squadron.

The D.III was in no real sense inferior to the D.V, which began to show up on *Jasta* rosters in the summer of 1917, and the D.Va, which came along in the autumn. Although the latter two models were not great improvements over the D.III and even had some serious structural defects, they were the most active of all Albatros models in the war (after which they were given the new designation L.24). On the Western front alone not less than 1512 Albatros D.Vs and Vas were operational, with others being used on the Italian front, in Palestine and in Home Defense units, thus making up the bulk of German fighter force.

Apart from all other D models, mention must be made of the seaplane version, the W.4, which became operational in September 1916. About 120 Albatros seaplanes were built before the W.4 was withdrawn from production toward the end of 1917. It was used chiefly for coastal defense near German bases in Flanders, but it was also active in the Aegean, where it gave a very good account of itself until the Allies mustered superior aircraft which forced the Germans to switch to the two-seat Hansa-Brandenburg W.12.

In October 1917 deliveries of the new Fokker triplane began; this aircraft was welcomed enthusiastically by German fighter pilots, who soon preferred it to the Albatros. When the Fokker D VII came along, it was clearly the best fighter the Germans had ever had, and the Albatros was relegated to secondary duties.

Left: *Albatros D.V flown by the Bavarian fighter ace Eduard von Schleich of* Jasta *32. The emblem is the Lion of Bavaria.* (Museo Caproni, Taliedo)
Right: *Albatros D.V of* Jasta *27, with the new type of black cross which was introduced in April 1918. The pilot is Lieut. Helmuth Dilthey.* (Archivio Apostolo)

AIRCO D.H.2

Geoffrey de Havilland was 32 years old when he joined the Aircraft Manufacturing Co. of Hendon in 1914 as chief designer. He had worked for four busy years at the Royal Aircraft Factory, Farnborough, both as an engineer and as a pilot, and this valuable experience soon served him well at Airco, where he designed the D.H.1, some 80 of which were built and delivered to the Royal Flying Corps, beginning in early 1915.

The structural formula of the D.H.1 was clearly based on the F.E.2 which de Havilland had designed for the Royal Aircraft Factory and had as its most noticeable features an engine mounted behind the pilot driving a pusher propeller, and longerons converging towards the rudder shaft. The vehicle was no masterpiece aerodynamically, and the necessity for carrying a crew of two further hampered its performance. The weight of the second crew member, an observer-gunner seated in the forward cockpit with a movable Lewis machine gun, actually represented a good 10 per cent of the total weight. At first the engine was a 70-hp Renault, since the intended 120-hp Beardmore was not yet available. The D.H.1 prototype was fairly convincing from the point of view of stability and maneuverability, but it had little speed and its rate of climb was far from satisfactory. By the time the Beardmore engine was available other, more advanced fighter scouts had already been put into the sky, and so when finally production aircraft were available they were used exclusively in Home Defense training schools, except for a few machines which were despatched to the Middle East. They were never used by any RFC units assigned to the Western front.

Specifications

Power plant	Gnôme Monosoupape, 100 hp	Le Rhône, 110 hp
Wing span, *m*	8·61	—
Total length, *m*	7·68	—
Height, *m*	2·91	—
Wing area, *m²*	23·13	—
Weight, empty, *kg*	427·74	455·40
Total weight, *kg*	653·60	701·72
Maximum speed, *km/hr*	149·67	148·06 (at sea level)
Climb to 1829 *m, min-sec*	11:00	12:00
Ceiling, *m*	4267	—
Flight endurance, *hrs-min*	2:45	3:00

Top: *One of the earliest production versions of the D.H2, bearing the serial number 5943. These aircraft of the early batches had longer ailerons than the prototype*
Bottom: *Prototype of the D.H.1, which was test-flown at Hendon in 1915. The following model, D.H.1A, was used only as a trainer and by a few Home Defense units.* (Imperial War Museum)

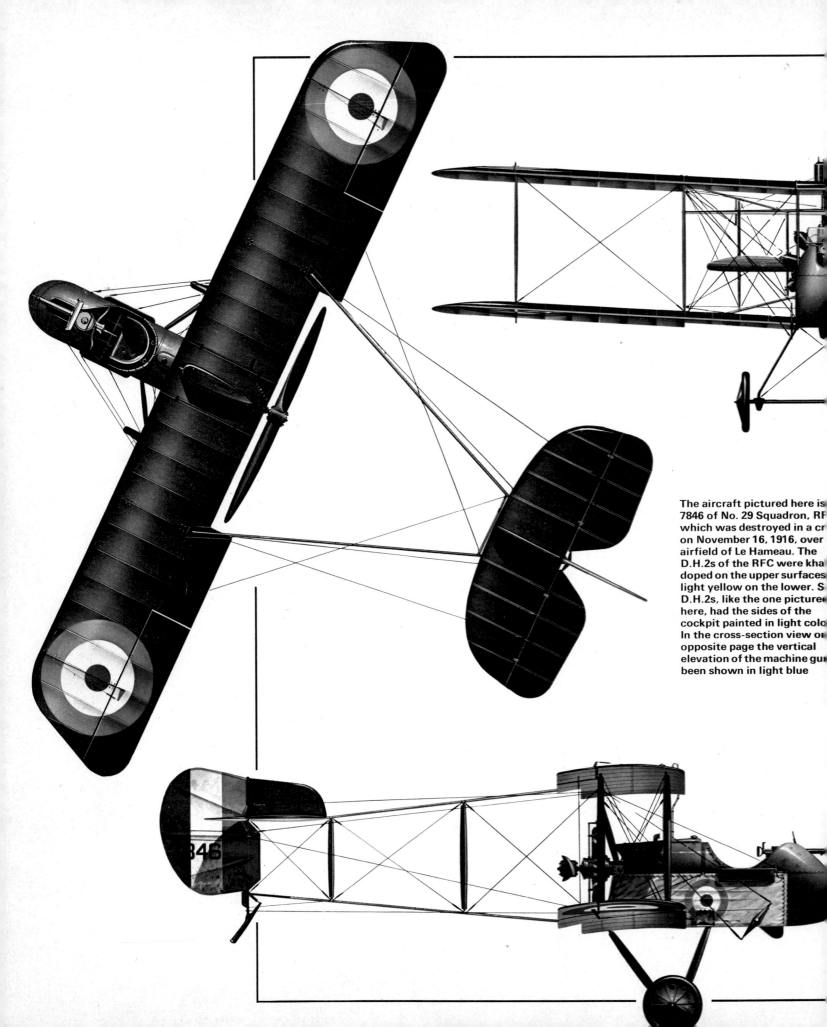

The aircraft pictured here is
7846 of No. 29 Squadron, RF
which was destroyed in a cr
on November 16, 1916, over
airfield of Le Hameau. The
D.H.2s of the RFC were kha
doped on the upper surfaces
light yellow on the lower. S
D.H.2s, like the one pictured
here, had the sides of the
cockpit painted in light colo
In the cross-section view on
opposite page the vertical
elevation of the machine gun
been shown in light blue

AIRCO D.H.2

784B

0   1   2 m

amedeo gigli

Top: *Prototype of the D.H.2, with the 100-hp Gnôme Monosoupape engine. This aircraft was test-flown in July 1915 and met with the approval of both engineers and military authorities*

Bottom left: *The first D.H.2s were sent to No. 24 Squadron of the Royal Flying Corps, based in France, early in 1916. This photograph shows one of the first D.H.2s taking off from the Beauval airfield. The pennant attached to the outermost starboard strut indicates that the plane is piloted by the squadron commander.* (Imperial War Museum)
Right: *D.H.2 No. 5923, an aircraft of the later series, with the four-bladed propeller which replaced the original two-bladed airscrew. The wingspan was also slightly increased on these later machines.* (Imperial War Museum)

Familiarity with the bugs which seemed innate in the D.H.1 led de Havilland to start work immediately on a one-seater version which was smaller and promised better performance. In the case of the D.H.1, de Havilland had been not only its designer but test pilot as well. For this reason he was probably well aware of the drawbacks of the skeletal fuselage with the pusher engine, but since at that time the British did not have any device permitting synchronization of machine gun fire with the propeller it was taken for granted that offensive firepower could be achieved only by positioning the gun ahead of the engine and propeller. The system was recognized as archaic, but de Havilland tried to make up for it by using a more powerful engine, by reducing the dimensions of the airframe and, especially, by lowering the all-up weight by eliminating the second crew member.

Design of the new aircraft was completed in late spring, 1915. By the middle of July the new machine, which carried the designation D.H.2, had completed the limited program of flight tests requested with satisfactory results. Pilots liked the new plane, and Government orders were immediately placed.

Technical description

The D.H.2 was a rather small aircraft, with rectangular, double-spar wings with a pronounced dihedral and the strongly raked wing tips popular at the time. The upper wing consisted of two out-

board sections fastened to the center section above the skimpy nacelle, while the two lower wing sections were attached to the sides of the nacelle. The upper and lower wings were joined by four pairs of vertical struts linked by steel wire bracing. The trailing edge had a rectangular cutout to accommodate the pusher propeller. The wing frames were entirely of wood, and covered with fabric.

The tail structure was quite similar to that of the D.H.1. The stabilizer, elevator and rudder were all of generous dimensions, while the fin was rudimentary. The cockpit was well designed and ensured good visibility; it was separated from the engine by a short length of the fuselage. The engine was left uncovered to facilitate servicing and to assist in cooling. Most of the fuselage and the tail elements were fabric-covered, with only the top decking of plywood.

The rear section of the D.H.2 was formed by two tubular steel beams joined to the rear wing spar at the point where the aft inboard strut was also attached; these beams converged towards the rudder hinge on the underside and were interrupted by the stabilizer leading edge on the upper side. The tail skid was positioned at the vertex of the lower converging beams and could be moved laterally by the pilot, thus offering a certain control during taxi-ing. The undercarriage had a wheel base of 1·77 m (69·6 inches), the axle being supported by V-type struts. The wheels were rather large.

The engine installed on the prototype and most production D.H.2s was the 100-hp Gnôme Monosoupape, a 9-cylinder rotary. The pusher propeller was a two-bladed wooden airscrew of 8 ft. 2½ in. in diameter. The main fuel tank was situated behind the pilot, and there was an auxiliary fuel tank, gravity-fed, fitted on the upper wing center section

or (especially on aircraft from the second and the last production series) under or over the port half wing.

Controls were the usual stick and pedals. There were ailerons on both upper and lower wings, spring-loaded to return them to their original positions with the controls centered.

The armament was a single movable 7·7-mm Lewis machine gun. In de Havilland's optimistic view this was to be mounted on brackets attached to both sides of the nacelle and the pilot was to set the gun up on whichever side might give him the better aim. The prototype D.H.2 was unarmed in its test flight, carrying only the port bracket.

A new system of fitting the machine gun was devised for the second D.H.2. It was secured to a central mounting which ensured ample fields of fire, but it was not much more satisfactory than the original installation, and British pilots embarked upon a vigorous campaign with their superiors to get the gun mounted in a fixed position, firing along the centerline of the nacelle. Experiments were also carried out with two Lewis guns bracketed one on either side of the cockpit. Another defect which plagued the D.H.2 armament was the limited capacity of the Lewis guns: the drums held only 47 rounds, and these were soon exhausted, thus necessitating feverish reloading during combat. Not until the end of 1915 were larger drums available (97 rounds), and at that point the fixed Lewis gun became standard equipment.

Maneuverability of the D.H.2 was excellent, in part due to the concentration of the bulk of the weight near the center of gravity, and this quality was immediately appreciated by the British airmen, who were not otherwise enthusiastic about an aircraft which they found of low stability and easily subject to tailspinning. Probably some of these criticisms of the D.H.2 were not entirely warranted; it may have been instead a case of the pilots' not feeling at home in so sensitive a plane after the stolid, rather lazy B.E.2. So far as the tail-spin is concerned, one must remember that at that time the entire question of tailspinning and what to do about it was far from being resolved, and the standard lesson in training dealt with avoiding spins rather than any rational scheme for getting out of them alive. Even so, already early in 1916 Maj. L. G. Hawker, commanding No. 24 Squadron RFC, demonstrated repeatedly that the D.H.2 could be intentionally put into a spin and brought out of it readily and safely once the pilot knew what was required.

Overall performance of the D.H.2 was not, however, particularly brilliant, since the high drag offered by the airframe with its abundant bracing lowered the maximum speed considerably and kept the plane from picking up speed even after prolonged nose dives. Thus the speed performance of the D.H.2 was necessarily limited, and this factor in itself added to the danger of tail spins.

On the positive side, the relatively low weight and the use of a very large diameter propeller gave the D.H.2 a higher rate of climb than practically any other aircraft of its day. It could climb to 2000 m (6000 ft) in 11 minutes and had a ceiling of 14000 ft. Certainly this excellent climbing ability and the plane's basic toughness were the outstanding features of the D.H.2, and it did not take the British pilots long to learn to exploit them superbly.

D.H.2s of No. 24 Squadron, RFC, at the air base in Beauval, France, where British pilots first got to know the new biplane which was to challenge German superiority in the fighter class. (Imperial War Museum)

Development of the D.H.2

Throughout the entire period of its production the basic design of the D.H.2 remained virtually unchanged. The only differences to be found among the approximately 400 D.H.2s built consisted of four-blade propellers on aircraft of the last few series, a slight increase in the aileron span, and the capacity of the fuel tanks, which increased from about 120 liters (26·4 gallons) with the Gnôme engine to 150 liters (32·9 gallons) on one machine that was experimentally powered with the 110-hp Le Rhône rotary engine. In spite of the higher horsepower of the Le Rhône engine the actual performance was less impressive than the Gnôme, to a great extent because of the increased weight, and flight endurance was only 15 minutes longer.

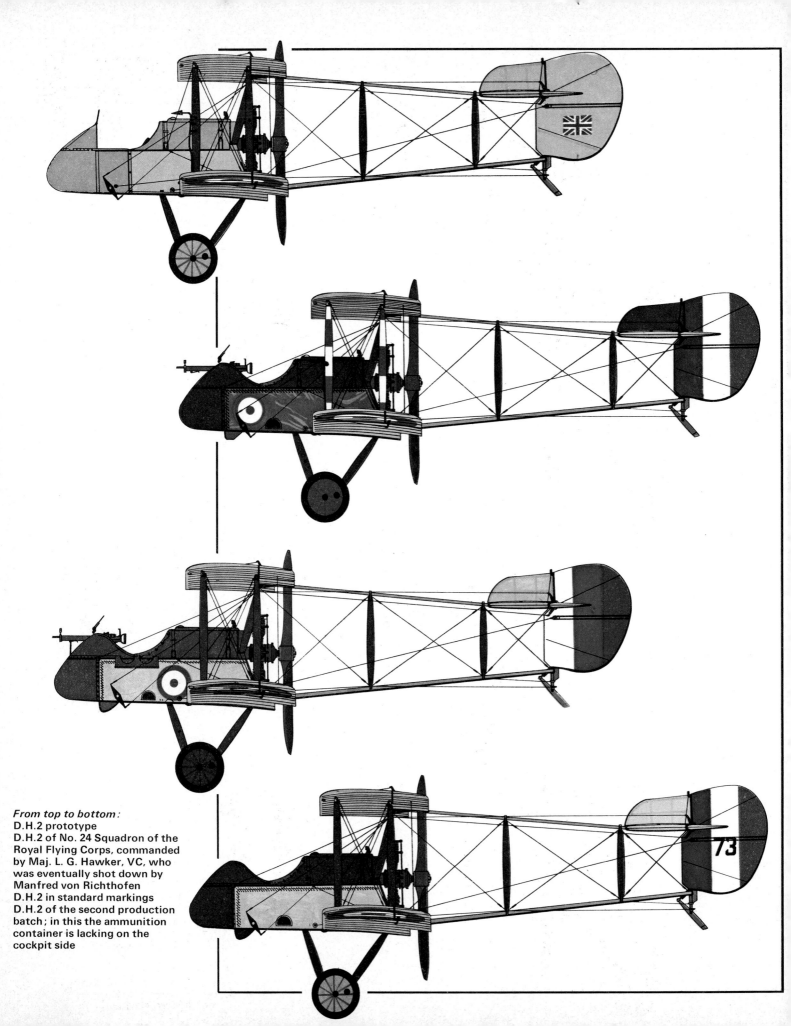

From top to bottom:
D.H.2 prototype
D.H.2 of No. 24 Squadron of the
Royal Flying Corps, commanded
by Maj. L. G. Hawker, VC, who
was eventually shot down by
Manfred von Richthofen
D.H.2 in standard markings
D.H.2 of the second production
batch; in this the ammunition
container is lacking on the
cockpit side

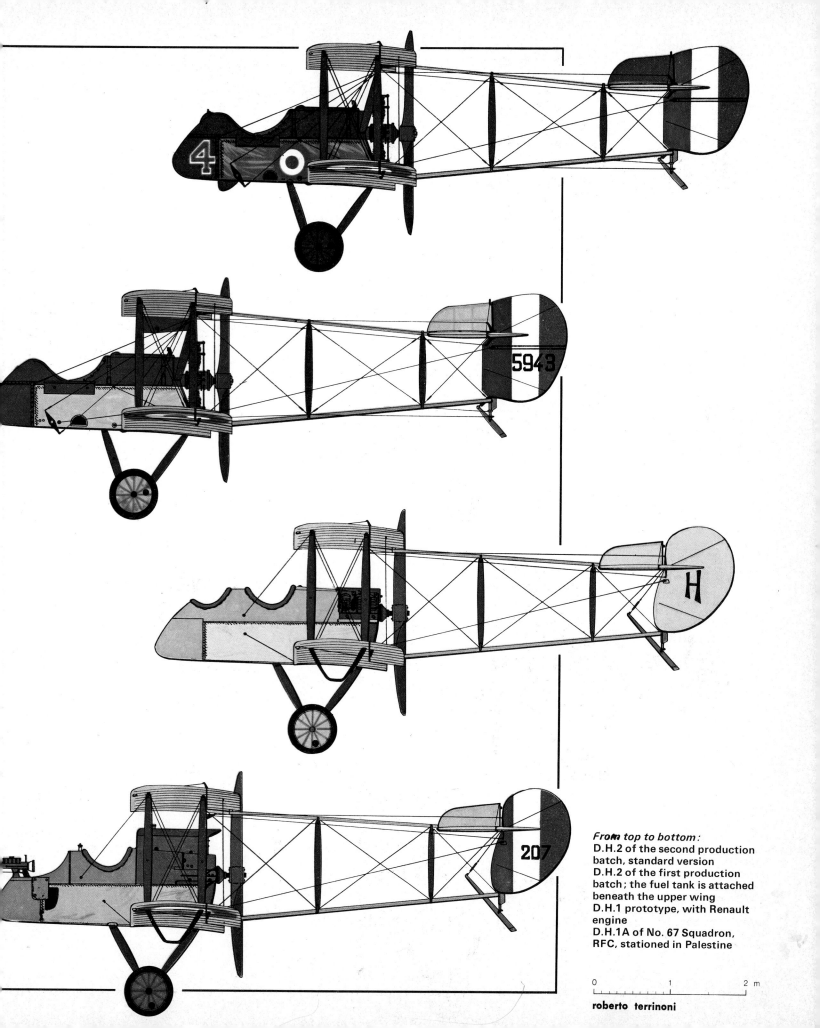

From top to bottom:
D.H.2 of the second production
batch, standard version
D.H.2 of the first production
batch; the fuel tank is attached
beneath the upper wing
D.H.1 prototype, with Renault
engine
D.H.1A of No. 67 Squadron,
RFC, stationed in Palestine

0   1   2 m

roberto terrinoni

Top: *The armament of the D.H.2 consisted of a Lewis machine gun on a movable mounting; the gun, a 7·7-mm weapon, was loaded and fired by the pilot.* (Imperial War Museum)

Bottom: *A D.H.2 forced down intact behind the German lines and captured by the enemy. This is an aircraft of the second production batch, but it is not possible to identify the unit markings*

How the D.H.2 was used in the War

The debut of the D.H.2, which was destined to become one of the great fighter scouts of World War I, was not very encouraging. After test flights had been made in England, the prototype was shipped during the latter half of July 1915 to No. 5 Squadron RFC, then based in France. The pilots of the 5th were asked to report on the plane's performance under operational conditions, but already on August 9 the aircraft failed to return from its mission, and the Germans let it be known that it had been forced down behind their lines and the pilot, Capt. R. Maxwell-Pike, had died of his wounds.

Even after the first production machines arrived at the front the beginnings of the D.H.2's career were not exactly satisfactory because of the problems of its armament and the low speed. Within a short time, however, the new fighting Scout proved itself a worthy foe of the feared Fokker monoplane, especially because of its excellent climbing performance.

One traditional explanation has been that the D.H.2 was built with the dangerous Fokker monoplane as its specific target in mind, but the truth lies elsewhere because the British biplane had been designed before the appearance of the Fokkers and it had completed its period of flight-testing precisely during the weeks when the Fokker was beginning to assert itself.

No. 24 Squadron RFC was the first to be equipped with D.H.2s, and in a little more than a year the 24th had downed 44 enemy aircraft in 744 encounters. It chalked up its first victory with the new biplane on April 2, 1916; the pilot was Lieut. Tidmarsh. The D.H.2s of Nos. 5, 11, 18, 29 and 32 Squadrons RFC were engaged in many notable actions, among them the combat in which Maj. L. W. B. Rees, commander of the 32nd, earned the Victoria Cross when, alone, he attacked a formation of 10 enemy bombers, shooting down two of them and driving the others off. In another famous battle four D.H.2s of No. 24 Squadron took on 11 enemy aircraft and shot down three of them. D.H.2s of Nos. 24, 29 and 32 Squadrons RFC also played important roles during the Battle of the Somme and ensured Allied mastery of the skies.

The Royal Naval Air Service considered adoption of the D.H.2 as a naval aircraft, but the Airco product was outclassed in this respect by the Sopwith Pup and Triplane. The D.H.2 partially equipped Nos. 14, 111 and 47 Squadrons in Palestine and the Balkans, and it was also assigned to No. 22 Squadron, in Egypt, for training and reconnaissance. It was also used in the Home Defense by Nos. 6, 10 and 15 Squadrons. The role of the biplane in the last-named activity was limited, but it did cause something of a stir when Capt. R. H. M. S. Saundby shot down the Zeppelin L.48 in collaboration with another pilot.

The proverbial toughness of the D.H.2 saved many a pilot from death, but the lack of reliability of the Gnôme Monosoupape engine also got a number of pilots into serious trouble. In some cases the furious little engine literally 'shot' its cylinders, and if one of these murderous missiles happened to hit any part of the tail structure, taps it was for plane and pilot. The Monosoupape's chronic ailments, together with the heavy limitations of speed and armament, meant that by the end of 1916 the stock of the D.H.2 was definitely in decline. Such up-to-date and powerful machines as the German Albatros D.I and D.II and the Halberstadt D.II and D.III brought about the final downgrading of the D.H.2, which was thenceforth assigned to less dangerous missions and to training.

An example of how things were in those months of the war is provided by the long, hard duel fought on November 23, 1916, between Maj. Hawker, VC (who had emerged safely from nine previous duels), and the German pilot of a red Albatros D.II fighter. The British biplane was more maneuverable than the enemy's Albatros, but it was inferior in both maximum speed and rate of climb. In the event Manfred von Richthofen, flying the crimson Albatros, booked his 11th victory in this furious dogfight, in which Maj. Hawker died.

The day of the D.H.2 had reached its twilight. This was tragically underlined less than a month later. On December 20, 1916, five Albatros tangled with six D.H.2s of No. 29 Squadron. Only one D.H.2 escaped, while all five Albatros pilots got home.

A few D.H.2s were used for a short while longer on the French front (von Richthofen claimed his last D.H.2 in the last days of March 1917) and in the autumn of 1918 they were definitely retired from the Royal Flying Corps.

GOTHA G.I–G.V

Specifications

	G.I	G.II	G.III	G.IV	G.V
Power group	D.III	D.IV	D.IVa	D.IVa	D.IVa
	2 × 160 hp	220 hp	260 hp	260 hp	260 hp
Upper wing span, *m*	20·30	23·70	23·70	23·70	23·70
Lower wing span, *m*	19·70	21·90	21·90	21·90	21·90
Length, *m*	12·10	12·20	12·20	12·20	12·20
Height, *m*	3·70	3·90	3·90	3·90	3·90
Wing area, *m²*	82·00	89·50	89·50	89·50	89·50
Weight, empty, *kg*	1800	2180	2380	2415	2740
Total weight, *kg*	2800	3190	3620	3650	3975
Maximum speed, *km/hr*	130	135	135	135	140
Ceiling, *m*	2700	—	—	5000	6500
Flight endurance, *hrs-min*	4:00	4:00	3:45	4-6:00	6:00
Number of machine guns	1	2	2–3	2–3	2–3

'*On June 13, 1917, at one o'clock in the afternoon, German time, London was bombed under good weather conditions by a squadron of German heavy bombers under the personal command of the squadron commander Capt. Brandenburg.*'

This was the concise war bulletin issued by the German High Command to confirm the first aerial bombardment of London, which was also the first long-range strategic mission carried out by Gotha bombers.

The mission had its origins far back in the summer of 1914, when Oskar Ursinus, ex-director of a popular aviation magazine, *Flugsport* (Flying Sport), launched the project of building a twin-engined seaplane of biplane configuration, with the upper wing mounted through the fuselage and the lower suspended below the fuselage by means of struts. Engine positions were to be so close that the tips of the two propellers almost touched.

The outbreak of the war caused suspension of the project for a civilian seaplane, but Ursinus revised his project, transforming the aircraft into a land plane. With the collaboration of Maj. Friedel, commander of *Fliegerersatzabteilung 3* (Pilot Replacement Unit) at Darmstadt, and other military personnel, Ursinus constructed a prototype, to which was given the designation B.1092/14 (the G of later designations was not yet used). The new aircraft was test-flown in January 1915. Ursinus's design had many things to recommend it

161

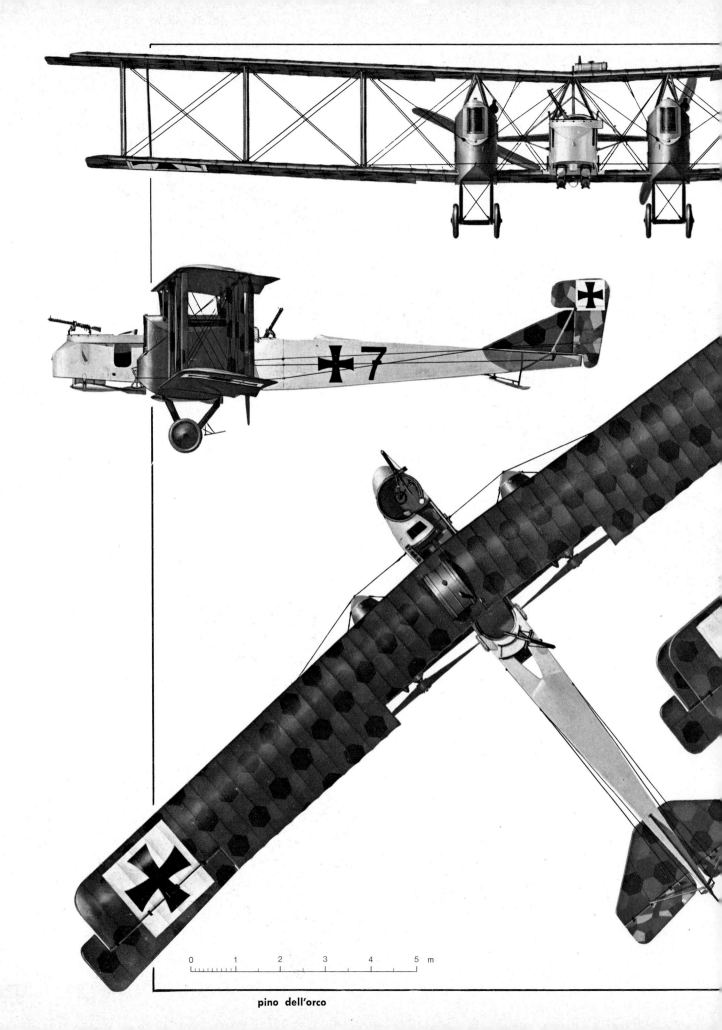

0   1   2   3   4   5 m

pino dell'orco

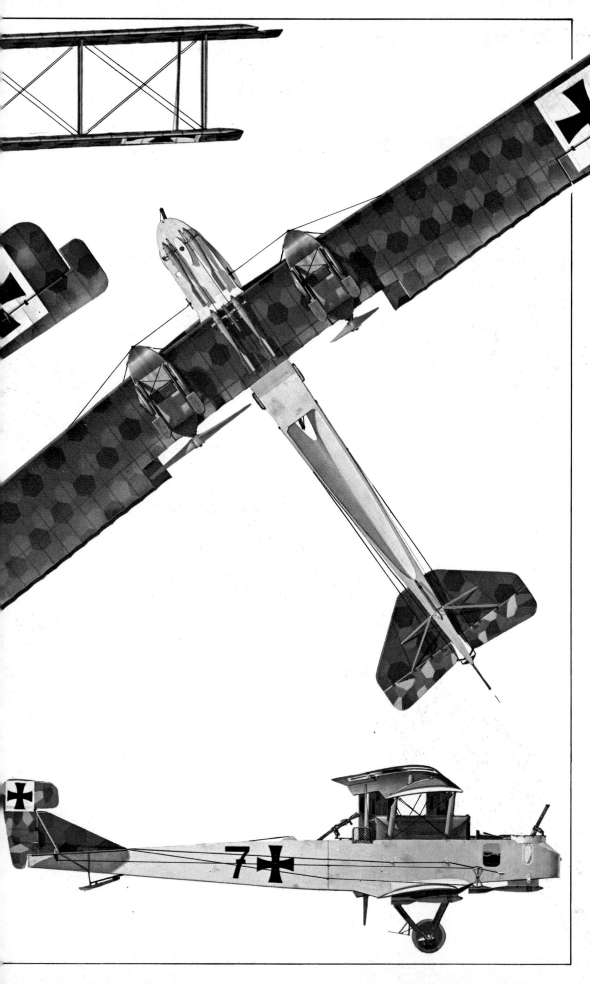

Gotha G.IV of *Kagohl 3,* serial No. unknown. The aircraft flown by this German bomber wing sported various markings and colorings. The engines were 260-hp Mercedes D.IVas. Note the light blue color which was typical of German and Austrian bombs, except for a few which were painted dark green. The large opening in the fuselage permitted a good field of fire downward for the gunner handling the rear machine gun, which was mounted behind the propellers. Such a gun position was typical of the Gotha G.III, IV and V

—good visibility, a broad field of fire for the defensive armament, and the possibility of flying on a single engine because of the close position of the two power plants. A distinct disadvantage, however, was the high position of the fuselage, which hampered smooth control in flight.

The project was approved by the military authorities in spite of its defects, and the contract for series production was passed on to the *Gothaer Waggonfabrik,* which for some time had specialized in aircraft with more than one engine.

Hans Burkhardt, chief engineer of Gothaer, simplified and improved Ursinus's design, and the first production machine of the G.I series came off the line on July 27, 1915. About 20 of this version were built, and they were active at the front until October 1916.

Toward the end of 1915, as the last G.Is were being completed, Burkhardt was assigned to the design of a new bomber capable of carrying at least 300 kg (660 lb) of bombs on long-range missions. This project became the G.II.

Technical description

The first G.II bomber differed substantially from the original design of Ursinus, and it was the true forerunner of the entire line of multi-engined aircraft built from its day through 1919.

The wings consisted of three sections, with the wooden spars and ribs covered with doped fabric. The upper and lower center sections had a long, narrow rectangular cutout in the trailing edge to permit installation of the two pusher propellers. The rectangular wings had a slight but very evident sweepback.

Two 220-hp Mercedes D.IV engines were mounted between the wings, driving either two- or four-bladed propellers. Their huge nacelles also contained the fuel and oil tanks, which were fitted beneath the engines. Another gravity tank was mounted on the upper center section.

The long, slender fuselage was built around a framework of oak and spruce braced with steel wires and covered with rough gray fabric; only the nose was sheathed in plywood. The tail elements consisted of tubular frames covered with fabric.

The undercarriage was of the traditional type but with two chassis, each equipped with two wheels; a strong tail skid served also as a brake.

The crew consisted of the pilot on the port side, the bomber-gunner in the nose, with a second gunner behind him. There was a narrow passage along the starboard side of the fuselage, serving as a connecting link between the three accommodations. At first the bomb rack beneath the fuselage could take 14 bombs weighing 10 kg (22 lb) each. Later, as bombs became bigger and more powerful, they were attached outside with interchangeable clips which permitted varying them to suit the needs of the individual mission.

About ten G.IIs were sent to the front, but because of the low efficiency of the 220-hp engine these bombers were fitted with two 260-hp Mercedes D.IV units. From this modification developed the G.III, which (apart from the engines) differed from its predecessor only in having a stouter fuselage and increased armament with a third machine gun mounted on the floor of the rear gunner's cockpit and free to fire downward.

The Gothaer built 25 G.IIIs in the period just before the appearance of the new, and greatly improved, G.IV (April-December 1916).

Development of the Gotha Bombers

The twin-engined G.IV was not greatly different from the G.III in basic design, but it did have a gallery along the rear section of the fuselage which gave passage to the rear gunner so that he might cover the aircraft from the tail. Normally the rear gun was used for this purpose, but a fourth gun

From top to bottom:
One of the earliest Gotha G.Is, 9/15, of Kagohl 2, Sonderstaffel 1. *After a crash this aircraft was immediately removed from the roster*
Another G.I, 10/15, also assigned to Sonderstaffel 1. *This aircraft continued in service until the end of 1915*
A view of a Gotha G.IV showing the slightly swept-back wing and the passageway between the pilot's and gunner's cockpits
Gotha IV. This version of the Gotha bomber became operational in March-April 1917, and with these machines Kagohl 3 *carried out the first daylight raids on London*
Lower right: A view of a Gotha G.V showing the position of the forward gunner. (Archivio Apostolo and Museo Caproni, Taliedo)

Gotha G.IV in flight. (Museo Caproni, Taliedo)

could be carried, although it meant some tradeoff in bomb load. The most obvious difference between the G.IV and the earlier model was the presence of ailerons on the lower wing. The fuselage was wholly wooden-skinned and partially waterproof, so that if forced down it could float for several hours.

An initial order for 35 Gotha G.IVs was soon increased to 50, bolstered by about 100 planes to be manufactured by the LVG and another 80 by Siemens-Schuckert. Of these total orders, 30 bombers were expected by February 1917, but this planned series production suffered a setback because of the scarcity of some materials and the unsatisfactory test flights of the first production plane.

A few Gothas built by Siemens-Schuckert in Berlin were modified in an effort to improve performance, with 245-hp Maybach engines mounted on one or two G.IVs, driving tractor propellers; on others an experimental Siemens supercharger, while still other machines underwent structural reinforcing. One entire batch was equipped—perhaps for the first time ever—with Flettner trim tabs. In

October 1917 a 20-mm Becker cannon was experimentally fitted on one aircraft, probably for use in downward firing against targets.

Meanwhile at the Gotha factory the G.V was under development, with improvements based on the suggestions of pilots and the military. The chief innovation on the G.V was the removal of the fuel tanks from the engine nacelles (a dangerous place to store fuel!) to the fuselage rear sections.

All bombs were racked externally, beneath the fuselage and lower wing.

Generally speaking the performance of the G.V was not greatly superior to that of the G.IV, and a higher maximum forward speed was achieved only at a sacrifice in rate of climb. Insufficiently seasoned structural materials and an increase in the supplementary equipment brought about a gain of about 400 kg (880 lb) over design total weight. The engines delivered 15 hp less than rated because of the low quality of the fuel, which resulted in a drastic lowering of overall performance.

The first G.Vs had good climbing speed (5500 m in 1 hr). With auxiliary fuel tank, reinforced airframe and extra equipment (oxygen system, navigational instrumentation, generator-operated heater, ammunition, etc.) the G.V was designed to operate with an overload of 140-160 kg (308-352 lb), with a consequent reduction in operational ceiling. These negative factors were, indeed, such that the first night mission with a G.V was carried out at an altitude of only 2000 m (6500 ft).

The final versions to see action were the G.Va and the G.Vb, which differed from previous models in only a few details of inside arrangement and,

in the case of the G.Vb, in the undercarriage, each half of which was equipped with four wheels. These two later versions also had a shorter nose and twin fins. They were put into production in March 1918, and flown to the front in June.

Gotha continued to build reconnaissance and bombing aircraft during the final months of the war and in the postwar period. Gotha G.VII and G.VIII had tractor propellers; they were designed by Rösner, but Burkhardt did the designs for the G.X. Hans Burkhardt, incidentally, also designed the G.VI, the first asymmetric aircraft design ever to come from the drawing offices, but its develop-

Top: *Improved Gotha G.V bombers took part in the bombing missions over London in the autumn of 1917.* (Archivio Apostolo)
Right, center: *Gotha G.Vb; note double landing gear and twin rudder.* (Museo Caproni, Taliedo)
Right, bottom: *With the Gotha G.VII the basic formula changed. Note the tractor propellers and the shortened nose.*
Lower left: *Detail showing how bombs were carried on the Gotha G.V. The lozenge design on the fuselage was widely used in 1917 and 1918.* (Archivio Apostolo)

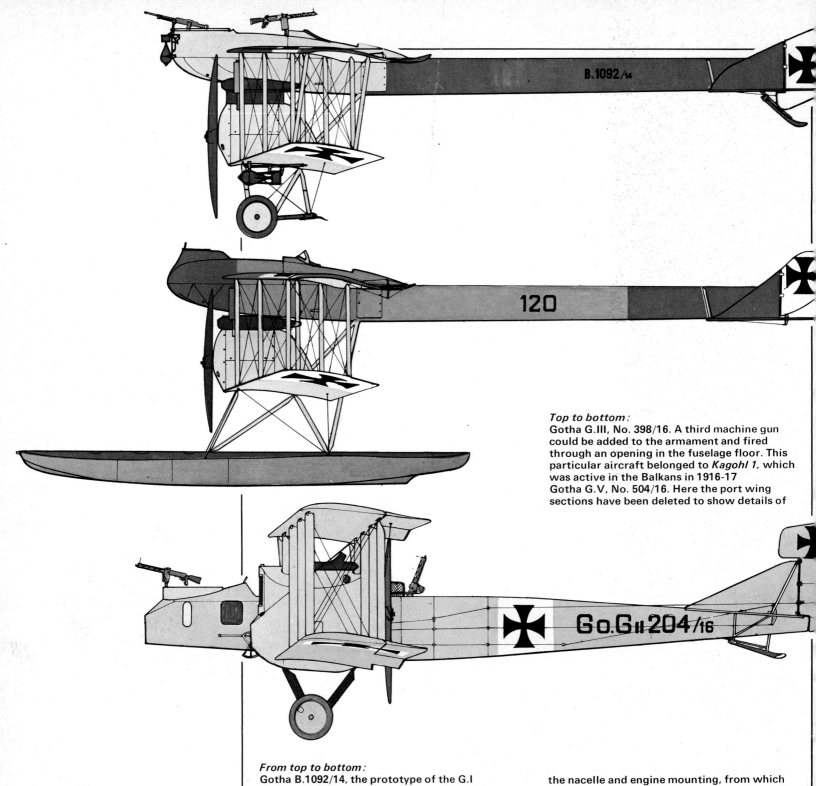

Top to bottom:
Gotha G.III, No. 398/16. A third machine gun could be added to the armament and fired through an opening in the fuselage floor. This particular aircraft belonged to *Kagohl 1,* which was active in the Balkans in 1916-17
Gotha G.V, No. 504/16. Here the port wing sections have been deleted to show details of

From top to bottom:
Gotha B.1092/14, the prototype of the G.I designed by Oskar Ursinus with considerable help from Maj. Friedel (the nose monogram incorporates the initials U and F). This was the first German multi-engined bomber and could carry some small bombs, two of which were suspended from the extreme nose. This machine saw action with *Feldfliegerabteilung 28* on the Eastern front in 1915 and inspired the design of the G.I.
Gotha UWD, Naval No. 120, accepted by the German Navy in February 1916 and eventually used as a training plane for torpedo launching.
Gotha G.II, No. 204/16. Note the four-bladed propellers and the shape of the rudder, which differs from the rudders of later versions in that it has a vertical trailing edge

the nacelle and engine mounting, from which the fuel tanks had been moved for reasons of safety. This machine, probably of *Kagohl 3,* carried national markings only on the underside of the lower wing
Gotha G.V, No. 547, typical of the final form of the G.V. This machine, which may have been from *Kagohl 3,* was forced down behind the French lines in 1918. The color scheme is conjectural
Gotha G.Vb, No. 935/16, a version with twin fin/rudder assembly. Note the Flettner trim tabs on the upper wing and the modified under-carriage (known as *Stossfahrgestell* or 'shock undercarriage') designed to facilitate night landing. The national markings are of the simplified type used until the end of 1918

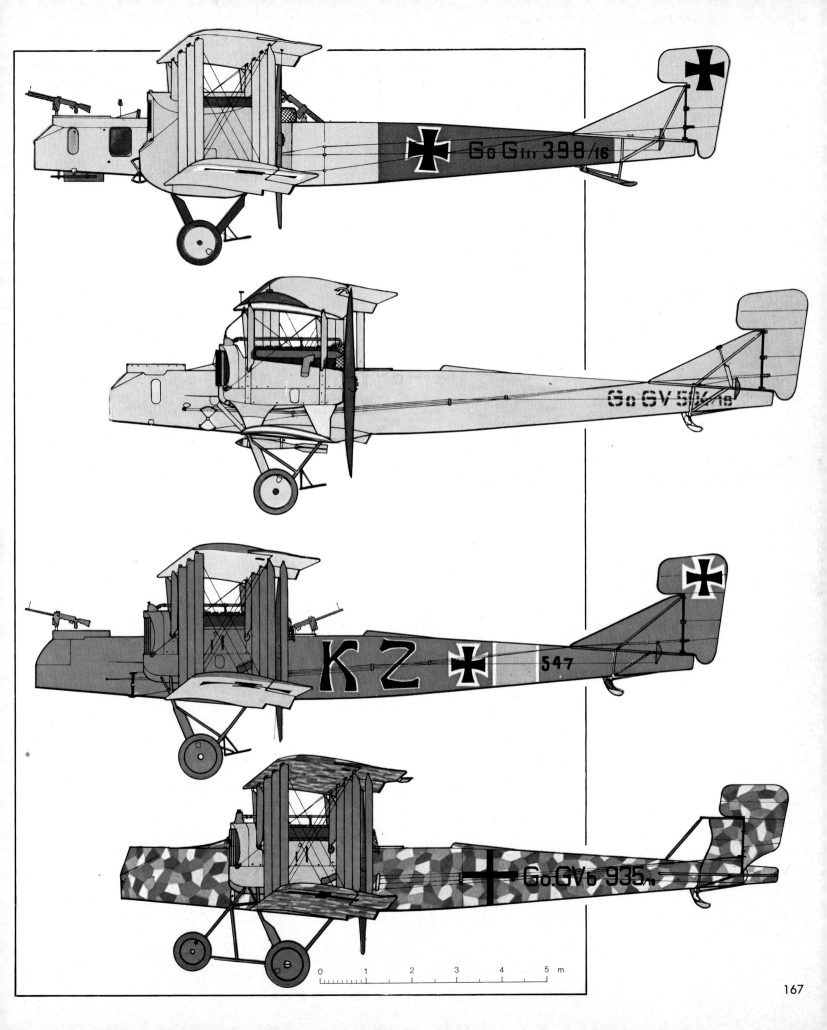

Go Gfr 398/16

Go GV 584/16

KZ ✠ 547

Go.GVb 935/16

0 1 2 3 4 5 m

Top: *Gotha G.V bomber, which differed from previous models by having ailerons on both wings. In this photograph the gravity fuel tank mounted on the upper wing is clearly visible.* (Archivio Apostolo)
Bottom: *Gotha G.VIII, which differed from the G.VII only in its slightly longer upper wing span. The engines were two 260-hp Maybachs.* (Museo Caproni, Taliedo)

How the Gotha Bombers were used in the War

The G.II and G.III began operations on the Balkan front with *Kagohl 1* (an early name for what was later called *Bombengeschwader),* based at Hudova. They played an important part in the destruction of a railroad bridge at Černavoda, and this cut in the railroad allowed the Germans to block reinforcements and supplies to the Rumanian troops. The success of these early operations gave considerable impetus to the development of bomber aircraft.

The G.III was used by *Kagohl 2* on the Western front with good results, although a sizeable number of aircraft were lost (chiefly through accidents, not through enemy action). Two of these Gothas

fell into Allied hands, one in the St-Michel sector through the efforts of the well-known French fighter pilot Guynemer, the second in British-held territory. Both machines were examined carefully by the engineers and military of both Allied nations.

By the end of 1916 the Germans had become aware of how costly and how useless it was to attack England from Zeppelin dirigibles, and the decision was made to utilize the new bombers. Thirty G.IVs were readied in February 1917 and assigned to the project known as *Türkenkreuz* (Turkish Cross). On May 25, 1917, the first of a series of daylight bombing sorties took off and headed for London under the command of Capt. Ernst Brandenburg, commander of *Kampfgeschwader 3* (later to be called *Bombengeschwader).* These raids did very little damage, but they did make it necessary for the British to recall two fighter squadrons for defense of the capital. The reinforced defense in turn forced the Germans to abandon their daylight missions and resort to night bombing. These missions continued until May 1918, when losses in men and aircraft became prohibitive and *Türkenkreuz* was abandoned.

ment was interrupted by the conclusion of the war.

Total production of these large bombers by the Gothaer Waggonfabrik amounted to approximately 300 machines.

In August 1917 the huge Gotha G.V bombers were delivered to *Bogohl 3* (another new designation for the bomber wing). It was hoped that the arrival of these new aircraft would allow resumption of the daylight raids over London, but the new plane also proved to be inadequate when faced with the heavy British defensive reaction.

Generally speaking the huge Gothas showed good maneuverability in spite of their size, and their defensive armament also proved successful at warding off Allied attacks. Most Gothas which went down were hit by anti-aircraft fire rather than falling prey to fighters, but a good proportion of them also crashed because of accidents, particularly in night landings. Their stability was good when fully loaded, but considerably less so after their bombs were dropped and their fuel tanks nearly empty.

In the period from September 3, 1917, to May 19, 1918, the G.IVs and G.Vs of *Bogohl 3,* supported by the bombers of *Riesenflugzeugabteilung 501,* flew 19 night missions against London, with a total loss from all causes of 60 aircraft.

When the cross-Channel sorties were canceled, the bombers of *Bogohl 3* were used against French targets during the spring offensive of 1918.

Many of the Gothas built under license by Siemens-Schuckert between late 1917 and early 1918 were used for training, for by that time the G.IV was obsolescent as a heavy bomber. These trainers were powered by 180-hp NAG C.IIIs or 185-hp Argus As.IIIs.

Beginning in February 1918 some 30 G.IVs built by the LVG with 230-hp Austrian Hiero engines were delivered to the Austrians who used them against the Italians and on other missions. These machines were armed with Schwarzlose machine guns.

HANDLEY PAGE 0/100-0/400

Specifications

	0/100	0/400
Power group	Rolls-Royce Eagle II 2×266 hp	Rolls-Royce Eagle VIII 2×360 hp
Wing span, *m*	30·48	30·48
Length, *m*	19·16	19·16
Height, *m*	6·70	6·70
Wing area, *m²*	153·10	153·10
Weight, empty, *kg*	3760	3856
Total weight, *kg*	6350	6350
Maximum speed (at sea level), *km/hr*	122	156·9
Rate of climb, *min-sec*	2:10 to 300 m	27:10 to 1981 m
Ceiling, *m*	2130	2591

Frederick Handley Page was born at Cheltenham in 1885. In 1909 he founded Handley Page Ltd., after several years' experience in aeronautical engineering, during which he had supplied parts to various clients. In 1908 he had built a glider of the *canard* type with characteristic sweepback.

The first aircraft built by the new Handley Page Ltd. were the monoplane A H.P.1, nicknamed 'The Bluebird' for its grey-blue fabric covering, and the biplane B H.P.2, built principally in an effort to determine the effect on stability of suspending the engine and cockpit beneath the two wings. Other biplanes followed, all autostabilized with swept-back wings—the C H.P.3, D H.P.4 (nicknamed 'The Yellow Peril' or 'Antiseptic' for its particular shade of yellow); the F H.P.6 and, finally, the G H.P.7, which gave a very good account of itself in test flights in so far as autostabilization was concerned.

The design of this last-named biplane was the first important work of a designer who was to gain deserved praise in years to come, George R. Volkert. This great engineer, a product of the Northampton Institute, was later to design the four-engine Halifax bomber of World War II fame. At the time we are speaking of, G. R. Volkert was

only 26. He had only recently joined Handley Page when, in 1914, the beginning of hostilities interrupted his work on the L/200 H.P. 8, a large biplane powered by a Salmson engine of 300 hp and the first attempt Handley Page Ltd. had made in the field of large aircraft. However, the projected L/200 H.P. 8 was to be the visiting card which served to present Handley Page to Cdr. Murray Sueter, director of the Air Department of

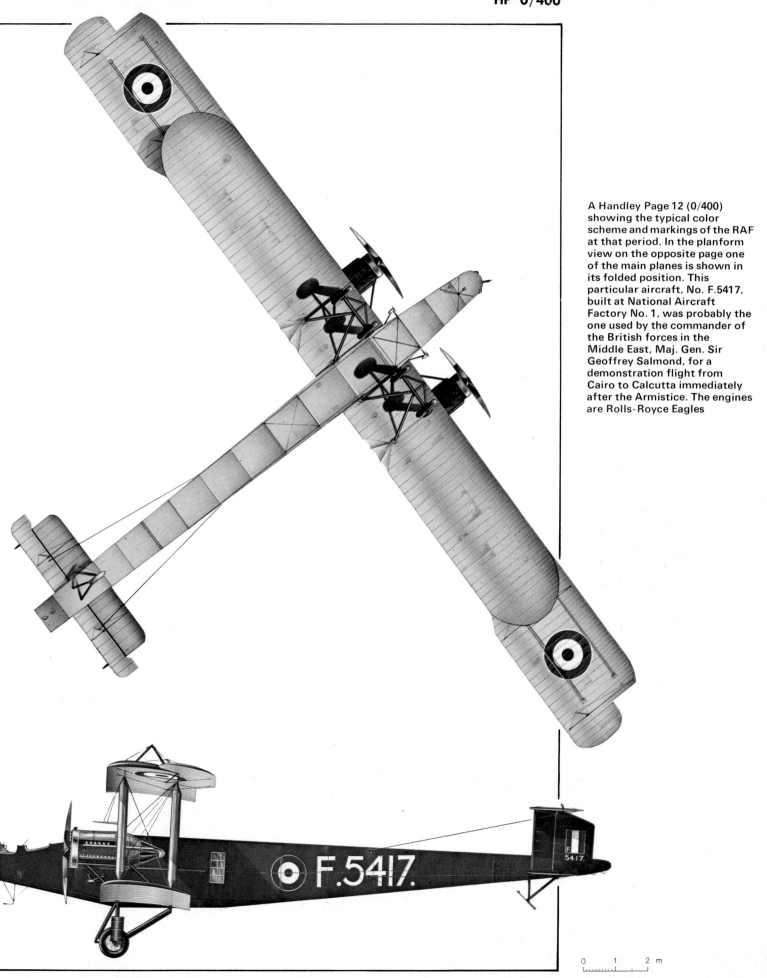

A Handley Page 12 (0/400)
showing the typical color
scheme and markings of the RAF
at that period. In the planform
view on the opposite page one
of the main planes is shown in
its folded position. This
particular aircraft, No. F.5417,
built at National Aircraft
Factory No. 1, was probably the
one used by the commander of
the British forces in the
Middle East, Maj. Gen. Sir
Geoffrey Salmond, for a
demonstration flight from
Cairo to Calcutta immediately
after the Armistice. The engines
are Rolls-Royce Eagles

0   1   2 m

vincenzo cosentino

the Admiralty. The Admiralty was vitally interested in big, multi-engined aircraft capable of long flights with heavy useful loads, and it had set up an Admiralty engineering section which was already working on a huge three-engined plane of more than 35-m span; in spite of its apocalyptic designation of A.D.1000, this machine was to prove a ghastly fiasco.

Obviously, for the Admiralty frame of mind at that time the L/200 H.P. 8 and the two twin-engined planes, the M and N, powered by two 120-hp Beardmore engines which Handley Page and Volkert first proposed were too small and too light. Sueter gave the young engineers a detailed specification of the sort of thing he was looking for—a 'paralyzing' aircraft of great size capable of carrying out strategic missions of vital importance to the war effort, not just 'a toy'. The year 1914 was drawing to a close, and Admiralty officials felt they didn't have any time to waste. Handley Page and Volkert got busy.

Technical description

In answer to the Admiralty's request the two engineers designed the 0/100, which, progressively improved by a number of modifications which were not radical changes, became the 0/400. The final version was ready by the end of 1917 and was a big two-engined biplane, with a biplane stabilizer and a triple rudder. The two rectangular wings, of equal chord, were joined by four pairs of vertical struts, and two truss structures, which served as inboard struts, also supported the engine nacelles, which were mounted midway between the upper and lower wings.

The upper wing, equipped with fully balanced ailerons, had considerably longer span than the lower, which was without control surfaces but had rounded wing tips. The wings were of box-spar construction, with wooden ribs. They were built in three sections—a center section, which was connected to the fuselage by a truss of steel-tubing, two sections for each main plane in the upper wing, and two sections for each main plane of the lower wing. The whole wing assembly was fabric-covered. The wing back spars, at the point corresponding to the engine nacelles, had connected to them the hinges of the main plane sections, which could be folded back parallel to the fuselage for transport (the smaller span of the lower wing enabled its wing tips to clear the tail structure when the wings were stowed).

The final design of the tail structure was reached after a series of changes. It consisted of twin stabilizers, which could be adjusted on the ground, and of four elevator components, each pair corresponding to one of the stabilizer panels (see drawing). Over a long period of development, with progressive reductions in the dimensions of the various elements, the stabilizers and elevators ended up looking rather strange and not particularly elegant. The vertical elements included a single central fin with twin rudders.

The fuselage was rectangular in cross section. It was a wooden truss structure, almost wholly fabric-covered, with longerons and spacers of spruce reinforced by steel wire bracing. For ease of fabrication the fuselage was also built in four sections, the first of which contained the cockpit, the second the bomb bay.

The engine nacelles were supported on struts of steel tubing; they were well designed from the aerodynamical point of view, and rather elongated by the two fuel tanks of 545 liters (120 gallons) each mounted aft of the engines. As time went on various engines were tried out, but certain basics were invariably observed, such as the use of four-bladed counter-rotating propellers, mounting of the engines forward of the interplane bracing, and the fitting of radiators in front of the engines.

The engines used were of various types, even on the prototype, which had its original 120-hp Beardmores replaced by 250-hp Rolls-Royce Eagle IIs; the latter in a beefed-up version were fitted on 40 production aircraft. Another half dozen 0/100s were powered by 320-hp Sunbeam Cossacks.

The undercarriage of the 0/100 was a rather complicated affair, with a wood-faired steel-tubing tripod for each (port and starboard) pair of wheels attached to the forward spar of the lower wing between the fuselage and the engine nacelle. The wheels measured 80 or 90 cm ($31\frac{1}{2}$-36 inches) in diameter.

The defensive armament of the Handley Page bomber consisted of one or two 7·7-mm Lewis machine guns mounted in the nose and a second position with either one or two identical Lewis guns plus another one for rear and downward defense, this last gun firing through a slot in the fuselage flooring at the level of the lower wing trailing edge. Original specifications had called for extensive sheet-steel armoring, which was abandoned after its installation on the prototype proved to add excessive weight (550 kg, or 1200 lb).

The bomb load carried by the 0/100 was high for that day, well above the weight required by the specification, and consisted of 16×51-kg (112-lb) bombs instead of the 6×46-kg (100-lb) bombs required by the Admiralty Air Department. The bomb-bay doors were held closed by a spring attachment and opened by the weight of the bombs on their release.

The development of the first British heavy bomber was rather long and troublesome, and in spite of the tight schedule which Frederick Handley Page imposed on his staff (9½ hours per day, 7 days per week), the first prototype, No. 1455, did not appear at the Hendon airfield until December 18, 1915. A few bugs were ironed out, and during the next few days the prototype made a few brief flights. It was immediately obvious that the original radiators wouldn't do (they were mounted above the engine nacelles and almost touched the upper wing), and the rudders were too streamlined and had to be replaced by others of greater chord.

On January 10, 1916, the 0/100 prototype flew from Hendon to Eastchurch, in spite of some engine trouble. As regular flight testing got under way numerous defects became apparent, a particularly serious one being the very noticeable vibration of the fuselage at speeds above 130 km/hr (80 mph), which was so powerful that it caused serious damage to the fuselage. The second prototype had a longer nose, an open rather than enclosed pilot's cockpit, and a central fin which was introduced to compensate for the directional instability (a tendency to yaw) which the designers attributed to the extended nose. In this second prototype there were still violent vibrations, but their onset was at a higher speed, and the situation was considered on the whole not to be unacceptable, although strengthening of the fuselage on production machines was considered necessary.

Development of the Handley Page 0/100 and 0/400

There were not very many 0/100s completed, since it was succeeded almost immediately by the improved 0/400. The prototype of the 0/400 was built by appropriateley modifying a 0/100, No. 3138, and the first test flights were made in September 1917. The 0/400 was externally practically identical to the 0/100, differing essentially in the fuel system, which was completely revised on the basis of experience gained with the 0/100. The engine nacelle tanks were eliminated, thus shortening the nacelles, and in place of the 590-liter (130-gallon) tank originally used two tanks of equal capacity were installed in the fuselage. Two auxiliary tanks mounted in the center section of the wing leading edge, with a combined capacity of 127 liters (28 gallons), were gravity tanks through which fuel pumped from the fuselage tank was fed to the engines; the two fuel pumps were driven by two small propellers mounted on either side of the nose slightly ahead of the leading edge of the lower wing.

Overall fuel capacity, then, was 1307 liters (288 gallons), as. against 1680 liters (370 gallons) in the 0/100, but in spite of the reduction in fuel weight the flight endurance remained 8 hrs, sufficient for carrying out fairly long-range missions. Two bomb racks fitted on the underside of the fuselage added to the total weight of bombs which could be carried.

Another minor change on the 0/400 was the center fin, which was set slightly further back.

About 400 of this new version were built in England by Handley Page Ltd. and other local firms; about 107 were turned out (for the most part simply assembled from British parts) by the Standard Aircraft Corp. of Elizabeth, N. J., on behalf of the US Army Air Service, which, however, never used the British bomber in combat.

Temporary delays in delivery of Rolls-Royce Eagle engines caused Handley Page to turn to other power plants, among them the 125-hp Sunbeam Maori, 260-hp Fiat A-12bis, 350-hp Liberty 12-N; the last-named was an American engine installed on American-assembled 0/400s,

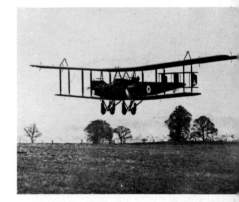

Top to bottom:
An 0/400, No D 8345, coming in for a landing. This plane was built by British Caudron. (Archivio Igino Coggi)
An 0/400 of No. 48 Squadron of the RAF in flight over the River Rhine near Bonn in May 1919.
The last series production 0/400, No. D 8350, built by British Caudron and used in 1919 as a transport. Named 'The Vulture', on May 1, 1919, it became the first 0/400 to be given a civil registration (G-EAAE). (Archivio Igino Coggi)
Bottom left: *A 0/400 with Rolls-Royce Eagle engines is towed with its mainplanes folded back*

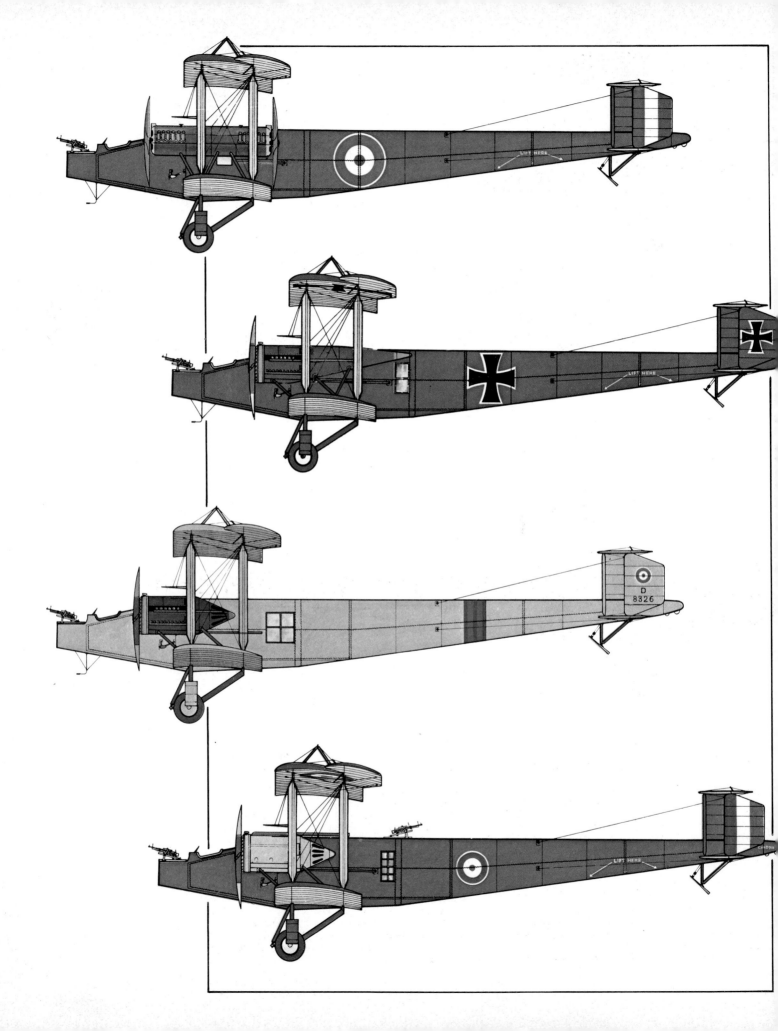

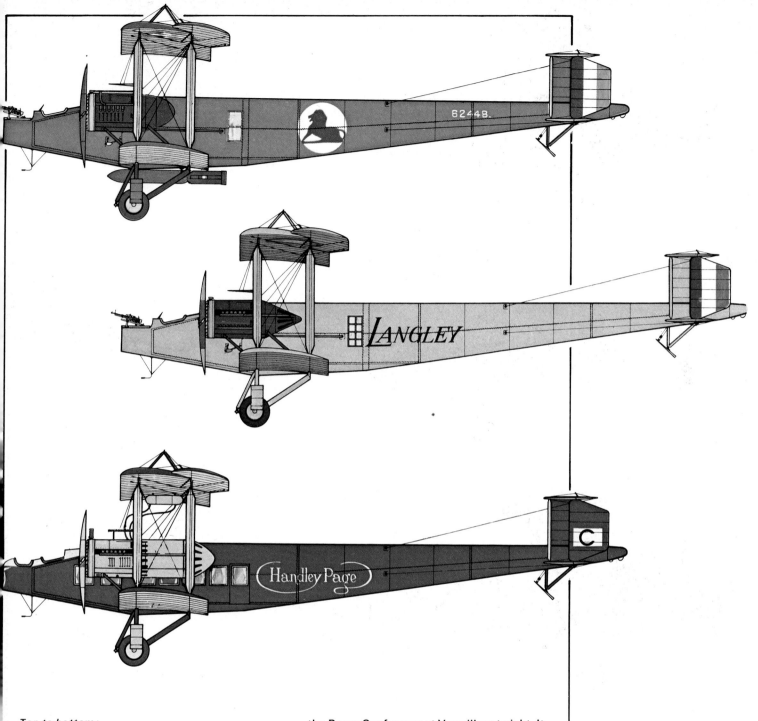

Top to bottom:
One of the prototypes of the H. P. 11 (0/100), with four 200-hp Hispano-Suiza engines working in pusher-tractor pairs
The third production 0/100 which was sent to France for delivery to the 5th Wing of the RNAS at Dunquerque. Landed by mistake on a German-held airfield, the plane, known as 'The Amazon', was repainted with German markings

An 0/400, No. D8326, of the 86th Communications Wing of the RAF, equipped as a passenger plane for the British sovereign. It was known as 'The Silver Star'. The fuselage was refitted to give comfortable passage to six passengers. This aircraft was also used to transport government personnel to and from

the Peace Conference at Versailles at night. It is powered by Rolls-Royce Eagle engines

A 0/400 of the US Air Service used for experimental bombing trials with large bombs at the Aberdeen Proving Grounds in 1921. It is powered by Liberty engines
The first 0/400 to have American markings. The US received eight of these aircraft, with components for the assembly of 100 more by the Standard Aircraft Corp. of Elizabeth, N.J. However, because of the cessation of hostilities, these machines were never assembled
A 0/400 fitted out for one of the first civil air operations of the postwar period. Note the windows in the fuselage, showing position of passenger seats

0 1 2 m

Top: *An H. P. 0/400 equipped for transport service takes off. This is an RAF plane, J 2250, built by the Birmingham Carriage Co. With windows in the fuselage, it was designated as H. P. 20. (Archivio Apostolo)*
Bottom: *A 0/400 photographed in 1920 at the Heliopolis airport near Cairo. No. 70 Squadron of the RAF had been assigned to Egypt as part of the Colonial Police, and until 1921 it was largely equipped with 0/400s. (Archivio Apostolo)*

which were capable of carrying 1361 kg (3000 lb) of bombs. Both the 0/100 and 0/400 were used to study problems whose solutions were to be incorporated on the Handley Page V/1500, such as a nacelle with two engines operating in tandem, which was tested in November 1917 on the 0/100 No. 3117, powered by four 200-hp Hispano-Suizas.

How the Handley Page Bombers were used in the War

The operational debut of the Handley Page 0/100 was not encouraging: the third plane delivered to the Royal Naval Air Service was flown from England to France by a pilot who made the mistake of landing at an airfield held by the Germans!

The first British unit to receive the 0/100 was the V Wing of the Royal Naval Air Service, based at Dunquerque; the first three machines were assigned there. The next four were delivered in April 1917 to No. 7 Squadron of the RNAS, also based at Dunquerque, and at least one machine was delivered to the III Wing of the RNAS at Luxeuil.

The earliest operational missions to which the 0/100s were assigned were maritime patrols, and on April 23 1917 three bombers of No. 7 Squadron RNAS, each armed with 14 × 30-kg bombs, attacked five German torpedo-boat destroyers (TBDs) off Ostend, scoring several direct hits and seriously damaging another boat. On April 26, in a similar mission, a 0/100 was shot down by anti-aircraft fire, showing for the first time how vulnerable it was to defensive gunfire; from then on the Handley Page was used almost exclusively under the cover of darkness.

On the night of March 16-17, a 0/100 of the III Wing, RNAS, raided the railroad station of Moulin-les-Mets, and other night missions followed, directed against submarine and light seacraft bases and facilities at Bruges, Ostend and Zeebrugge, against enemy industrial centers, the railroad network of southern France and Flanders, and against the airports of St-Denis Westrem and Gontrode, takeoff bases for Gotha raids on England.

The Gotha bombing raids over England were one of the factors which hastened activation of the 0/400s. These new planes joined the 0/100s of A Squadron, which had come under the 41st Wing in October 1917 at Ochey in France, and formed the nucleus of a strategic air arm which was later to become the RAF Independent Force assigned to the bombing of German industrial targets. As new aircraft arrived new squadrons were formed—Nos. 97, 100, 115, 215 and 216; and it was two 0/400s of No. 215 Squadron which began the air offensive against Germany. On the night of August 25-26 1918, they raided the Badische Anilin u. Sodafabrik at Mannheim, dropping bombs and strafing with machine guns.

On a few occasions as many as 30 bombers attacked a single target, and with very substantial results since bombs were getting bigger (including one 748-kg bomb, i.e., a 1650-pounder). Handley Pages of Nos. 7 and 14 Squadrons RNAS took part in repeated attacks against the railroad system used by the Germans for support of their last effort on the Western front, and at the same time bombers of the RAF were joining naval aircraft in raids on Ostend and Zeebrugge and the vital communications center of Bruges.

The successes rung up by the Handley Page 0/400 were gained at considerable losses, however, due in part to German anti-aircraft fire but mainly to crashes or other accidents, which destroyed more than 70% of the 69 bombers lost by the Independent Force from June to November 1918.

Only one 0/400 was used operationally outside the European theater. It was assigned to the 1st Squadron the Australian Flying Corps and flew both transport and bombing missions in Palestine.

The high useful load and the ample space available in the 0/400s suggested their use as transport aircraft and two of these machines, equipped to take 12 passengers each, were utilized to fly back pilots used in ferrying British-built aircraft to France. Later eight more machines were assigned to No. 1 Squadron and used on liaison work carrying VIPs between England and France during the Versailles Peace Conference. Still other 0/400s were used in test-flights over new commercial routes by Handley Page Ltd., thus providing background material for the development of the 0/700, of which about 15 were eventually built. In 1920, as the RAF was undergoing postwar reorganization, the 0/400s which were still around were retired, and thus ended the career of the only British heavy bomber used operationally in World War I.

Of the 0/400s built under license in the United States, some were eventually transferred to and used by the fledgling Chinese air force.

FOKKER D.VII

The Fokker D VII was one of the best fighter scouts of any air arm in World War I. The aircraft shown here is No. F.461/18, built at the Fokker plant. (Bundesarchiv)

Specifications

Power plant	1 × BMW IIIa 185 hp
Wing span, *m*	8·90
Length, *m*	6·95
Height, *m*	2·75
Wing area, *m²*	20·5
Weight, empty, *kg*	700–735
Useful load, *kg*	180
Total weight, *kg*	880
Maximum wing loading at take off, *kg/m²*	42·9
Maximum speed at about 1000 *m*	200
Climb to 1000 *m, min-sec*	1:45
Climb to 4000 *m, min-sec*	10:15
Ceiling, *m*	7000

Towards the end of 1917 the German *IdFlieg* (German abbr. for 'Inspectorate of Flying Troops') invited proposals for a new fighter scout equipped to compete with the recent new Allied aircraft and to succeed the Dr.1 triplane, then irremediably outclassed. The only condition was that this new fighter had to utilize the 160-hp Mercedes D III engine. The winner of the amazing total of 31 prototypes submitted for comparative trials at the Adlershof airfield near Berlin was the Fokker D.VII, one of nine submitted by Fokker. Anthony Fokker was determined not to lose this opportunity to submit a new winner which might be a worthy successor to his monoplanes and triplanes. The D.VII prototype, known by the designation V.11, was a sesquiplane, a 'one-and-a-half winger', with a decided difference in span between upper and lower wings, and it won a clear victory over all the other models submitted.

The design complies in every way with the concept of the simple aircraft formula defended by Reinhold Platz, now known to be its true creator, although Fokker claimed the design for himself. The V.11 was clearly based on the Dr.I triplane, from which it took virtually intact the fuselage and tail structure. In the original version the aircraft had lacked stability and was not easy to pilot, and when Fokker heard from Manfred von Richthofen, who took part in the tests at Adlershof, confirmation of the defects which he had already found, he decided that radical action was necessary. He spread the word that the V.11 needed a few repairs as a result of a hard landing, then he took advantage of a weekend to assemble a few of his best workmen (who were at Adlershof as a maintenance crew) and by dint of incredibly hard and fast work succeeded in lengthening the fuselage by about 40 cm (16 inches).

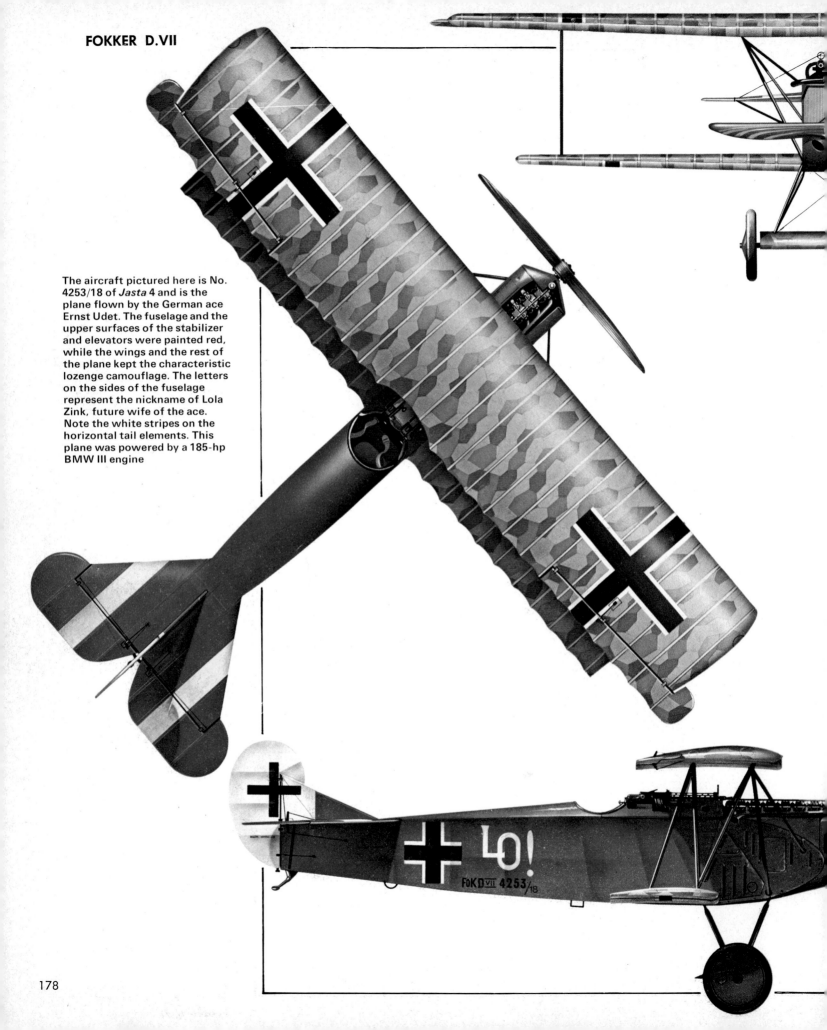

FOKKER D.VII

The aircraft pictured here is No. 4253/18 of *Jasta* 4 and is the plane flown by the German ace Ernst Udet. The fuselage and the upper surfaces of the stabilizer and elevators were painted red, while the wings and the rest of the plane kept the characteristic lozenge camouflage. The letters on the sides of the fuselage represent the nickname of Lola Zink, future wife of the ace. Note the white stripes on the horizontal tail elements. This plane was powered by a 185-hp BMW III engine

178

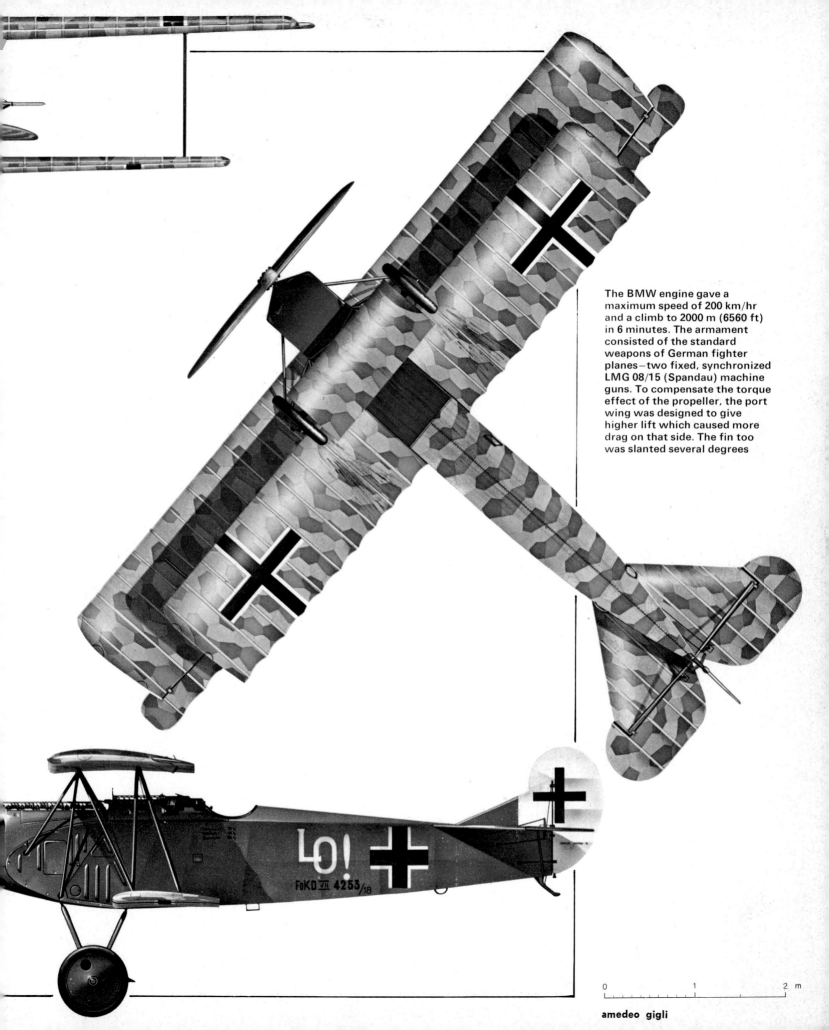

The BMW engine gave a
maximum speed of 200 km/hr
and a climb to 2000 m (6560 ft)
in 6 minutes. The armament
consisted of the standard
weapons of German fighter
planes—two fixed, synchronized
LMG 08/15 (Spandau) machine
guns. To compensate the torque
effect of the propeller, the port
wing was designed to give
higher lift which caused more
drag on that side. The fin too
was slanted several degrees

FoKD VII 4253/18

LO!

0   1   2 m

amedeo gigli

Fokker's hunch paid off. Von Richthofen's original report on the V.11 had been substantially negative, and Fokker invited him to try it again, confiding that over the weekend he had 'improved the controls'. The Red Baron tried the V.11 again and landed to report on it with enthusiasm. His prestige as a fighter pilot was such that his favorable opinion won the day for Platz's design, and it was thenceforth known as the D.VII (D indicated a single-engine single-seat fighter scout of the German Imperial Air Force).

If today greater credit is given to Reinhold Platz as designer of the D.VII, Anthony Fokker's share must not be underestimated. His skill as a test pilot contributed a great deal to the day-to-day development of Platz's design and the building and perfecting of the prototype. The doughty Dutchman also had a talent for dealing with military authorities which the quiet and retiring Platz did not have.

From top to bottom: *A Fokker D VII delivered postwar to the Italians, photographed at the* Centro Sperimentale (*Experimental Center*) *of Montecelio near Rome.* (Archivio Apostolo)
A Fokker D VII piloted by the German ace, Lieut. Kurt Wüsthoff. (Archivio Apostolo)
Fokker D VII of Jasta 53. (Archivio Apostolo)
Fokker D VII in a typically weird livery such as German pilots used in World War I

The fine qualities of the new fighter scout were greeted enthusiastically by other German pilots, who were willing to overlook its relatively poor performance at altitude (the British S.E.5a and the French SPAD XIII had far superior rates of climb). Moreover, the inferiority of the D.VII from that point of view was not to last long, for already during the Adlershof competition Fokker and Platz had foreseen the possibility of installing a more powerful BMW engine. The new power plant was built in the new factory founded by the Triestine financier, Camillo Castiglioni, and it soon enabled the D.VII to show truly exceptional performance.

Technical description

The production D.VII was essentially identical to the V11 prototype, incorporating the improvements made at Adlershof. As in many previous planes, the fuselage was a braced box-girder structure of welded steel tubing, of quadrangular cross-section, with the steel tube diameter gradually decreasing

from nose to tail to lighten the overall structural weight. The traditional Fokker tail construction of welded steel tubing covered with fabric and rigidized by wire bracing remained almost unchanged.

The two wing mainplanes were rectangular, each in a single piece, and of rather thick aerofoil section. Both two-spar wings were of all-wood construction, covered with doped fabric. The trailing edge was of wire, with the characteristic dentellated form. The upper wing was attached by streamlined struts to the fuselage longeron heads and nacelle. The lower wing was designed so that the spars could pass through the fuselage by means of a special cutout in the lower longerons. Upper and lower wing spars were joined by N-struts quite close to the lower wing tips. A false dihedral effect resulted from the fact that the wings tapered in thickness towards the tips; upper surfaces were perfectly flat, and British pilots eventually came to call the D.VII 'old straight wings'. Stabilizer, rudder and ailerons were all balanced and rounded; the ailerons, rather small, were only on the upper wing.

The overall structure of the D.VII was very strong, light and rigid, giving it a decided structural superiority over practically all other World War I fighters. Its toughness pleased the German front-line pilots, and their confidence was well founded: in spite of violent maneuvers in battle, daring nose dives and hits from enemy fire, the D.VII rarely conked out. The Fokker factory was notorious for the carelessness with which it sometimes assembled its aircraft, but Platz's design was such that even the production D.VIIs from the Fokker plant were seldom victims of the accidents which plagued the Dr.1 triplanes and the E.V-D.VIII monoplanes.

The undercarriage Vs were of streamlined steel tubing, and there was an aerofoil lifting surface enclosing the axle, as on the Dr.I triplane. The shock-absorbers were not of the elastic-cord type then generally in use but incorporated spiral springs, a modification imposed by the scarcity of rubber in Germany. The stout ash tail skid was also connected to the fuselage by two spiral springs.

At first the D.VII was powered by the 160-hp 6-cylinder Mercedes D.III in-line engine, but as soon as it became feasible the manufacturers began to install the 185-hp BMW IIIa, which could be boosted to as high as 240 hp for short spurts. This was also a 6-cylinder in-line engine, water-cooled and with a special carburetor. The greater power of the BMW engine enabled the D.VII to return a vastly superior performance to what it could do with the Mercedes. The D.VIIF, as it was known when powered by the BMW, had a maximum speed rating of 200 km/hr and a rate of climb which took it up to 6000 m (20000 ft) in less than 20 minutes.

The automobile-type radiator mounted just behind the two-bladed wooden propeller kept the D.VII from rivaling the Albatros from the esthetic point of view, but its simple, efficient circulation did ensure it against the problems that plagued other aircraft with more complicated cooling systems. Even when trying out other types of engines the position of the radiator remained unchanged, although larger radiators were needed with BMW engines than had been the case with the Mercedes.

The pilot enjoyed fairly good visibility because of the shorter and narrower lower wing and a rather small cutout in the trailing edge of the upper wing above the cockpit. Apparently the shallowness of the cutout inconvenienced the taller pilots.

Instrumentation was meagre, in part because of the small size of the cockpit, and included only a tachometer, fuel pressure gauge, fuel and oil level gauges and compass; an altimeter was fitted only rarely. The metal fuel tank was in the forward section of the fuselage and was divided into three sections—one of 8 liters for oil, a 60-liter main fuel tank and a 30-liter reserve fuel tank. The BMW engine ran on a gasoline-benzene mixture, a recourse dictated by the lack of gasoline and the relative abundance of benzene, a coal-tar distillate.

Controls included pedals, a control stick with grips for both hands, machine gun trigger, ignition, spark advance and starter booster coil. An emergency manual fuel pump was installed on the port side of the cockpit. Armament consisted of a pair of the classic 7·92-mm LMG 08/15 machine guns, with 500 rounds each, fitted with a synchronizer giving a rate of fire of 600 rounds per minute through the propeller.

a slightly longer fuselage, a prominent curving fin (the V.11 had no fin) which was eventually to diminish to the narrow triangular fin characteristic of the D.VII. Production aircraft with Mercedes engines and those with BMW engines (practically indistinguishable except for the difference in power plant) made up the bulk of series D.VIIs. There were, in addition to these, derivative types and experimental variants, among them the V.21, with slightly raked wing tips and a special high-compression-ratio Mercedes engine; in spite of a slightly lower empty weight, its performance was generally lower than that of the D.VII. On the V.22 the wings had been restored to the initial rectangular planform, introducing a slight dihedral to the upper wing. There was a curious four-bladed propeller with the blades set at distances of 60° and 120° (a Jaray-type airscrew, roughly like an **X**). However, this variant did not prove to be appreciably better than the series-production model. The V.24 was a D.VII flown in 1918 with a 240-hp Benz Bz IV engine; although climb rate was considerably improved, overall performance was not satisfactory because the increased engine weight hampered low-speed flight and maneuverability.

Another variant which did not get anywhere was designed by the *Allgemeine Ungarische Maschinenfabrik A.G.* of Budapest. It had a slightly shorter fuselage and a 210-hp Austro-Daimler engine. Fear of an eventual shortage of steel tubing led the Albatros factory, which was building its rival's planes under license at the behest of the government, to build a D.VII with a wooden airframe covered with plywood. In the event no shortages occurred, and only one wooden' D.VII was ever completed.

Top: *Fokker D VII of the Swiss air force in the 1920s*
Center: *This Fokker D VII is equipped with an Austro-Daimler engine; note the lack of the characteristic BMW radiator*
Bottom: *One of the earliest Fokker D VIIs, built by the Ostdeutsche Albatros Werke. Note the unusual fuselage markings.* (Archivio Apostolo)

Development of the Fokker D.VII

The V.11 led to the development of the V.18, a heavier and possibly more rugged second prototype built before the beginning of production, featuring

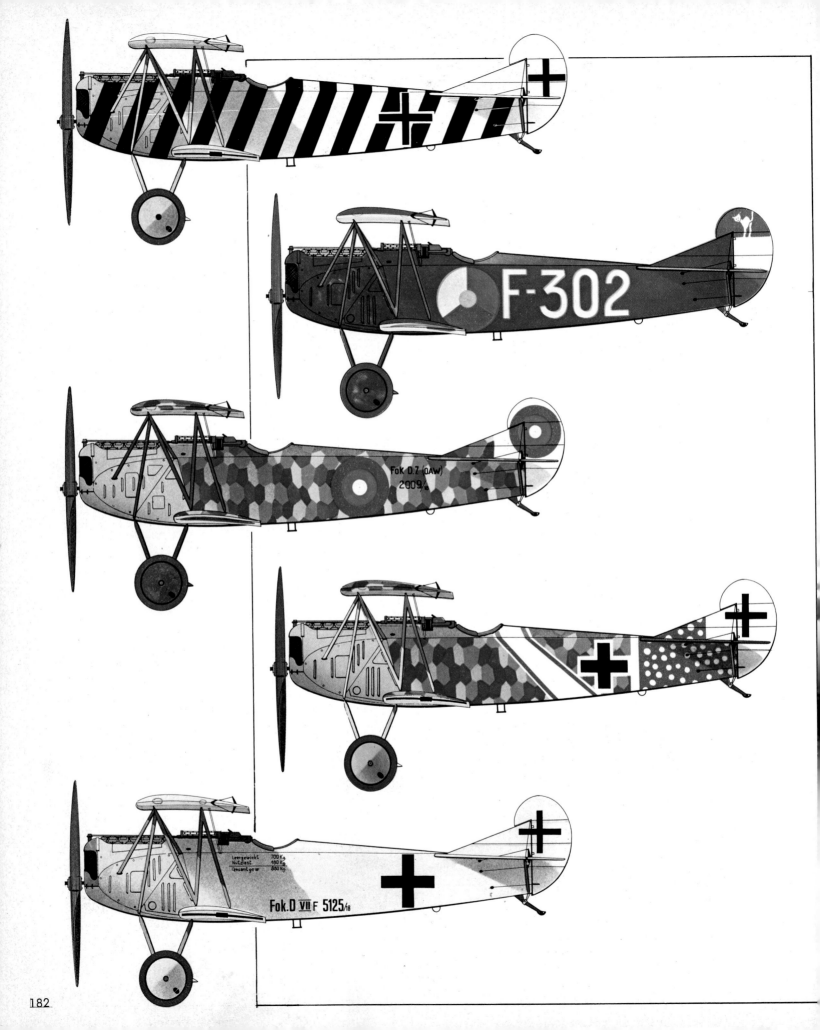

Fok. D.Z (OAW)
2009/18

Leergewicht 700 Kg.
Nutzlast 160 Kg.
Gesamtgew 850 Kg.

Fok.D VII F 5125/18

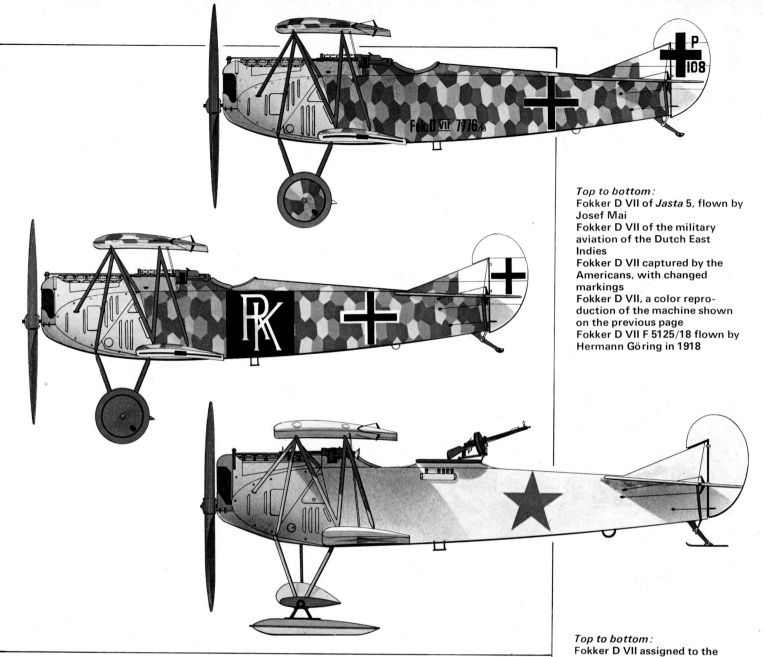

Fok. D VII 7776/18

Top to bottom:
Fokker D VII of *Jasta* 5, flown by Josef Mai
Fokker D VII of the military aviation of the Dutch East Indies
Fokker D VII captured by the Americans, with changed markings
Fokker D VII, a color reproduction of the machine shown on the previous page
Fokker D VII F 5125/18 flown by Hermann Göring in 1918

Top to bottom:
Fokker D VII assigned to the United States by the Armistice Commission
Fokker D VII used in the summer and autumn of 1918
Fokker V38 developed from the D VIII, No. C.1 (two-seat reconnaissance biplane), powered by a 185-hp BMW IIIa engine. Aircraft of this type equipped one of the earliest units of the new Soviet Russian air arm. The D VIII was produced after World War I and used by the Dutch, American, Soviet Russian and Danish air services. The Danes manufactured the machine under license, and used it extensively until 1940

Insignia on D VII used by German police in postwar period

Georg von Hantelmann of *Jasta* 15

Lieut. Windisch, commander of *Jasta* 66

Lieut. O. von Beaulieu-Marconnay, of *Jasta* 19

Personal insignia of a pilot belonging to *Jasta* 74

***Oberleutnant* Rudolph Berthold, commander of *Jasta* 11**

0   1   2 m

roberto terrinoni

An experiment was made with a synchronized 12-mm heavy machine gun in place of the usual 7·92-mm gun to be used against aircraft and armored vehicles, and another with a Siemens machine gun with the interrupter synchronized with the propeller by a small electric motor.

In the summer of 1918 there appeared another two prototypes, the V.34 and V.36. The V.34 differed from the D.VII by having a small trapezoidal rudder in place of the rounded, comma-like control surface which had been a hallmark of so many Fokker models and installed without a vertical fin. The V.36 restored the traditional fin and rudder assembly but differed by having the fuel tank in the axle fairing. One reason for this unusual positioning of the tank was that the advanced development of tracer bullets and incendiaries meant that a single bullet could destroy an aircraft, since burning fuel either finished off the pilot or the fabric of the wings or tail. This undercarriage tank was used on various other Fokker machines but never on the D.VII.

Top: *Detail showing workmen of the Albatros plant assembling a Fokker D VII; the plane has the characteristic lozenge camouflage motif on the fuselage*
Bottom: *Fokker D VIIs were flown by many of the leading German fighter aces. In this photograph, Ernst Udet and his D VII*

The V.35 was simply a conversion of the D.VII into a two-seater by taking advantage of the space freed between pilot and engine by moving the fuel tank to the undercarriage axle fairing. From this variant there was derived the V.38, a liaison and reconnaissance aircraft of greater size and weight than the D.VII; it also was powered by the 185-hp BMW engine, which limited its performance. No military orders were ever proffered for the V.38 because of the Armistice, but some 70 machines of this type were built and crated up, and secretly taken to Holland after the war.

How the Fokker D.VII was used in the War

The first D.VII to reach front-line pilots was delivered in April 1918 to *Jagdgeschwader* 1, which was commanded by Manfred von Richthofen, and soon the several factories ordered to build the new fighter scout under license brought Fokker production up to such a rhythm that a good many other fighter units could be re-equipped with them.

Of the 2000 Fokker D.VIIs ordered, about 1000 were delivered to the *Jagdgeschwader* 1, 2 and 3 which included *Jastas* 2, 4, 6, 10, 11, 12, 13, 15, 19, 26, 27 and 36, plus some 40 separate and independent squadrons.

The firms involved in the production of the D.VII included, besides the Fokker plant itself (which built about 370 of them), the Albatros Werke of Johannisthal and the Ostdeutsche Albatros Werke of Schneidemühl; the AEG of Henningsdorf was to have been added to this list.

In action the D.VII soon proved to be the best plane the Germans had produced and better than most opposing fighters.

A D.VII piloted by Ernst Udet was also the first fighter scout to come off best in an encounter with an armored vehicle. Udet attacked a British tank six times, subjecting it to a concentrated fire and finally forcing it to overturn as it was trying to negotiate a rail bed.

An indication of the respect that the D.VII inspired on the opposing side: before long the Allies were convinced that the German *Jastas* had roughly twice as many of the 'straight wings' as they actually did have. Another tribute can be found in Article IV of the Armistice which detailed that the war materials to be handed over to the Allies should include '. . . *especially* all machines of the Fokker D.VII type . . .' In spite of the great compliment implicit in this condition, German airmen evaded it in various ways—either by gently crashing on landing or by concealing their planes. By bribery and other tricks Anthony Fokker managed to cart off to Holland, where production continued after the Armistice, six train loads of spare parts and raw materials, as well as 400 engines, and about 120 D.VIIs in crates (everything coming from the Schwerin plant, and all of it German military property), thus keeping it from the victorious Allies.

Fokker's talents as a businessman and operator, bolstered by the unquestionable quality of the aircraft, ensured a long postwar career for the D.VII. Belgian, Dutch and Polish airmen flew the Fokker sesquiplane for many years, as did the fledgling air arms of Denmark, Italy, Spain, Sweden, Switzerland and (after 1930) Germany. The splendid climbing ability of the D.VII made it particularly valuable in weather research.

Official records show that after the Armistice the US Army brought not less than 142 Fokker D.VIIs to the States where they were used as advanced fighter-trainers for some time—apart from influencing the American aircraft designers for a dozen years or so (and starring in several Hollywood epics).

SVA

Specifications

	SVA 3	SVA 4	SVA 5	SVA 9	SVA 10	SVA 10
Power plant	SPA 6A 220 hp	SPA 6A 220 hp	I.F.V.6 270 hp	SPA 6A 200 hp	SPA 6A 200 hp	I.F.* 200 hp
Wing span, *m*	7·75	9·18	9·18	9·18	9·18	9·24
Length, *m*	8·13	8·13	8·13	8·13	8·13	8·18
Height, *m*	2·65	2·65	2·80	2·65	2·65	2·65
Wing area, *m²*	22	26·90	26·90	26·90	26·90	27
Weight, empty, *kg*	665	700	665	690	730	894
All-up weight, *kg*	890	975	975	990	1036	1294
Maximum speed, *km/hr*	220	220	238	220	210	215
Climb to 3000 *m, min-sec*	11:00	10:00	8:00	14:00	11:00	15:00
Climb to 4000 *m, min-sec*	—	16:15	14:00	36:00	23:50	—
Flight endurance, *hrs*	3–4	4	3–4	3–4	3–5	4:15
Ceiling, *m*	5000	5000	7000	4500	5500	5800

* Isotta-Fraschini

Top: *One of the first long-distance flights featured this SVA (left), piloted by Mario Stoppani, who flew from Turin to Udine and back.* (Museo Caproni, Taliedo)
Bottom: *SVA 6575, the first of the SVAs to be delivered to the 91a Squadriglia, on August 21, 1917, by the test pilot Guidi.* (Museo Caproni, Taliedo)

The series of SVA (Savoia-Verduzio-Ansaldo) aircraft marks a milestone in the development of Italian aeronautical engineering, with the passage from the empirical phase to calculations based on precise scientific criteria of the aerodynamic and structural characteristics of the final product. With the SVA it became possible for Italian designers to work out on paper the eventual qualities of their aircraft before actually building the prototype. And through their work on the SVAs, Italian aeronautical engineers began to catch up with the more advanced technologies of France, England and Germany.

Some critics have argued that the SVA never completely fulfilled the design objectives, since as a fighter plane it was in fact defective and inferior to the SPAD. However, its performance as a bomber and reconnaissance aircraft was above reproach and called forth the reluctant admiration of the enemy. A final seal of the SVA's efficiency is provided by the simple fact that it remained in active service from 1917 until 1935.

In 1916 aircraft design was controlled essentially by the *Direzione Tecnica dell'Aviazione Mili-*

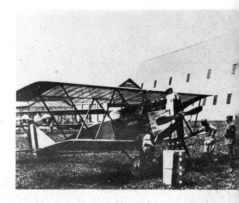

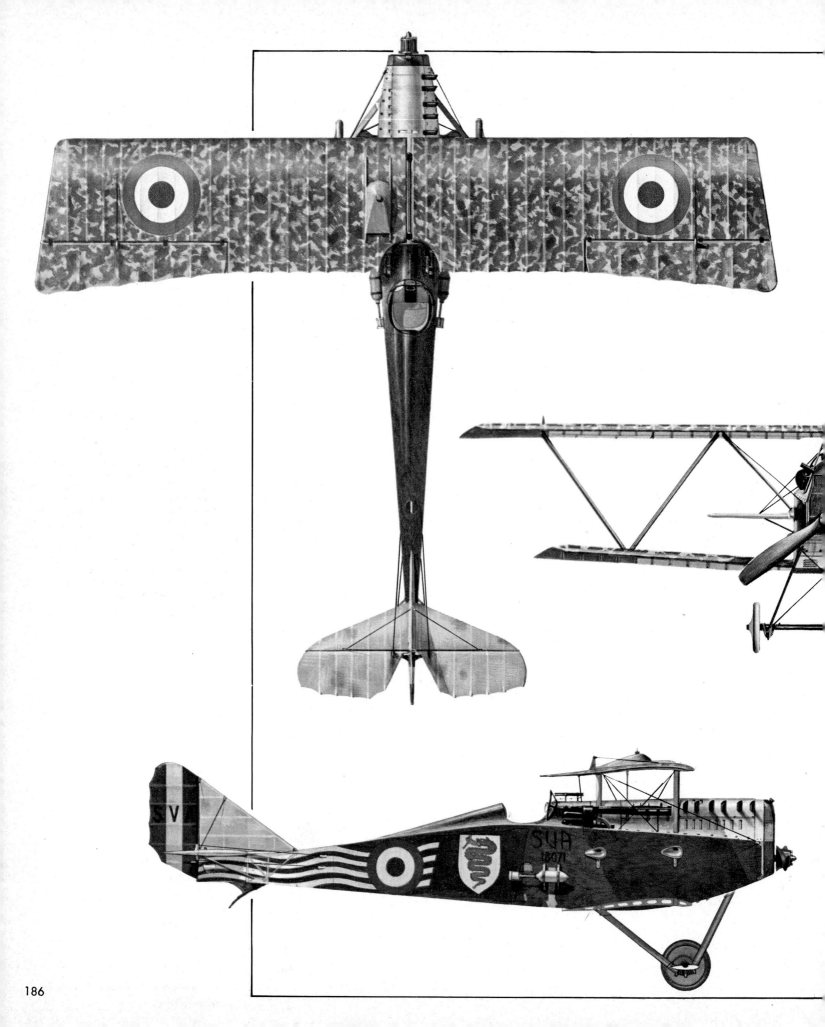

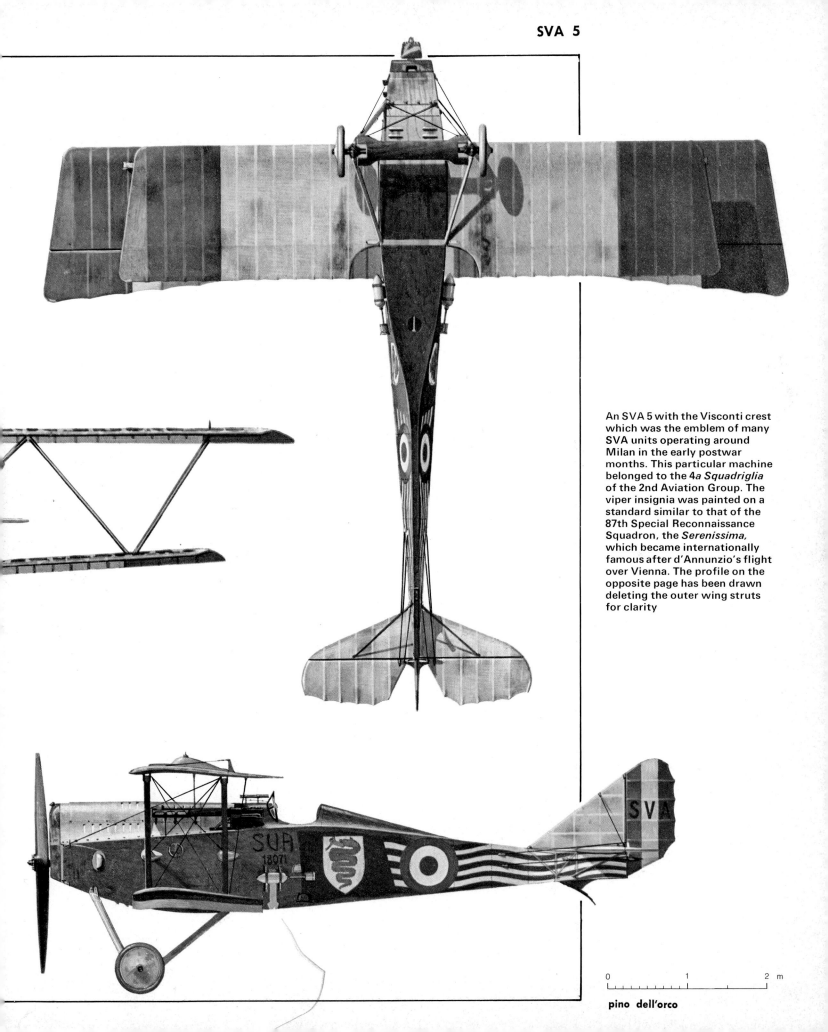

An SVA 5 with the Visconti crest which was the emblem of many SVA units operating around Milan in the early postwar months. This particular machine belonged to the 4a *Squadriglia* of the 2nd Aviation Group. The viper insignia was painted on a standard similar to that of the 87th Special Reconnaissance Squadron, the *Serenissima,* which became internationally famous after d'Annunzio's flight over Vienna. The profile on the opposite page has been drawn deleting the outer wing struts for clarity

pino dell'orco

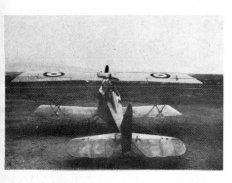

Top left: *The SVA 3 was essentially the same as the SVA 4 but with a reduced span (7·75 m instead of 9·18 m), a modification intended to improve maneuverability.* (Archivio Bignozzi)
Center: *One of the earliest SVAs; note the absence of the circular cutout at the center section of the upper wing, added later for improved upward visibility.* (Archivio Apostolo)
Top right: *The SVA 10, a two-seat reconnaissance biplane which continued the general single-seat design. It was armed with a Lewis machine gun.* (Archivio Apostolo)
Bottom: *SVAs of the Italian* Prima Sezione *(First Section), a unit which carried out many reconnaissance sorties over the Istrian coast.* (Aeronautica Militare Italiana)

tare (Air Force Engineering Command), a body which included the best technical talents of the day. In 1915 the Italians had built a series of biplanes, the Savoia-Pomilio, which were far from brilliant in their performance; after this experience, the DTAM recognized the need for designing a new aircraft based on sound structural and aerodynamic principles.

Such research was carried out in the summer of 1916 by Umberto Savoia and Rodolfo Verduzio, assisted by Celestino Rosatelli. All structural details were carefully calculated, and when the design was complete it was turned over to the Ansaldo Corp. of Genoa.

In December 1916 Ansaldo began building the prototype, which differed from the blueprints in its improved tail structure and the adoption of a single front radiator, similar to an automobile radiator, instead of two radiators mounted between fuselage and upper wing, as in the original design. In spite of the many initial difficulties, the 200 workmen at the Ansaldo plant at Borzoli Mare were able to complete the prototype by March 1917, to a great extent through the work of an engineer named Brezzi, a particularly energetic man who was also the director of the Ansaldo plant.

The first SVA was transferred from Borzoli to an airfield at Grosseto, where it was test-flown by Sgt. Mario Stoppani on March 19, 1917. In the following weeks the SVA was put through a series of rigorous tests and certain defects were corrected while the testing staff awaited the arrival of other machines from the Ansaldo factories at Borzoli and Bolzaneto.

During the summer the first batch of SVAs was tested by military pilots, who found them wanting in maneuverability but in compensation found them capable of higher speeds than they had been able to achieve with the Hanriot HD.1 and SPAD VII fighters. Similar results were reported from the front, where the SVA had met the slower but more agile enemy planes. The decision was quietly made to assign the SVA to missions where its virtues could

be used to the best advantage and its defects became less critical and so it became a reconnaissance aircraft and bomber, in the modest 1917 sense of the word.

Technical description

The SVA was a biplane, originally a single-seater with a two-bladed tractor propeller, and with the whole airframe built entirely of wood. From the very beginning the SVA had a characteristic appearance, due to the use of a series of diagonal interwing struts and the nearly total lack of wire bracing. The wings were of double-spar construction, extraordinarily thin (and intentionally so, to maximize efficiency while minimizing drag). Another identifying characteristic was the flared upper wings. Both mainplanes were covered with fabric, either linen or silk, and the struts were of streamlined steel tubing. One detail which distinguished the first SVAs from those built later was the presence on the latter of rounded cutouts in the trailing edge of the two wings, above the cockpit and at the wing roots, to improve visibility upwards and on landing. Only the upper wing had ailerons. The tail structure was similarly of wood and fabric, with a variable-incidence stabilizer which could be set on the ground according to the load carried. Some SVAs had tailplanes of tubular steel structure.

The fuselage was of curious construction, of a rectangular cross section ahead of the wings and a triangular cross section aft of the cockpit. This design improved downward visibility in flight. The fuselage, a truss structure covered with plywood, was especially sturdy, and the design had been carefully worked out in an effort to achieve optimal aerodynamics.

The pilot's cockpit was roomy and comfortable, and its instrumentation normally included a tachometer, an oil pressure gauge, a fuel gauge, a magneto selector, a choke and fuel mixture control.

The undercarriage was a simple structure of metal tubing bolted directly to the fuselage longerons. The tail skid consisted of a metal spring section.

Except for one version (the SVA 10, which was powered by an Isotta-Fraschini V.6 engine), all SVA models had the reliable and efficient 6-cylinder SPA 6A in-line, a water-cooled power plant developing 205 hp at 1600 rpm (220 hp) on later models. The juncture between engine and fuselage was perfectly faired above and below: the surface of the aluminum cowling was broken only by the six exhaust pipes on the starboard side.

Normal armament consisted of two Vickers machine guns (or sometimes only a single gun mounted on the port side of the engine cowling), synchronized to fire through the propeller.

Two photo-reconnaissance cameras could be mounted behind the engine, immediately aft of the fuel tank.

Development of the SVA Scouts

It was apparent from the very beginning that the SVA was a promising operational aircraft within the limits described above. Its development followed two separate paths once the SVA had entered the production phase and as alternate versions were considered experimentally.

In September 1917 the Ansaldo firm had absorbed the SIT *(Società Italiana Transaerea* of Turin), providing a third plant working on the new aircraft by the spring of 1918. At the same time the Ministry of War invited other firms to participate in the SVA production—Savoia at Bosisio, AER at Orbassano, Moncenisio at Condove —to fulfil a total order for more than 1000 machines.

Until the spring of 1918 the SVA was produced in two basic versions: the SVA 4, a direct descendant of the prototype, equipped with photo-reconnaissance cameras and carrying sufficient fuel for four hours' flying time; and the SVA 5, which was the version produced in largest numbers. The SVA 5 was also armed, and had a flight ensurance of six hours.

The SVA 3 was practically identical with the SVA 4, except for its wing span, reduced from 9·18 to 7·75 m to increase maneuverability. The few SVA 3s produced were used together with 4s and 5s.

At the request of the Royal Italian Navy and in collaboration with Col. Guidoni, the Ansaldo Co. evolved a seaplane version of the SVA 4 (designated ISVA) which had tubular floats with special flaps to assist in take-off. Tests were satisfactory, but the aircraft was hard to fly and, especially, to land. Despite this, 50 ISVA floatplanes were built.

A two-seater version, much more successful, widened the SVA's operational scope. In preparation for the new versions a number of interesting events had been organized in the late summer, fall and winter of 1917. The first was an 110-km (684-mile) flight, Turin-Udine-Turin, flown by Stoppani in 5 hours. The second event was a 600-km (373-mile) flight, Turin-Rome, in 2 hrs 50 min. In both flights the average speed was 220 km/hr (136·7 mph), an extraordinary achievement for the time. Maj. Lombard also made an impressive 580-km (360-mile) flight from Milan to Foggia.

Designs for the SVA 9 and 10 were prepared at Borzoli towards the end of 1917, and testing of the prototypes began in April-May 1918. These two-seaters kept most of the features of the single-seat version except for substantial changes in the fuselage. The SVA 9, designed as a training plane,

had dual controls, no armament and a smaller fuel tank. The SVA 10 was designed as a photo-reconnaissance aircraft, with the observer behind the pilot. The aircraft was armed with a flexible Lewis machine gun in the rear cockpit. Some SVA 10s were also equipped with a radio transceiver for communications with the base. The SVA 9 and SVA 10 had the same range. Initial production concentrated on the SVA 9, which was in fairly wide use in various training commands by the summer of 1918.

A boosted version of the SVA 5 was also built in 1918, powered by a 250-hp Isotta-Fraschini V.6 engine. With this engine the SVA 5 could achieve 235 km/hr (146 mph), and returned an excellent overall flight performance with outstanding climbing capability.

Another experimental engine tried out in the spring and summer of 1918 was the 220-hp Lorraine-Dietrich. Several machines fitted with this engine were built, but the Lorraine-Dietrich version did not go beyond the prototype.

How the SVA was used in the War

On February 28, 1918, four SVAs from the *Prima Sezione* (First Section) of the Italian air arm, consisting of three aircraft carrying a pair of 25-kg (55-lb) bombs each and one machine with reduced wing span equipped with vertical aerial photographic cameras took off from the airfield of Ponte San Pietro. The pilots were Capts. Palli and Palma di Cesnola, Lieut. Orsini and Sgt. Arrigoni. After a 250-km (155-mile) flight over the Alps they reached Innsbruck in Austria, where they dropped their bombs and shot up the railroad marshaling yards. After three hours' flight they were back at their base.

This bombing of Innsbruck, the first successful such action of any appreciable importance, clinched the reputation of the SVA with Italian pilots, and soon each of the six army commands had its own 'Sezione SVA' (SVA group). In addition to these, there had also been activated early in 1918 a special squadron, the 87a *Squadriglia,* under the High Command.

This strategic reconnaissance unit flexed its muscles with a series of flights along the Alpine valleys known as Val di Non, Val d'Adige, Passo della Mendola and Valsugana, then on May 21 1918 it carried out its first long-range mission. Two SVAs piloted by Arturo Ferrarin and Antonio Locatelli penetrated to Lake Constance on the Swiss-German-Austrian border, where they photographed the important industrial center of Friedrichshafen.

Other important missions were carried out by the 1a *Squadriglia* as well as the 97a *Squadriglia,* which was renamed the *'Serenissima'* and had the St. Mark's crest of Venice *('la Serenissima Repubblica')* as its emblem. Natale Palli, flying with the 1st SVA Section, made many solo flights over the towns of the Istrian Peninsula and along the Dalmatian coast, sometimes ranging as far as

Top to bottom:
Several SVA 4s were converted into seaplanes, and 50 machines, equipped with cylindrical floats, were ordered. (Aeronautica Militare Italiana)
Another SVA equipped with floats of a different design from those usually found on the seaplane version. (Fototeca Storica Nazionale)
An SVA operated by the Soviets. This photograph was taken in 1924. (Archivio Bignozzi)
An SVA 4 at the front. Note that the starboard machine gun has been removed to accommodate photo-reconnaissance cameras. (Aeronautica Militare Italiana)

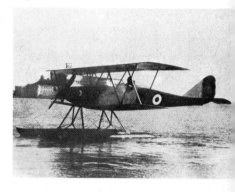

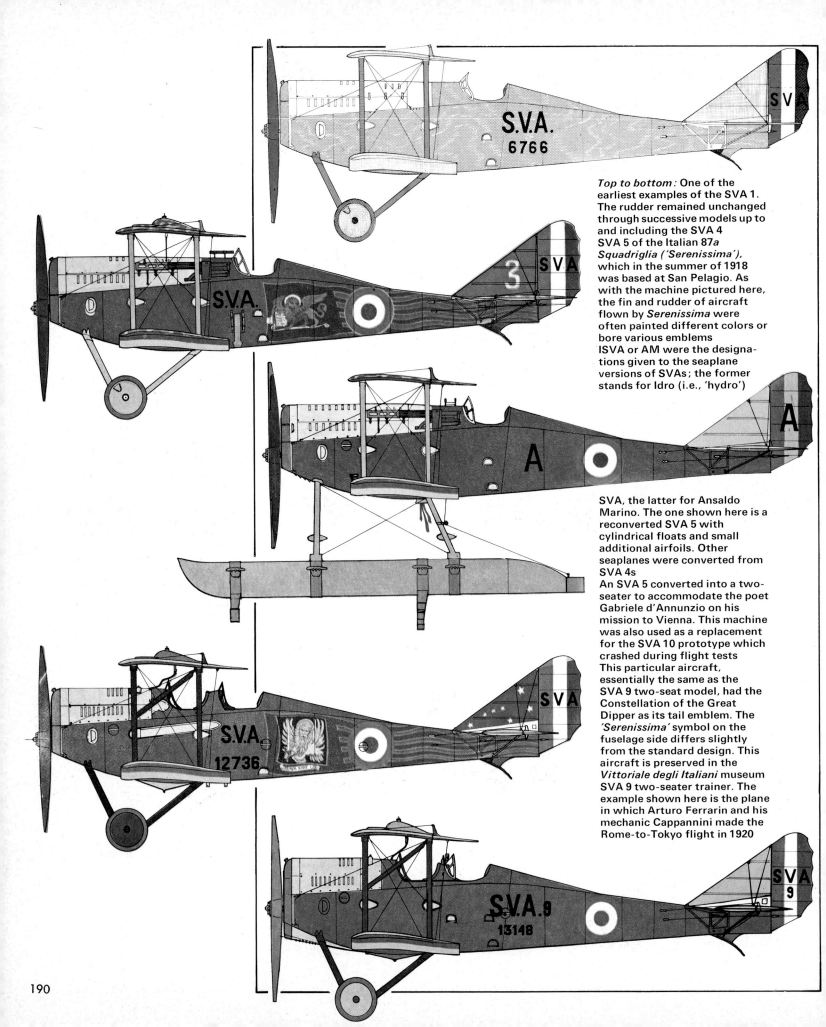

Top to bottom: One of the earliest examples of the SVA 1. The rudder remained unchanged through successive models up to and including the SVA 4

SVA 5 of the Italian 87*a* *Squadriglia* ('*Serenissima*'), which in the summer of 1918 was based at San Pelagio. As with the machine pictured here, the fin and rudder of aircraft flown by *Serenissima* were often painted different colors or bore various emblems

ISVA or AM were the designations given to the seaplane versions of SVAs; the former stands for Idro (i.e., 'hydro') SVA, the latter for Ansaldo Marino. The one shown here is a reconverted SVA 5 with cylindrical floats and small additional airfoils. Other seaplanes were converted from SVA 4s

An SVA 5 converted into a two-seater to accommodate the poet Gabriele d'Annunzio on his mission to Vienna. This machine was also used as a replacement for the SVA 10 prototype which crashed during flight tests This particular aircraft, essentially the same as the SVA 9 two-seat model, had the Constellation of the Great Dipper as its tail emblem. The '*Serenissima*' symbol on the fuselage side differs slightly from the standard design. This aircraft is preserved in the *Vittoriale degli Italiani* museum

SVA 9 two-seater trainer. The example shown here is the plane in which Arturo Ferrarin and his mechanic Cappannini made the Rome-to-Tokyo flight in 1920

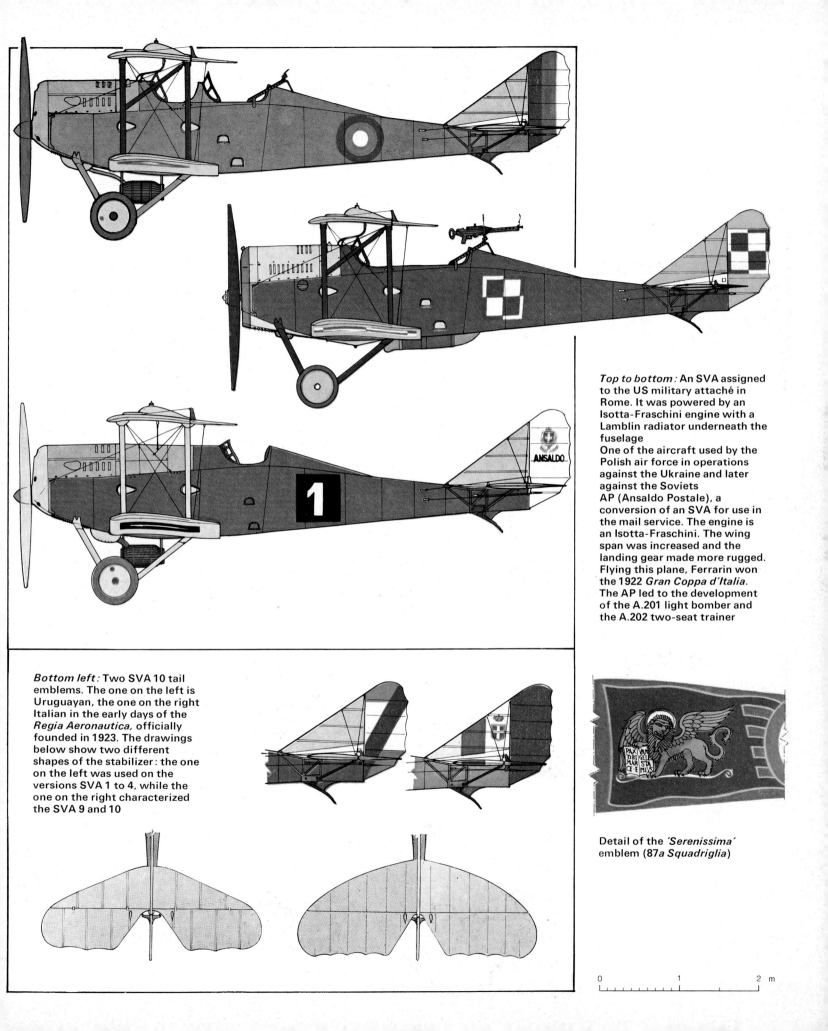

Top to bottom: An SVA assigned to the US military attaché in Rome. It was powered by an Isotta-Fraschini engine with a Lamblin radiator underneath the fuselage

One of the aircraft used by the Polish air force in operations against the Ukraine and later against the Soviets

AP (Ansaldo Postale), a conversion of an SVA for use in the mail service. The engine is an Isotta-Fraschini. The wing span was increased and the landing gear made more rugged. Flying this plane, Ferrarin won the 1922 *Gran Coppa d'Italia*. The AP led to the development of the A.201 light bomber and the A.202 two-seat trainer

Bottom left: Two SVA 10 tail emblems. The one on the left is Uruguayan, the one on the right Italian in the early days of the *Regia Aeronautica*, officially founded in 1923. The drawings below show two different shapes of the stabilizer: the one on the left was used on the versions SVA 1 to 4, while the one on the right characterized the SVA 9 and 10

Detail of the *'Serenissima'* emblem (87a *Squadriglia*)

0   1   2 m

From top to bottom:
Aircraft of the 87a Squadriglia ('Serenissima') which received worldwide attention for its 1918 flight over Vienna. It was based at San Pelagio airfield
Two photographs of SVA 5s taken at San Pelagio in the summer of 1918. (Aeronautica Militare Italiana)
An SVA 9 two-seater as used shortly after the end of the war for postal service. This photograph was taken at Centocelle in 1919. (Aeronautica Militare Italiana)
Bottom right: *SVAs of the 56a Squadriglia at the Mirafiori airport in 1923.* (Aeronautica Militare Italiana)

500 km (310 miles) from his base. The 87*a Squadriglia* often flew in formation as an escort to Caproni bombers, and among the most impressive of these sorties was the historical bombing of the military installations at Pola.

The international fame of the SVAs was established, however, in the famous 'Vienna Raid' dreamed up by Gabriele d'Annunzio, a rather extravagant poet of the time who fancied himself a warrior. He had wanted to have 'his' raid flown by Caproni trimotor bombers, but the scheme was opposed by the Italian High Command, since to use such heavy aircraft would mean exposing valuable crews to unnecessary dangers. At the same time, using the SVA two-seaters would have complicated the whole scheme beyond the point of minimum feasibility.

However, when d'Annunzio got to know what the SVA 5 was capable of performance-wise he began to plan his exploit around these biplanes. The big problem was to give two-seaters of the SVA 5 variety a flight endurance of 7 hours, the time necessary to get to Vienna and back. Ansaldo got interested in the problem and solved it by equipping an SVA 9 with a special fuel tank holding 300 liters (66 imperial gallons), enough to get the poet to his dream objective and home.

Eleven modified SVAs set out on the morning of August 9, 1918, from the airfield at San Pelagio. Eight of these arrived at the target, piloted by Palli, Locatelli, Massoni, Allegri, Censi, Sarti, Granzarolo and Finzi, with d'Annunzio riding along with Palli. Sarti was forced to make an emergency landing in enemy territory, while the others went on to take reconnaissance photographs of Vienna and to toss out propaganda leaflets which d'Annunzio had written in his customary high-flown prose.

This flight, which seems only picturesque today, had an extraordinary psychological effect on the enemy. Apart from that by showing what they could do, the SVAs had marked a milestone in the development of military aviation which impressed both Allies and the enemy.

In the autumn of 1918 operational use of the SVAs was increased, and new squadrons were added to the Italian air arm: the 56th, 57th and 84th Reconnaissance and Bombing Squadrons and two *sezioni* equipped with SVA two-seaters. At the same time, other SVAs were being flown by pilots of the 111*a* and 116*a Squadriglie* in Macedonia and Albania.

The Italian Navy, which had acquired seaplane versions of the SVA (ISVA), based them at Venice, Varano, Brindisi, Valona, Civitavecchia, Taranto and Bolsena, and used these machines as escorts to their ships and for long-range reconnaissance. This navy group later became known as the 'Squadriglia San Marco' (St. Mark's Squadron), named after the patron saint of Venice. The Navy was also the only branch of the Italian military service to use SVA fighters, basing some at Brindisi and La Spezia as port defense and others at Jesi, Ferrara and Grottaglie to protect dirigible hangars. Other SVAs were assigned to the 193*a Squadriglia Mista* ('Mixed Squadron') at S. Vito dei Normanni and at Valona. All of these units participated in the intense campaign of reconnaissance and bombing which was carried out in the autumn of 1918, against enemy troop concentrations and supply routes to the front.

In these late campaigns, Italy lost some of her most famous pilots: Locatelli, forced down in enemy territory and captured; Allegri, killed in a collision with Lieut. Vianini; Contratti, shot down in a dogfight with four Austrian fighter planes. During the decisive Battle of Vittorio Veneto the SVA squadrons took an active part in the action, especially in the strafing of enemy ground troops and installations.

At the time of Armistice (November 4, 1918, in Italy) there were several hundred SVAs in service, and new ones were arriving from the factories at the rate of about 250 per month. By the end of 1918 a total of 1200 SVAs and 50 ISVAs, the seaplane version, had been built. In the winter following the war production was reduced to a few machines built at *Cantiere* (Plant) No. 5. All of these planes took part in the postwar development of the SVA concept.

SVAs took part in many civilian air races and other events in the postwar period, and some Italian feats merited the attention of other nations: Locatelli piloted his SVA over the Andes, while Ferrarin and Cappannini flew from Rome to Tokyo, a distance of 18000 km (11000 miles).

These feats were good for public relations, and soon SVAs had been sold to Argentina, Brazil, France, Lithuania, Latvia, Holland, Peru, Poland, the Soviet Union, Spain and the United States.

When production of SVAs was terminated in 1928, a total of 2000 had been built. The final version was the SVA 10. These aircraft were active until 1929 in police work, and along mail routes and general communications in Africa, where they were successful although they had not been designed with tropical conditions in mind.

ZEPPELIN STAAKEN R.III,VI,XIV,L

The VGO I in its original form, with four tail fins and tapered nacelles

Specifications

	R.III	R.VI	R.XIV	L
Power plant	Mercedes 6×160 hp	Maybach 4×245 hp	Maybach 5×245 hp	Mercedes 4×260 hp
Wing span, *m*	42·20	42·20	42·20	42·20
Length, *m*	24·50	22·10	22·50	22·20
Height, *m*	6·80	6·30	6·30	7·38
Weight, empty, *kg*	8600	7920	10350	8400
Total weight, *kg*	11600	11850	14450	11800
Total wing area, *m²*	332	332	334	360
Maximum speed, *km/hr*	120	135	130	125
Climb to 2000 *m, min-sec*	29:00	—	—	58:00
Climb to 3000 *m, min-sec*	—	43:00	70:00	—
Ceiling, *m*	3000	4320	3700	2500
Range, *km*	—	—	1300*	—
Flight endurance, *hrs-min*	6:00	7 to 10:00	—	10:00

*With 1000 kg of bombs

Count Ferdinand von Zeppelin gave his name not only to the huge, efficient airships familiar to everyone but also to the most successful among the very large aircraft of World War I. Indeed they were the only *Riesenflugzeuge* (giant aircraft) which were capable of operating over England with little chance of their being downed by anti-aircraft fire.

For the origin of these huge airplanes we must go back to a project for a six-engined seaplane which the German aeronautical pioneer Helmuth Hirth designed as his entry in the contest sponsored in 1913 by the London *Daily Mail*. The prize was £10000 for the first air crossing of the Atlantic. The Bosch firm financed Hirth's project, but the beginning of the war naturally also meant an end of the whole contest idea. Count Zeppelin, however, thought that Hirth's design had the poten-

tial leading to the development of long-range bombers. As a result a corporation was set up by Robert Bosch and Gustav Klein, Director of the Bosch factories, called the VGO (*Versuchsbau GmbH Gotha-Ost*—Gotha East Experimental Constructions). The chief designer was Alexander Baumann, assisted by a group of fine technicians, among them a pioneer in the field of metal constructions, Adolph Rohrbach. Claudius Dornier also joined the team, at first doing some experimental work on large metal aircraft (particularly seaplanes) in a hangar near Lake Constance. In rented offices at Gotha-Ost the construction of the first large aircraft with a wooden airframe started in September 1914, one month before Siemens-Schuckert began their parallel development and before the military authorities had even approved the project. This lack of military approval eventually caused various disagreements and delays, and the first flight of the VGO.I took place only on April 11, 1915.

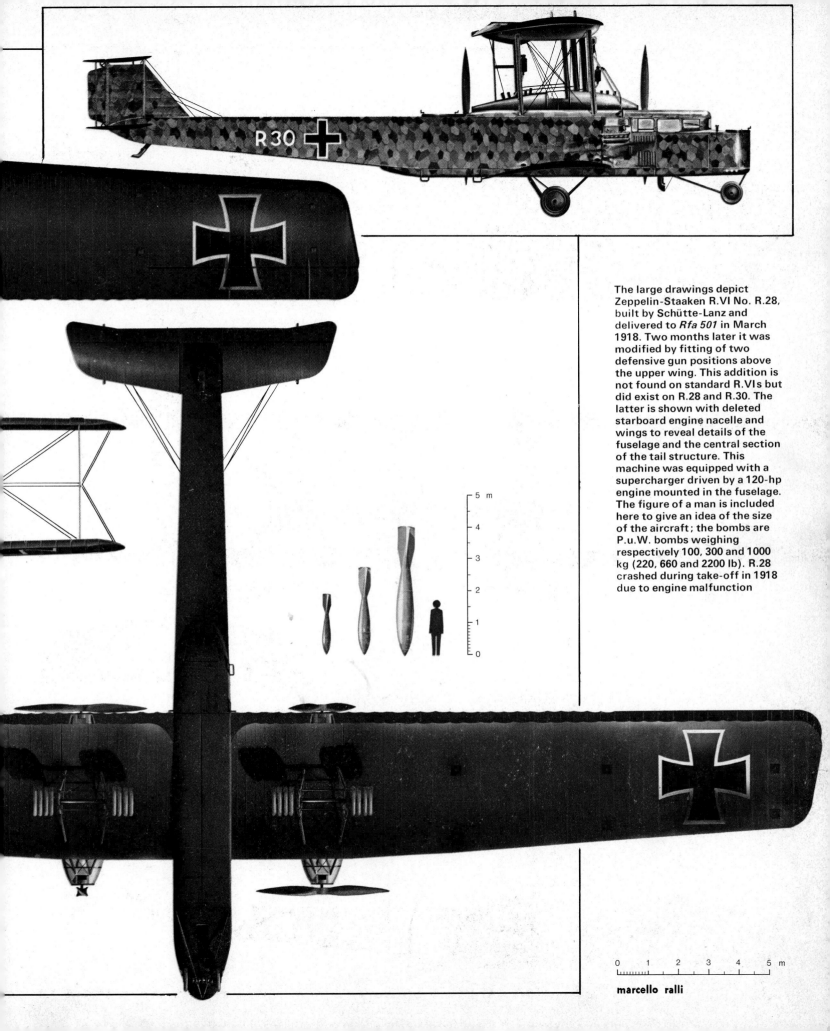

The large drawings depict Zeppelin-Staaken R.VI No. R.28, built by Schütte-Lanz and delivered to *Rfa 501* in March 1918. Two months later it was modified by fitting of two defensive gun positions above the upper wing. This addition is not found on standard R.VIs but did exist on R.28 and R.30. The latter is shown with deleted starboard engine nacelle and wings to reveal details of the fuselage and the central section of the tail structure. This machine was equipped with a supercharger driven by a 120-hp engine mounted in the fuselage. The figure of a man is included here to give an idea of the size of the aircraft; the bombs are P.u.W. bombs weighing respectively 100, 300 and 1000 kg (220, 660 and 2200 lb). R.28 crashed during take-off in 1918 due to engine malfunction

5 m
4
3
2
1
0

0 1 2 3 4 5 m

marcello ralli

The VGO.I above had been rebuilt after an accident. It now has only two fins of slightly larger area, and machine guns have been fitted on the nacelles
Above, right: An R.IV which survived the hazards of war. It is shown here at Kassel in April 1919, with the post-1918 form of cross visible on the tail structure
Bottom: The command cockpit photographed in flight from the gun position of the upper wing center section

Technical description

The Giants were rather orthodox in basic design in so far as the external appearance was concerned, but when one has a closer look at these products of the factory at Staaken, the Berlin suburb which succeeded Gotha-Ost as the manufacturing plant, it is immediately apparent that they involved a level of technical know-how which today seems surprising.

One of the basic criteria at Staaken was that for aircraft of the R class the engines should be generally accessible for minor repairs in flight. Engines were invariably mounted in groups of at most two, a different scheme from that used in the original Hirth project for a trans-Atlantic seaplane, where the designer planned on mounting all six engines in an 'engine room' in the hull and to drive the propellers via transmission gears. On the large bombers the engines varied from three in the VGO.I and II to four in the R.VI, R.XVI and seaplane versions, to five in the R.V, VII, XIV, XV and finally to six in the VGO.III and the R.IV. Only in the four-engine models were the propellers driven by a single engine (the engines were mounted in tandem pairs). On the other versions the lateral nacelles each contained two engines working in tandem to drive a single propeller, which, except in the case of the R.V, was of the pusher type. On the R.V the arrangement of the side engines was identical to that in the R.VI, with the addition of a centrally mounted engine in the nose of the fuselage, as in normal aircraft. On the R.III (which was originally the VGO.III) the tractor propeller was driven by a side-by-side pair of engines. On two aircraft of the R.VI series a fifth engine had been added mounted in the fuselage, and used to drive a supercharger to feed the propulsion engines at higher altitudes.

Airframes were basically of wooden construction. The fuselage was normally a fabric-covered, braced box-girder structure of quadrangular section. The upper longerons were of spruce, the lower of ash, with bracing elements of steel tubing, and diagonal braces for the center and forward sections. The nose section was covered with plywood, while the rest was fabric-covered.

The extraordinarily long-span wings were of normal construction, with ash main spars for the upper and spruce for the lower. The wing ribs were of spruce with steel-tubing compression elements between the spars at the junction of each of the eight pairs of interplane struts. The two wings were of equal span, wing area and planform, with a slight taper of the leading edges. There was a very slight negative stagger, that is, the upper wing was mounted slightly behind the lower. The outer sections of the lower wing had a slight dihedral. Ailerons were fitted only on the upper wing and were unbalanced except on the three R.VIs built by Aviatik, on the R.30 of this series and on the R.XIV and R.XV. The ailerons were of tubular steel frame covered with fabric. The stabilizers were two fixed planes set at a 6° angle of incidence variable on the ground; the stabilizer frames were of spruce. The elevators and rudders consisted of fabric-covered duralumin frames. On the R.XIVa the elevators were shaped as aerofoils.

The undercarriage was composed of eight wheels on either side (reduced to four on some R.VIs), in groups of four. On the earliest machines and in all with a nose propeller, a third set of two wheels, mounted like what today would be called a nose landing gear, served for taxi-ing and on-the-ground support. On the R.VI and subsequent versions this nose fixture served only as protection against nosing over. On the seaplanes the wheels were replaced by two enormous floats measuring about 13 m (43 ft) in length. The crews of these bombers were quite large and usually consisted of a pilot and co-pilot, navigator, wireless operator, two or three flight mechanics, a fuel control hand and sometimes, but rarely, one or two gunners. The actual number varied depending on the particular mission, but normally there were a total of seven aircrew.

Instrumentation was particularly extensive and sophisticated for the time: in addition to all normal flight instruments these Giants were also equipped with the Bamberg repeater compass, gyroscopic artificial horizon (initially the Anschütz type, from 1917 on the Drexler), pilot-mechanic intercom unit, a powerful wireless for a primitive form of directional navigation (used because of the lack of trained astro-navigators), and finally an efficient electrical bomb release system, developed by Oskar Wilke.

The bomb load was carried inside the center section of the fuselage, beneath the fuel tanks. On the R.VI it included as many as 18×100-kg (220-lb) bombs in three rows of six each. Bombs of 300-kg (660 lb) or more protruded slightly from the hold. Normally the bomb load was between 1000 and 1200 kg (2200 and 2640 lb), but on short-range missions it might be as much as 2 metric tons while on very long range missions it would decrease proportionately. For example, on a mission of 900 km requiring 3200 liters of fuel, the bomb load was reduced to 750 kg.

Standard defensive armament for R aircraft had been set at three machine guns, as often as possible captured Lewis guns being preferred by the German airmen. On Staaken aircraft the number of guns was usually greater, sometimes running to seven weapons. Of such a battery, two might be mounted in a dorsal defensive position, four others at the opposite ends of the nacelles from the propellers or concealed in the upper wing sections, and another one mounted on the floor of the fuselage, behind a clever two-jawed hatch, for vertical defense. On the R.VI and the seaplanes the available nose space permitted mounting a frontal defense machine gun, while on the R.V, to protect the nose section, a supplementary gun position, known as the *Schwalbennest* or 'swallow's nest', was installed in the center section of the upper wing leading edge. In 1915 20-mm cannon had been experimentally mounted on the Gotha G.I, and the Staaken engineers planned to use them on their new machines, but so far as is known this plan was never realized.

Development of the Zeppelin Staaken Planes

The VGO.I was powered by three 240-hp Maybach HS engines, cooled by three pairs of Hägele und Zweigle radiators and fueled from fuselage tanks, in the case of the central engine, and nacelle tanks for the beam engines. Difficulties in tuning up the powerful engines (which had been used on dirigibles but under far less demanding conditions than on the giant planes) delayed delivery of the aircraft ordered by the naval aviation authorities. During the delay an accident led to the original version being rebuilt with certain improvements. Another accident in September 1916 again made it necessary to rebuild the aircraft, and for a second time an improved version resulted, this time powered

by five 245-hp Maybach Mb.IVa engines with a supercharger; this solved the principal problem, which was that of inadequate power. The VGO.II, essentially the same machine, was powered by three Maybach HS engines. It was first test-flown on October 25, 1915.

In the same month work was begun on the VGO.III, in which the engine horsepower was increased to 960 (as compared to 720 hp of its predecessors) supplied by six engines consisting of three pairs of the reliable 160-hp Mercedes D.IIIs. An attempt was made to mount a light Becker cannon in a dorsal position, but the effect of the recoil on the airframe was such as to discourage use of this weapon. When the classification R was introduced, the VGO.III, armed with five machine guns, became the R.I.

When the production plant was transferred to Staaken, the official name of the firm was changed to *Flugzeugwerke Staaken*. The last Giant built at the Gotha East works was probably the R.IV, which was flown for the first time on August 16, 1915. It was similar to its predecessor except that the beam engines were replaced with the 220-hp Benz Bz.IVs. Combined horsepower was thus raised to 1200, which made the new version very promising indeed. The R.IV was the only Giant with paired engines which enjoyed a long operational career. After serving on the Eastern front, it even took part in the raids on London.

There was a tradeoff for this enormous power, and this was the delay due to the complexities of coordinating the transmission systems. This same difficulty plagued the R.V, the first of which were completed late in 1915 and early in 1916, but with the first aircraft delivered only in September 1917. In this case all propellers were of the tractor type, driven by five 245-hp Maybach Mb.IVa engines.

The R.VI was the first of the giant Zeppelin aircraft to be produced in series: 18 were built, plus seaplane versions, by the parent corporation (which by then was known as the Zeppelin-Werke-Staaken), six by Aviatik, seven by Schütte-Lanz, and four by the Ostdeutsche Albatroswerke. With four 245-hp Maybachs mounted in pairs (or, in some cases, 260-hp Mercedes D.IVas), there was a free nose section of new design, featuring an enclosed cabin and a frontal machine gun position. The engines were equipped with electric or mechanical starters, and on the Albatros-built

The two most typical Zeppelin Giant configurations. Below, left: an R.VII and R.VI (No. R.26)
Below, right: An R.IV preparing for take-off, with the starboard propeller already turning. Note the camouflage pattern

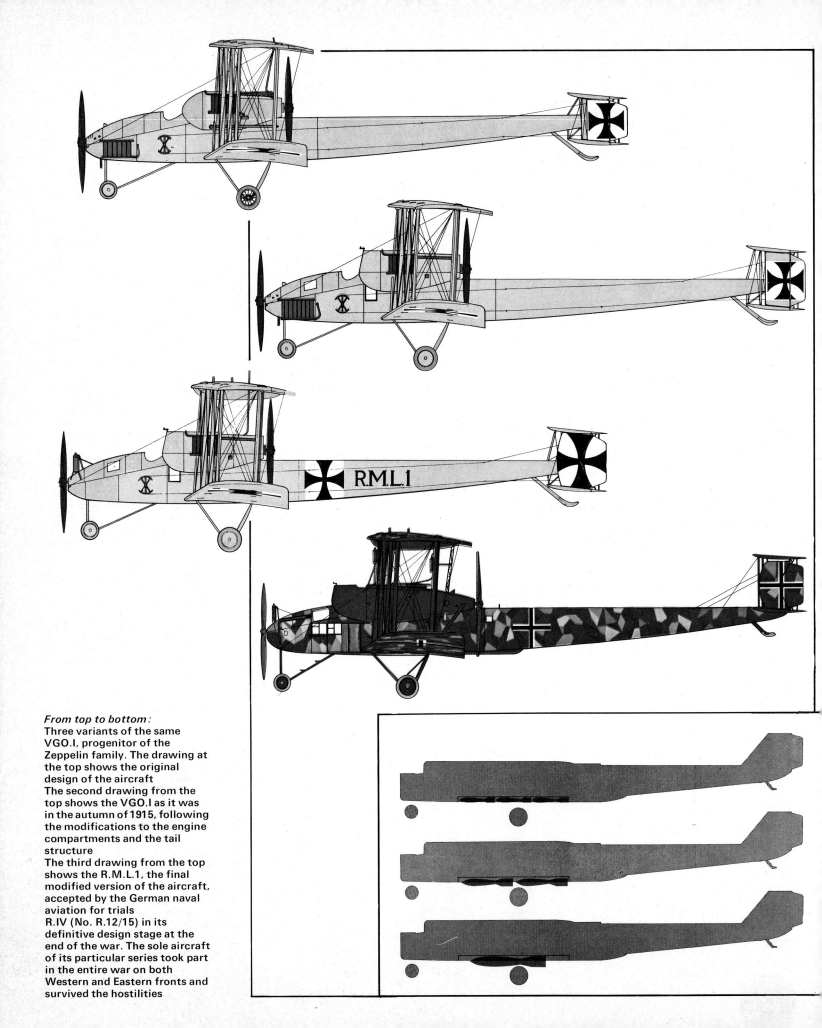

From top to bottom:
Three variants of the same
VGO.I, progenitor of the
Zeppelin family. The drawing at
the top shows the original
design of the aircraft
The second drawing from the
top shows the VGO.I as it was
in the autumn of 1915, following
the modifications to the engine
compartments and the tail
structure
The third drawing from the top
shows the R.M.L.1, the final
modified version of the aircraft,
accepted by the German naval
aviation for trials
R.IV (No. R.12/15) in its
definitive design stage at the
end of the war. The sole aircraft
of its particular series took part
in the entire war on both
Western and Eastern fronts and
survived the hostilities

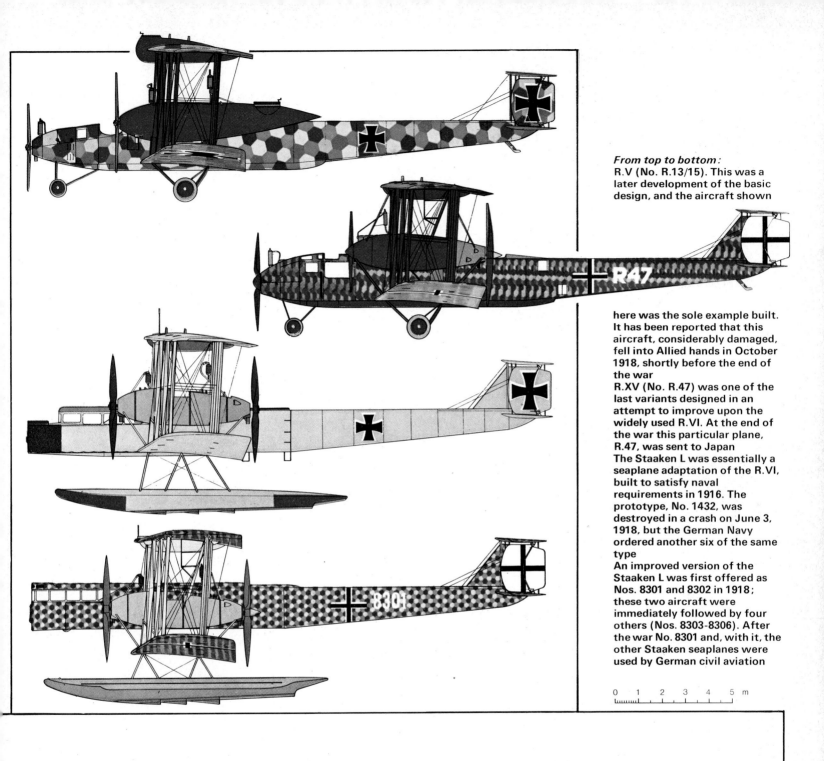

From top to bottom:
R.V (No. R.13/15). This was a later development of the basic design, and the aircraft shown here was the sole example built. It has been reported that this aircraft, considerably damaged, fell into Allied hands in October 1918, shortly before the end of the war

R.XV (No. R.47) was one of the last variants designed in an attempt to improve upon the widely used R.VI. At the end of the war this particular plane, R.47, was sent to Japan

The Staaken L was essentially a seaplane adaptation of the R.VI, built to satisfy naval requirements in 1916. The prototype, No. 1432, was destroyed in a crash on June 3, 1918, but the German Navy ordered another six of the same type

An improved version of the Staaken L was first offered as Nos. 8301 and 8302 in 1918; these two aircraft were immediately followed by four others (Nos. 8303-8306). After the war No. 8301 and, with it, the other Staaken seaplanes were used by German civil aviation

0 1 2 3 4 5 m

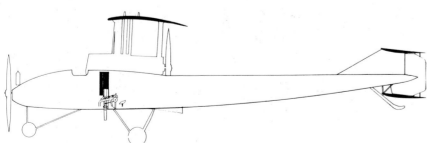

Schematic, bottom: The three profiles of the R.VI on the opposite page show arrangement of the bombs, 18 of which could be accommodated internally if they were of the 100-kg (220-lb) variety. Bombs weighing 300 and 1000 kg (660 and 2200 lb) had to be racked in part externally

The schematic drawing on this page shows how the 130-mm cannon was intended to be mounted in the VGO.II for downward firing

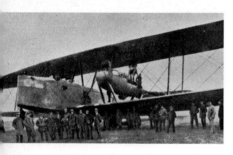

Top: *No. R.31, one of 18 R.VIs built*
Center: *One of the last of the
Zeppelin giants, R.XIVa, No. 84/17,
on the manufacturer's airfield.*
(Museo Caproni, Taliedo)
Bottom: *A Staaken XVI, No. 49/17,
built by Aviatik.* (Museo Caproni,
Taliedo)

Giants the rotor hubs were protected by special spinners. Fuel was stored in from eight to ten 245-liter tanks, and there was, in addition, a 155-liter (35-gallon) gravity tank mounted on the upper wing with a quick-release device.

The first R.VII was delivered on July 3, 1917, only to crash a month later. Basically, it was simply a rehash of the R.IV. The R.XVI, of which three were ordered from Aviatik, was slightly larger than the R.VI with more powerful engines — two 220-hp Benz Bz.IVs and two 530-hp Benz Bz.VIs (developing a total of 1500 hp — a record power for an aircraft during the entire war). A single example of this aircraft flew before the end of the war.

In 1917 there was a return to the five-engined concept, in the R.XIV (of which 5 were completed) and the R.XIVa (3 built). The XIVa was a lightened version, intended for high-altitude work. The same number of R.XVs were built, identical except for slight aerodynamic improvements. On these aircraft the engines were, once again, the Maybach Mb.IVa, fitted with reduction gears on the R.XIVa.

Of the seaplanes, the Type L (of which only Naval No. 1432 was built) was virtually an R.VI except for its enormous (13-m-long) duralumin floats, which were divided into 12 water-tight compartments. This giant floatplane was delivered and at least three additional machines were completed (of which one was later reconverted for land use), all of which incorporated improvements already used on the R.XIV. The distinguishing external characteristic of this type was the fuselage, which was mounted at the midpoint of the separation between the upper and lower wings. The dorsal machine guns were intended to be replaced by 20-mm Becker cannon.

How the Zeppelin-Staaken Giants were used in the War

Perhaps because they had been impressed by the Russian *'Ilya Mouromets'*, the Germans first used the Zeppelin R planes on the Eastern front.

The Siemens-Schuckert R.1, the first to reach the front, could not become operational for a considerable time. For this reason the honor of being the first actively fighting Giants went to the VGO.II, the first R plane accepted by the military (Serial No. R.9/15), which joined the *Rfa 500 (Riesenflugzeugabteilung* = Giant Aircraft Detachment) at Alt-Auz (Vecauce, in Latvia) in February 1916. It took part in various operations, after which it was retired to training. In action it worked together with the first Giant of the German naval air arm, the VGO.I (No. RML.1), which was active with the *Marine Kommando LR.1* at least from August 12 to 24, 1916, before returning to the factory to be converted into a five-engined machine.

According to some sources the first night bombing successfully carried out by the German Giants was on the Northeastern front, August 13, 1916, the aircraft involved being the VGO.III No. R.10/15. This aircraft took part in five or six raids around Riga in Latvia, was then retired to training and finally crashed on January 17, 1917, the first of

the Giants to meet its end this way. In the *Rfa 500* it was replaced by R.IV No. R.12/15, which in August or September 1917 was transferred to *Rfa 501* in Belgium, where in December it was joined by R.V No. 13/15.

Rfa 500 and *501*, each equipped with six aircraft, moved into their bases at respectively Custinne in France in February 1918 (apparently with the specific plan of bombing Paris) and at Scheldewindeke and other minor airfields in the vicinity of Gand and Ostend, as early as August 1, 1917. The mission of *Rfa 501*, integrated with *Bombengeschwader 3*, was to give support to Gotha squadrons in their bombing missions over London, planned by the summer of 1915 and actually begun in the summer of 1916. The Giants began their incursions over England in 1917. For the attacks beyond the Channel the R aircraft used were all from the Staaken plant and included a number of versions. The machines actually employed operationally were: R.12 (R.IV), R.13 (R.V), R.25, 26, 27, 28, 29, 30, 32, 38 and 39 (R.VI). The first combined raid on London was carried out by two Giants working together with 25 Gothas on the night of September 28-29 1917. From that night on, Staakens dropped 27190-kg of bombs on England, including three 1000-kg missiles, in a total of 11 missions flown over a period of eight months.

In the periods when it was not possible to bomb England, the Rs carried out actions behind the French lines. At least 24 missions were flown over France and Belgium by the Giants of *Rfa 500* and *501*, all of them tactical in nature (that is, within a range of 100 km) with the exception of some missions over Le Havre, Deauville and Rouen. No Giants were lost in operations against England, although two had technical troubles, but with no casualties. On the Continent the R.XIV No. R.43 was shot down by a night fighter piloted by Capt. Yuille of No. 151 Squadron RFC, and R.VI No. 37 was brought down by French anti-aircraft fire. No. R.31, which was an R.VI, also went down in flames, but it was never established whether this was because of anti-aircraft damage or fire aboard the aircraft. All in all, the wartime activity of the Staakens was highly successful, with 93·4 per cent of the missions successful as compared to 76·4 per cent for the Gothas.

The end of the war did not mean the end of these giant German aircraft. For some time they were used for tourist flights and occasional civilian missions in an effort to get commercial aviation under way. These flights were carried out with aircraft Nos. 30 and 8301 (the latter a seaplane). Another important mission of the giants was in transporting funds to the Ukraine, which knew a brief moment of independence between the Czarist and Leninist hegemonies. This resulted in numerous highly adventurous flights with three of the Rs, Nos. 39, 69 and 70. No. 70 made a forced landing in Rumania and was immediately confiscated by the local authorities. Later on, R.69 seems to have been turned over to the Italian government by way of reparations.

THE BRISTOL F.2A-F.2B

F2B of the first series. Fighters of this type were used in the last phases of World War I. (Archivio Igino Coggi)

Specifications

	F.2A Prototype 1	F.2A Prototype 2	F.2B	F.2B	F.2B
Power plant	R.R. Falcon 190 hp	Hispano-Suiza 150 hp	Falcon II 220 hp	Falcon III 275 hp	Hispano-Suiza 200 hp
Wing span, *m*	11·95	11·96	11·96	11·96	11·96
Total length, *m*	7·85	7·57	7·87	7·87	7·53
Height, *m*	2·84	2·89	2·97	2·97	2·89
Wing area, *m²*	36·14	36·14	37·68	37·68	37·68
Weight, empty, *kg*	783	668	∞900	∞900	∞900
Total weight, *kg*	1249	1122	1297	1292	1193
Maximum speed, *km/hr*	177 at s/l*	160 at 1219 m	179 at 3054 m	182 at 3054 m	169 at 3054 m
Climb to 3054 *m, min-sec*	14:30	19:00	13:15	11:50	15:05
Ceiling, *m*	4877	4419	6096	5486	5791
Flight endurance, *hrs-min*	3:15	6:00	3:00	3:00	—

* sea level

By spring 1916 the British and Colonial Aeroplane Co. Ltd. of Filton (which was to become the Bristol Aeroplane Co. Ltd.) had already delivered more than 400 B.E.2 two-seaters to the Royal Flying Corps, and a few more were to be delivered before production was terminated entirely. The B.E.2s were basically sound, but their day had passed and they were tragically unprepared to face the rigors of wartime service.

Fortunately for the British pilots and observers, as early as the summer of 1915 the War Office had listed a certain Capt. Frank Barnwell as being on 'indefinite leave without pay'. Toward the end of 1914 Barnwell had left British and Colonial to join the Royal Flying Corps as a lieutenant, largely because of his annoyance at the never-ending bickering and finagling which went on between the army and navy, a state of affairs which made it quite impossible (at least for Barnwell) to work efficiently.

Barnwell was an extraordinarily talented engineer. In 1914, little more than 20 years old, he had designed the small, efficient Scout. He was well aware of the shortcomings of the biplanes produced by Royal Aircraft, and also knew that nothing could be done to improve them. Thus inevitably the Filton plant put in a proposal to the War Office (which had also become aware of the B.E.2's limitations) for a two-seater equal-span biplane allocated the designation R.2A. The R.2A was to

201

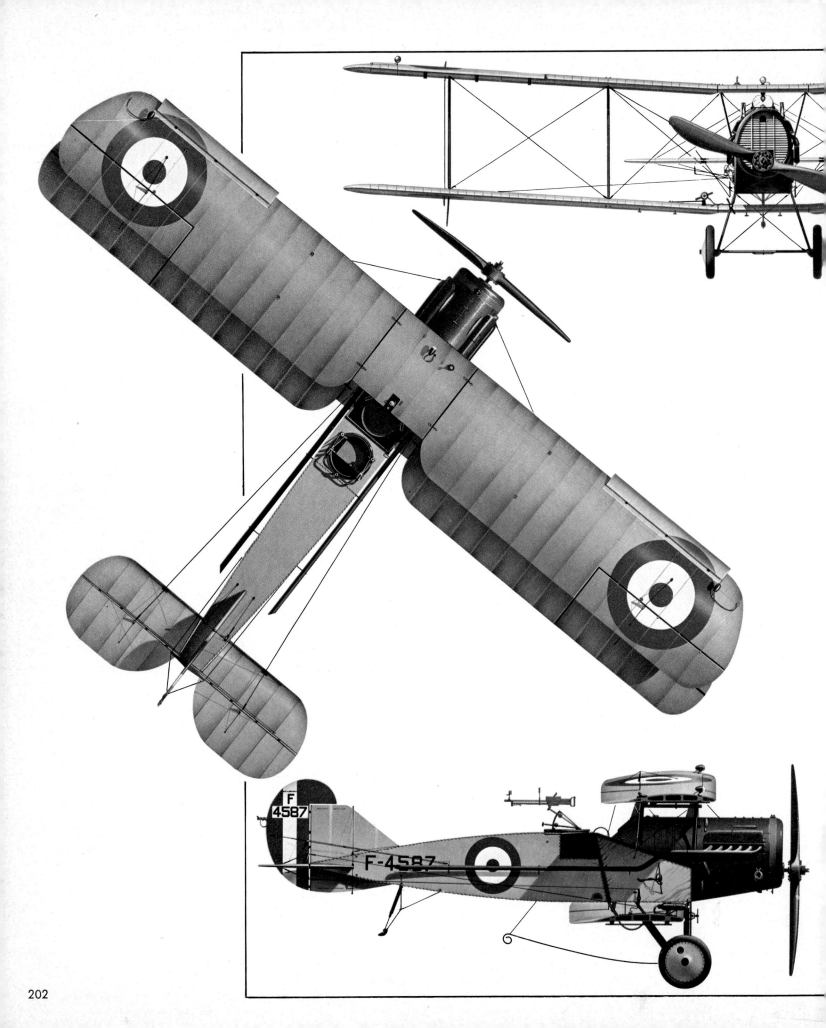

by unconsciousness or death of the pilot. The variable-incidence stabilizer, which could be adjusted in flight, made it possible for the pilot to set the plane on a course and fly at a desired speed with the controls freed—a rudimentary form of autopilot.

Many engines were used on the F.2B, but the most frequently installed power plant was the water-cooled Rolls-Royce V-12 Falcon I, II or III, developing 190, 220 and 275 hp respectively. The propellers were of wood, either two-bladed or four-bladed, their diameter ranging between 2·865 and 2·987 m. The engine was protected by sheet-aluminum cowling meeting the radiator in front, of roughly elliptical shape with cooling louvers to regulate air intake and exhaust manifolds—which in some cases were of truly impressive length.

Armament included a fixed 7·7-mm Vickers machine gun equipped with a Constantinesco C.C. synchronizer and an Aldis optical sight, plus either one or two Lewis guns of equal calibre on a Scarff No. 2 ring mount with a Norman sight in the rear cockpit. The fixed gun was mounted under the cowling forward of the pilot's seat on the aircraft center line, and this positioning of the weapon made it necessary to alter the construction of the fuel tank rather drastically. A maximum of 12 Cooper fragmentation bombs could be racked under the lower wing.

Development of the Bristol Fighter (F.2B)

Bristol Fighters were built in a number of different versions, of which the earliest (as distinguished from the recce plane) was the F.2A. Two prototypes were built, followed by 50 production

machines which were recognizable by the lack of covering on the center section of the lower wing. This structural peculiarity, which was adopted to permit greater downward visibility, was bad aerodynamics, however (even the addition of end plates at the lower wing roots helped little), and so this scheme was abandoned.

The first F.2A prototype was numbered A3303. It was test-flown on September 9, 1916, with rounded wing tips and powered by the 190-hp Rolls-Royce Falcon I engine cooled by two tall lateral radiators aligned with the front center-section struts. However, this arrangement seriously blocked the pilot's view, especially on landing, and was discontinued on all later aircraft, including A.3304, the second prototype. The latter was tested on October 25, 1916, powered by the 150-hp 8-cylinder Hispano-Suiza, after which it was considerably modified and became the first prototype of the F.2B.

The Bristol Fighter was eventually produced in a number of series, both by the proprietary firm and by various other British companies—Sir W. G. Armstrong, Whitworth & Co. Ltd., Gloucestershire Aircraft Co. Ltd., Austin Motor Co., National Aircraft Factory No. 3, Harris & Sheldon Ltd., and Standard Motor Co. Marshall & Sons received an order for 150 aircraft which was, however, canceled when the war ended. Production of the F.2B was so extensive, in fact, that Rolls-Royce could not manufacture their Falcon engines fast enough to keep up with the deliveries of airframes, and it became necessary to use other power plants— the 200-hp Hispano-Suiza, the Sunbeam Arab of the same horsepower, the 300-hp Hispano-Suiza, the 230- and 290-hp 6-cylinder Siddeley Puma and the 200-hp Wolseley Viper. Most of these other engines were unsatisfactory because of defects due to lowering of quality standards. Apart from that numerous changes in the radiator systems were necessary. The fortunes of the F.2B were definitely linked with those of the Rolls-Royce Falcons in their Mark I, II and III versions, which finally attained a rating of 290 hp.

It was only after the war, with the 300-hp 8Fb, that the Hispano-Suiza engine proved satisfactory when installed in the 40 F.2Bs built under licence by the SABCA in Belgium (Société Anonyme Belge de Constructions Aéronautiques). In the United States, installation of the 400-hp Liberty 12 engine proved disastrous, and of the 2000 machines ordered from the Curtiss Aeroplane and Motor Corp. of Buffalo, the Dayton-Wright Airplane Co. of Dayton and the Engineering Division of the Bureau of Aircraft Production, only about 80 were actually completed (including several of semimonocoque construction). The Liberty engine was simply too powerful; Barnwell himself, the designer, had advised against installing it, but it was not until three crashes had taken place that the gravity of the error was finally realized by the Americans.

In the late 1920s there were still Bristol F.2Bs on active service in the Middle East. Here one such aircraft of No. 208 Squadron, based at Ismailia on the Suez Canal, is flying over the pyramids. (C. A. Sims) Bottom left: An F.2B of No. 11 Squadron, RAF, captured by the Germans near Cambrai in the summer of 1917. (Archivio Apostolo)

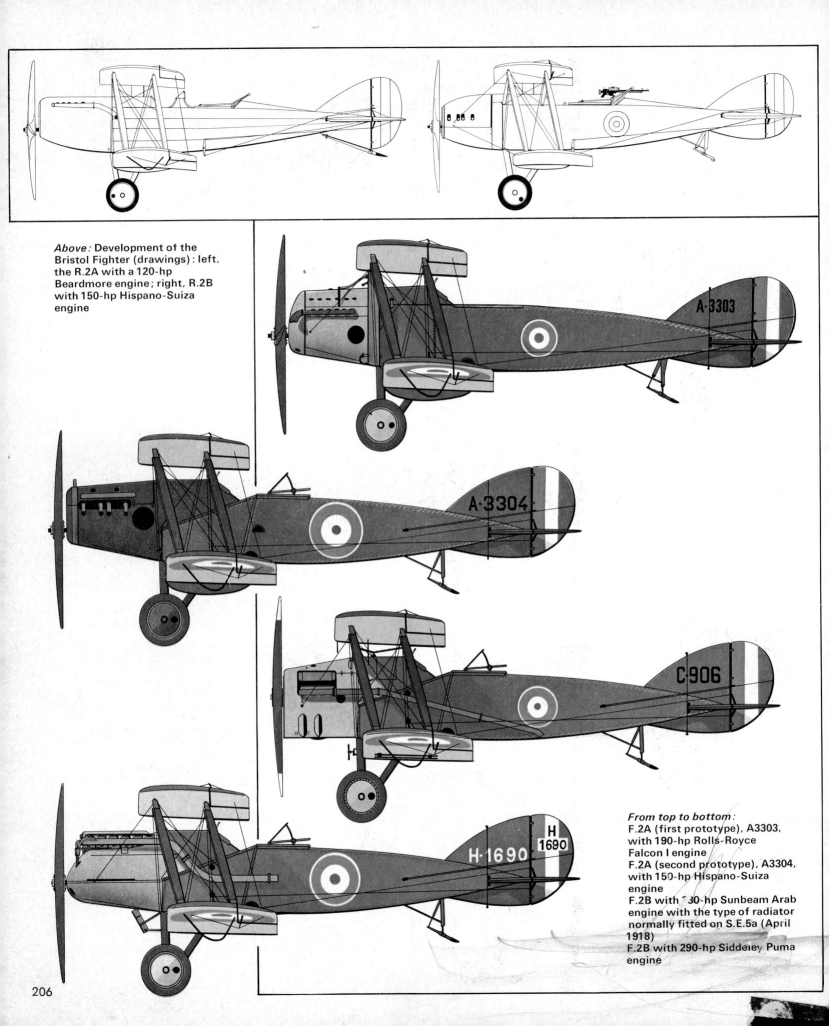

Above: Development of the Bristol Fighter (drawings): left, the R.2A with a 120-hp Beardmore engine; right, R.2B with 150-hp Hispano-Suiza engine

A·3303

A·3304

C·906

H 1690

From top to bottom:
F.2A (first prototype), A3303, with 190-hp Rolls-Royce Falcon I engine
F.2A (second prototype), A3304, with 150-hp Hispano-Suiza engine
F.2B with 130-hp Sunbeam Arab engine with the type of radiator normally fitted on S.E.5a (April 1918)
F.2B with 290-hp Siddeley Puma engine

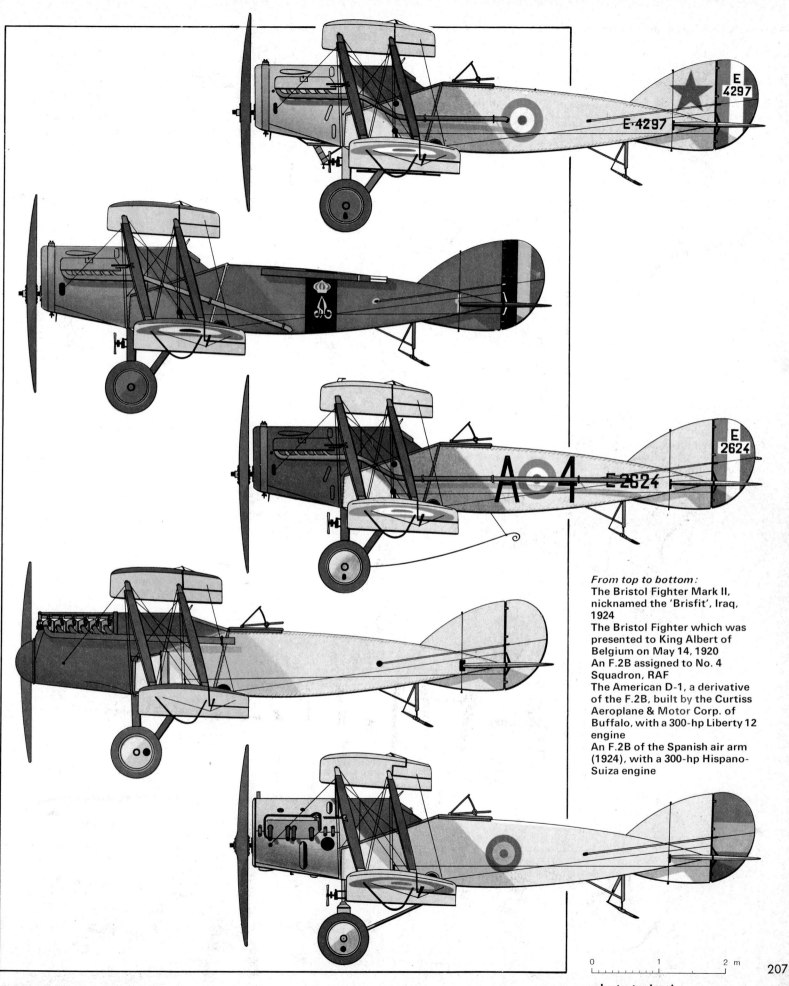

From top to bottom:
The Bristol Fighter Mark II, nicknamed the 'Brisfit', Iraq, 1924
The Bristol Fighter which was presented to King Albert of Belgium on May 14, 1920
An F.2B assigned to No. 4 Squadron, RAF
The American D-1, a derivative of the F.2B, built by the Curtiss Aeroplane & Motor Corp. of Buffalo, with a 300-hp Liberty 12 engine
An F.2B of the Spanish air arm (1924), with a 300-hp Hispano-Suiza engine

0   1   2 m

roberto terrinoni

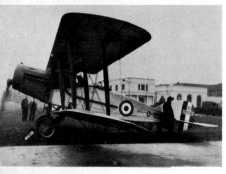

Immediately after the war a series of 215 F.2Bs were built (J6586-J6800) Above: J6586 was normally used for testing tropical equipment. (Archivio Coggi)
Bottom: The last F.2B to remain active—an exhibition aircraft maintained in prime flying condition by the Shuttleworth Collection in England. (Archivio Apostolo)

Bristol continued producing F.2Bs until 1927, even after the doughty little fighter had been relegated to such humdrum army support duties as recovery of messages and wireless sets. The final 30 machines, of the Mark III series, carried no guns and were completed with dual controls for use as trainers.

All told more than 5200 Bristol Fighters were built. Most of them, of course, went to equip the RAF and other military air arms, but a good number were also used in various experimental projects and for the development of and perfecting of techniques which were gradually adopted for later production aircraft.

How the Bristol Fighters were used in the War

Like some other British aircraft, the early life of the Bristol Fighter was rather disastrous. On the maiden flight of the first prototype, the test pilot, Capt. Hooper, reported that he had been unable to climb above 2000 meters. This floored the designers, until it was discovered that the problem was a malfunctioning altimeter! When the first F.2As were sent into action beyond the front lines early in April 1917 (Battle of Arras), the great painful surprise fell to the British, not the German airmen. On their first patrol No. 48 Squadron, RFC, lost four out of six machines, including the F.2A of the squadron leader, Capt. W. Leefe Robinson, holder of the Victoria Cross, who was taken prisoner. The Bristol fighters had been surprised by a group of five Albatros D.IIIs, which returned unharmed to their base. The German fighters belonged to *Jasta* 11 and were led by Richthofen, who accounted for two of the new Bristols. All in all it was not an auspicious beginning for the F.2As, and more was to follow, with the loss of another eight F.2As against only two German Albatros fighters shot down on another occasion.

Now the Bristol Fighter was a good aircraft, maneuverable and sturdy, but the British tactics had been faulty. They had considered the ring-mounted Lewis to be their most important weapon, and by maneuvering to give the observer a better chance to fire they had actually put themselves in a defensive position and were manhandled by the Albatros, which had assumed and kept the initiative.

The British learned their painful lesson quickly and well, and soon the F.2B pilots began to wage aggressive war, attacking with the techniques used by single-seater fighters and leaving all defense function to the rear gun. The close position of the two cockpits proved to be an advantage in that it allowed good communication between the two men and this led to some fine 'team' performances. A good illustration here was a Canadian pilot, Lieut. (later Maj.) A. E. McKeever, who, backed up by Sgt. (later Lieut.) L. F. Powell, destroyed 30 German planes in a 6-month period, from June 1917 to January 1918.

Production of the Bristols continued at such a rate that many squadrons were soon equipped with them—on the Western front, Nos. 11, 20, 22, 48, 62 and 88; then No. 139, which was particularly effective on the Italian front; the Australian No. 67 and, partially, No. 111 in Palestine; and Nos. 33, 36, 39, 76 and 141, assigned to Home Defense. Many F.2Bs went to other units which used them mixed with other aircraft types on reconnaissance and artillery spotting missions.

After the war the tough, reliable Bristols, by then available in quantity, found widespread uses at home and in the occupation forces in Germany and Turkey. In the Near and Middle East and in India the Bristol Fighter continued to be used for some years by the British forces but it also found new owners in the air arms of other nations, including Belgium, Greece, Mexico, Norway, Peru and Spain, as well as in Ireland and the Dominions. Between 1928 and 1931 young flying enthusiasts of the Oxford and Cambridge University Air Squadrons won their spurs on F.2Bs, and the RAF used them until 1932. In New Zealand some were still flying smartly as late as 1938.

Two of these 'Brisfits' are still in existence. One is exhibited at the Imperial War Museum in London; the other, in full flying trim, takes part in exhibitions at the Shuttleworth Foundation at Old Warden Aerodrome (as advertised) in Bedfordshire, still giving a good account of itself and doing honor to its creator, Frank Barnwell.